ADJUSTMENT OF
Insurance Loss Claims on Merchandise

ADJUSTMENT OF
Insurance Loss Claims on Merchandise

ACCOUNTING PROBLEMS AND PROCEDURES

By

Leo Rosenblum, Ph.D., C.P.A.

Assistant Professor of Accountancy
School of Business and Civic Administration
The City College of New York

KING'S CROWN PRESS

COLUMBIA UNIVERSITY, NEW YORK

1948

Printed and bound in the United States of America
by the Vail-Ballou Press, Inc., Binghamton, N. Y.

KING'S CROWN PRESS

is a division of Columbia University Press organized for the purpose of making certain scholarly material available at minimum cost. Toward that end, the publishers have adopted every reasonable economy except such as would interfere with a legible format. The work is presented substantially as submitted by the author, without the usual editorial attention of Columbia University Press.

To

the memory of

I. B. R. *and* S. J. R.

ACKNOWLEDGMENTS

I wish to express my appreciation for the assistance given me in the preparation of this book. Helpful interviews were granted, but anonymity was requested, by a number of insureds, adjusters, underwriters, and brokers. Miss Mabel B. Swerig, Librarian of the Insurance Society of New York, Inc., and Miss Thelma E. Reid, Assistant Librarian, made available the Society's vast collection, including the unpublished material referred to in this work. Acknowledgment is made to the publishers who have graciously permitted the reproduction of material within their copyrights.

My colleagues in the Department of Accountancy of The City College of New York were helpful in our many discussions. My friend, Alexander Brody, Ph.D., LL.B., of the Department of Economics, aided by reading and commenting upon parts of the manuscript. The first draft was carefully reviewed by Louis Rosenzweig, LL.B., before his retirement from the practice of law. Professors Ralph H. Blanchard, James L. Dohr, Paul H. Nystrom, and Edwin W. Patterson, all of Columbia University, made valuable suggestions. I am under great obligation to Professor Roy B. Kester, of Columbia University, for continuous counsel and encouragement during the development and completion of this book.

To my wife, Marjorie Lewitt Rosenblum, I owe much for her patience, understanding, and encouragement. Most of all, I am indebted to my brother, David I. Rosenblum, B.S., LL.B., who made himself available for many consultations, read the entire manuscript, and made important suggestions.

LEO ROSENBLUM

New York, N.Y.
July, 1947.

CONTENTS

Chapter 1

INTRODUCTION

THIS IS A STUDY in accounting theory and method in one area of insurance, namely, the adjustment of loss claims. That insurance is an important social mechanism requires no elaboration. It is universally regarded as a medium employed for the spreading of risk and the distribution of loss. Willett defines insurance as "that social device for making accumulations to meet uncertain losses of capital which is carried out through the transfer of the risks of many individuals to one person or to a group of persons. . . ."[1]

Through risk-bearing organizations, the hazards to which business men and others may be subject are distributed. It has been stated that:

> Insurance may be regarded as a business, a detailed mathematical-statistical science or a broad social device or technique. Essentially insurance is a formal social device for the substitution of certainty for uncertainty through the pooling of hazards. It may or may not be a business, it may or may not use the services of statisticians and actuaries; it is always a social device operating on the principles of pooling. Pooling allows the individual to substitute average loss costs for actual; a large group of hazard exposures is required to permit pooling. . . .[2]

Insurance is a stabilizing factor in business and in personal life. A casualty which might seriously impair the economic life of a business man may be cushioned by insurance:

> Instead of being confronted daily with the possibility that he may at one time be called upon to meet a large, perhaps ruinous loss (since he cannot hope to maintain reserves to meet all risks), he has a small certain loss. This small certain loss is so nearly constant from year to year that it becomes

1. Willett, Allan H., *Economic Theory of Risk and Insurance*, Columbia University, Faculty of Political Science. Studies in History, Economics and Public Law, Vol. 14, No. 2 (New York: Columbia University Press, 1901), p. 106.

2. Kulp, C. A., *Casualty Insurance* (Rev. Ed., New York: Ronald Press Co., 1942), p. 10.

for him simply an expense of production. He can calculate all the more accurately his manufacturing or distributing costs; he would be lucky indeed, if he were able to reduce all his costs of production to the same degree of accuracy.[3]

Out of funds assembled from the contributions, or premiums, of a group of participants, insurance indemnifies those who have suffered losses. The participants as a group can estimate the total loss fairly accurately and each member is assessed his share. Thus one whose property is insured against fire or burglary, for example, is relieved of anxiety about the possibility of destruction or loss of his possessions, and he may be spared many of the economic problems which would result from such event. In commercial losses, the almost immediate availability of indemnity reduces the period of interruption to business and the resulting cost.

There are some self-insurers. These plan, individually, to absorb such losses as they may suffer through fire, burglary or other casualty as costs of doing business. Periodically they set aside funds as a reserve against losses, basing the amounts reserved upon an estimate of losses to be expected. An uninsured firm which set aside no funds whatever to meet losses could not properly be called a self-insurer; it would be merely a firm with no insurance.

Self-insurance is relatively uncommon. In the field of fire insurance the practice is feasible only where there are a large number of properties, widely distributed. In health, accident and life insurance, self-insurance is even less common, since to operate safely and effectively, coverage of this type must embrace a very large number of individuals. In the absence of large numbers self-insurance is not practical.

It cannot be said that insurance is not costly. In addition to the total losses, the operating expenses of the insurance companies are an important factor. An added element exists as to property insurance. Carelessness in the handling of property often results from the knowledge that insurance is in effect. This tends to bring about an increase in the number of losses.[4]

Despite these cost factors, there is little doubt about the desirability

3. Kulp, C. A., *Casualty Insurance* (New York: Ronald Press Co., 1928), p. 14.

4. On the other hand greater care will presumably be exercised in the prevention of loss when the property is under-insured than when it is fully insured. *Infra*, p. 3a.

of insurance. In addition to its other advantages, a device which "furnishes a convenient and practicable method of paying for the consequences of hazard which men cannot or will not prevent performs a social service the value of which can hardly be exaggerated. . . ."[5]

The rationale of insurance is well-summarized by Josiah Royce:

> As experience shows, the insurance principle comes to be more and more used and useful in modern affairs. . . . It tends more and more both to pervade and to transform our modern social order. It brings into new syntheses not merely pure and applied science, but private and public interests, individual prudence, and a large regard for the general welfare, thrift, and charity. It discourages recklessness and gambling. It contributes to the sense of stability. It quiets fears and encourages faithfulness.[6]

The document evidencing coverage, the insurance policy itself, serves the purpose of defining the risk and enumerating the conditions under which the insurance is written. It secures the insurer against fraud and imposition in the event of loss, as to the cause and amount. From the point of view of the insured, the insurance contract serves to make clear the procedure of settlement of losses, and it gives the security and the benefit for which he pays.[7]

The insurance contract has been defined as follows:

> Any agreement or other transaction whereby one party, . . . called the insurer, is obligated to confer benefit of pecuniary value upon another party, . . . called the insured or the beneficiary, dependent upon the happening of a fortuitous event in which the insured or beneficiary has, or is expected to have at the time of such happening, a material interest which will be adversely affected by the happening of such event. A fortuitous event is any occurrence or failure to occur which is, or is assumed by the parties to be, to a substantial extent beyond the control of either party.[8]

It is clear, therefore, that the function of insurance is to indemnify or reimburse those who undertake risk and suffer loss. But the insured need not be placed in as good a condition financially as if no loss had occurred. The measure of loss in property insurance is the reproduc-

5. Kulp, C. A., *Casualty Insurance* (Rev. Ed.), *op. cit.*, p. 13.

6. Royce, Josiah, *War and Insurance* (New York: The Macmillan Co., 1914), p. x.

7. See Appleman, John Alan, *Insurance Law and Practice* (Kansas City, Mo.: Vernon Law Book Co., 1942), Vol. 12, § 7005, pp. 17–18, and Mowbray, Albert H., *Insurance* (3rd. Ed., New York: McGraw-Hill Book Co., Inc., 1946), pp. 43–44.

8. New York, Insurance Law, § 41.

tion value of the property at the time of the loss, after reduction for depreciation and obsolescence.[9] The maximum payment is the amount of the insurance coverage provided under the policy, and insurance companies are not required to reimburse for sentimental values.

Public policy dictates that no opportunity be given the insured to profit through the loss of his property:

It is a wise public policy, and a rule of obvious and simple justice, which limits contracts of insurance to liability only for indemnity of loss, and thereby relieves them from any element of wager, and precludes their use as a means of money making and profit. . . .[10]

This policy yields to recognition that loss of profits may be entailed and is in certain situations insurable without creating a condition of unjust gain. The observation of the court is not inconsistent with the situation that insurance may be obtained for loss of profits when business operations are interrupted because of some casualty, for example, a fire. Loss of profits insurance is obtained upon a special agreement between insured and insurance company, under which the insured pays an additional premium.

The insurance contract is a personal one. Consequently, as a general rule it cannot be transferred without the insurer's consent.[11] This condition results from the following circumstances. The character, history and background of an applicant for insurance coverage are significant factors in an insurance company's decision whether to accept or reject the risk. The care and protection given the property by an applicant who submits it for coverage likewise influence the insurer's decision, and often affect the premium rate. A change in ownership might render the risk less desirable to the insurer. Therefore, if the insured's interest in the subject at risk ceases, and the insurer has not acquiesced in a transfer of the policy, the coverage terminates.

9. In some states fire insurance companies are permitted to write replacement insurance on buildings and building service equipment. This coverage is also known as depreciation insurance. In the event of loss the insurer pays the cost of restoration, without deduction for depreciation.

10. Larner v. Commercial Union Assur. Co., Ltd., of London, Eng. (1926) 215 N.Y. Supp. 151, 154.

11. Life insurance contracts and marine insurance contracts are exceptions to this rule. It is noted, also, that the insurer may alter the personal nature of the contract, for example, by adding to a policy an "in trust or on commission" endorsement.

The types of insurance coverage available are many and diverse. For the purpose of this analysis, a few are enumerated. Policies are written covering loss from fire or death, accident or strike damage, boiler damage or transportation risks, burglary or sickness. Although the insurance contracts embracing the specific classes of risk differ from each other in detail, they are similar in principle. Each describes the types and amounts, or limits, of the risk insured, and the conditions under which the coverage is in effect. In each case the undertaking of the insurer is also expressed. For example, one type of burglary policy, that known as the Mercantile Open Stock Burglary Policy, contains the following statement of the insurance company's undertaking:

> To INDEMNIFY the Assured FOR ALL LOSS BY BURGLARY, of merchandise, furniture, fixtures and equipment, from within the Assured's premises. . . .
>
> To INDEMNIFY the Assured FOR ALL DAMAGE (except by fire) to merchandise, furniture, fixtures and equipment in the premises, caused by such burglary or attempt thereat. . . .

The company thus makes clear that only loss and damage resulting from burglary or attempted burglary are insured against. It is noted that such policies provide, as an exception from the coverage, that damage from fire, although caused in the course of burglary or attempted burglary, is excluded. Another section of the policy sets forth in dollars the maximum liability of the company on the risk. In another clause the following reservation is made:

> In no case shall the Company be liable for more than the actual cash value of the stolen or damaged property at the time of the loss or damage, nor for more than the actual cost of repairing or replacing such property. . . .

The above provision expresses the limitation of the company's liability to the cash value at the time of loss, or to the actual cost of repairing or replacing the property.

Another type of property policy, the New York Standard fire insurance policy, provides that the insured will be covered

> to the extent of the actual cash value of the property at the time of loss, but not exceeding the amount which it would cost to repair or replace the property with material of like kind and quality within a reasonable time after such loss, without allowance for any increased cost of repair or reconstruc-

tion by reason of any ordinance or law regulating construction or repair. . . .

This clause, too, expresses the limitation of the insurance company's liability to actual cash value. Likewise, it reflects the alternative limitation, noted in the above discussion of the burglary policy, of cost to repair or replace. As with the burglary policy, the insurance company's maximum liability on the risk is set forth.

From the above it is seen that the insurance contract is a contract of indemnity, that it is generally a personal contract, and that in it is set forth a series of concise statements of the undertaking on the part of the insurance company.

This study will analyze the accounting problems and procedures involved in the adjustment of insurance loss claims. The types of claims considered are those arising under policies covering risks to merchandise held as stock in trade.[12] The classes of losses reviewed are those attributable to fire, burglary and other casualties. Marine losses are excluded.

It is proposed, first, to consider the clauses in the insurance policy which affect the work of the accountant in loss determination, and to examine the legal background of these clauses. Illustrations of such provisions are those which outline the obligation of the insured to keep records and accounts, and to supply information concerning the loss. Second, the adequacy of methods of record-keeping employed by insureds will be reviewed. Generally, practices which facilitate estimating the amount of loss expedite settlement of the claim. Third, accounting procedures followed in arriving at the amount of loss and in detecting inflated claims will be analyzed and appraised. Methods distinctive to particular types of coverage and particular sets of circumstances will be identified. To illustrate, in a loss claim arising from a fire which destroyed the major part of an insured's miscellaneous stock of mer-

12. Webster defines merchandise as "The objects of commerce; whatever is usually bought or sold in trade; wares; goods." *Webster's New International Dictionary* (2nd. Ed., unabridged, Springfield, Mass.: G. and C. Merriam Co., 1945); Bouvier, as "A term including all those things which merchants sell, either wholesale or retail: as, dry goods, hardware, groceries, drugs, etc. It is usually applied to personal chattels only. . . . If used in an insurance policy to describe the goods of a merchant it may very properly be limited to goods intended for sale. . . ." Rawle, Francis, *Bouvier's Law Dictionary* (3rd. Revision, St. Paul, Minn.: West Publishing Co., 1914).

chandise, as well as many of his records, the accounting procedures employed to compute the amount of the loss would differ considerably from those made use of in a burglary loss involving a small number of items where all records were available.

This study will utilize material on actual loss claims. This material is found in published summaries of the work of adjusters and accountants. The author has also availed himself of considerable unpublished material embodying the experiences of a large number of individuals engaged in the settlement of loss claims. The facts in each claim are significant because they throw light on the accounting procedures employed in the solution of particular problems. Evaluation is made of the practices followed by the accountants.

The writer has also had the opportunity, in his practice as a certified public accountant, to participate in loss adjustment work. A series of case studies is presented based upon this experience. The significant features of the cases are assembled in a tabular summary. Specific case studies are cited at various places in this work in order to give concrete illustration of the points developed.[13]

Other phases of the problem of examination of records in loss claims will be presented. It will be seen, first, that the direction taken by the accountant's inquiries during the review of a claim is influenced by the unusual features of the claim or of the method of record-keeping; second, that as a result of an accountant's participation in insurance loss work over a long period, his experience contributes in cumulative fashion to the ability to decide speedily upon the audit procedure in a given case; [14] third, that in insurance adjustment work the tasks of adjuster, accountant, and lawyer are closely related.

The close relationship among the tasks of adjuster, accountant, and lawyer merits emphasis. The insurance company's adjuster generally

13. Appendix A comprises 56 case studies of actual loss adjustments involving accounting or auditing work. Cases #16, 20 and 35 merit particular attention because of the many points enumerated relating to the work of the accountant. It will be noted that in many of the cases where the bookkeeping records were distorted, the insured's financial condition and operating results were poor.

14. Compare Reed's comment relating to adjusters: "The adjuster is constantly observing, comparing, and remembering. Thus he accumulates an increasing store of knowledge, some of which becomes so buried in his memory that he uses it unconsciously. . . ." Reed, Prentiss B., *Adjustment of Fire Losses* (1st. Ed., New York: McGraw-Hill Book Co., Inc., 1929), p. 298.

engages an accountant in situations where data of some complexity must be obtained from books of account and related records. The accountant's interpretation of the significance and plausibility of sets of figures is sought by both adjuster and attorney for the insurance company. His observations are likely to suggest avenues of inquiry in cases where loss claims require further investigation. On the claimant's side, the insured, if a large concern, will generally have in its employ one or more accountants capable of assembling the data needed in presenting a claim. The small firm turns such work over to its independent public accountants. In an adjustment where the insured is represented by a broker, adjuster or attorney the insured's accountant consults and co-operates with this representative.

Chapter II

THE INSURANCE POLICY AND THE WORK OF THE ACCOUNTANT

The Accountant's Work

The tasks confronting the accountant for the claimant are:

One:—Assembling financial information, including inventory figures, concerning the loss, from the books of account and the related papers, vouchers and other records.

Two:—Preparing the accounting sections of documents to be submitted to the insurance companies.

Three:—Preparing other material for presentation at informal meetings, at examinations under oath and in court testimony.

In those circumstances where financial information must be submitted as a condition of the issuance of the policy the insured's accountant often assembles such data or supervises its compilation.

The duty of the accountant for the insurance company is generally to review or audit figures, rather than to assemble them. He has not had access to the insured's records during the period preceding the loss, except, perhaps, on rare occasions for such purposes as to verify the amounts at risk under reporting policies. The company's accountant, therefore, finds it necessary to test the authenticity of the claim by considering, among other matters, whether entries in the various records are consistent with one another. He may find the need to adopt, in part, the role of investigator as well as that of accountant. The scope and detail of his work will vary with the conditions encountered, including the circumstances under which the loss occurred, the financial condition of the insured, the adequacy of record-keeping, internal check and internal auditing, and the type of auditing or accounting service performed by the insured's independent accountants.

In theory, the work of loss-estimating is substantially the same whether performed by the company's accountant or the claimant's. In practice, the insurance company's representative, because of his lesser familiarity with the insured's records, must undertake a more exhaustive examination. This frequently includes checking the information obtained from the books and related records against that obtained from some or all of the following sources: minutes of the examination under oath, proof of loss, inventory of damaged or missing goods, appraiser's estimates, and declarations or proposal.

In assembling figures relating to a loss, the claimant's accountant rarely undertakes new, detailed tests of consistency, designed particularly for the point under consideration. But such tests are almost invariably undertaken by the insurer's accountant. Where the claimant's internal accountant or independent accountant would generally accept as correct loss data taken directly from the records, and not improbable or incorrect on their face, the insurance company's accountant, on the other hand, would make counter-checks of such data and related comments by the insured, against other material submitted.

To illustrate, a loss claim arose because of water damage to a quantity of neckties at a manufacturer's premises.[1] An audit by the insurance company's accountant revealed that the claimed cost of production per dozen of one of the lots involved, namely, a large quantity of untried, experimental merchandise, was a sum equalling or exceeding the sales price per dozen of ninety-five per cent of the regular line of neckties sold during the year preceding the loss. In the same case, the dates of the final process in the manufacture of the experimental lot, namely, the stamping of emblems upon the neckties, were the same as, or very close to, the dates, some months past, when similar quantities of merchandise had been shipped to a west-coast wholesaler, affiliated with the insured, for sale to retailers. This showed that the experimental merchandise included in the claim was not new stock. It had been carried over from the previous season, and had not been manufactured recently, as claimed by the insured, for sale during the forthcoming season.

In another situation, a condition of unreliable record-keeping was revealed by checking serial numbers of items of merchandise reported

1. See Appendix A, Case 54.

stolen, against the combined stock book-physical inventory record, and against purchase and sale records.[2] Many items said to have been stolen were not listed in the latest inventory preceding the loss, although the items were stated to have been purchased prior to the date of this inventory-taking. Items reflected in sales records as having been sold—and not subsequently returned by customers—before the most recent inventory date, nevertheless appeared in the listing of physical inventory of that date and in the claim list.

Although books of account are said to speak for themselves, under certain circumstances the same set of figures or conditions will take on different meanings to different readers or interpreters. For example, a dress manufacturer made claim for the disappearance of finished garments, based upon the loss indicated by comparing the balance compiled from a perpetual inventory record, with the physical inventory figure.[3] It developed that there were almost daily differences between physical inventories and figures assembled from the perpetual inventory records. Obviously, such differences cast doubt upon the validity of the perpetual inventory record.[4]

The Insurance Policy Clauses Which Facilitate the Accountant's Work

Audit of the amount of the merchandise loss sustained by a claimant may be facilitated by insurance policy requirements such as clauses prescribing record-keeping, and provisions compelling supply of information about the loss. Typical requirements are that the insured:

1) Submit declarations, or an application or "proposal," in connection with the insurance coverage sought.
2) Keep records and accounts.
3) Prepare an inventory of merchandise stolen, damaged or destroyed, as well as that not stolen or damaged, stating original cost, cash value and amount of loss claimed.

2. Appendix A, Case 32. 3. *Ibid.*, Case 9.

4. In this connection note Montgomery's comment that the adjustment of businessmen's fire loss claims is aided by the existence of periodic accountants' reports for the claimants. "If the accounts are in good shape, and if the latest inventories have been supervised or tested by independent accountants, the insured are in a materially better position to deal satisfactorily with insurance adjusters." Montgomery, Robert H., *Auditing Theory and Practice* (6th. Ed., New York: Ronald Press Co., 1940), p. 6.

4) Exhibit books, papers and vouchers.

5) Submit a proof of loss.

6) Present himself and his associates for examination under oath.

All of these provide tools for loss claim verification and thus contribute to the solution of the accounting problems which arise in estimating or verifying the amount of loss; proper audit of the insured's claim requires the correlation of financial and other data assembled from many sources. A closer analysis of these claims and their legal background follows.

Declarations, Application or Proposal

Like all other property insurance policies, the issuance of policies on merchandise is based upon oral or written statements, or both, concerning the items at risk, made by, or on behalf of, the prospective insured. Among the simplest of these statements is a brief description of the property, such as is finally incorporated in the policy itself. Somewhat more extended is the series of observations by the insured, generally called Declarations, incorporated in blank spaces provided in the burglary policy. These represent facts needed by the company in determining the desirability of the risk and in computing the premium rate; [5] the information includes indication of the protective devices to be furnished by the insured and data on the burglary loss history of the insured.[6]

Much more comprehensive is the written application. This application, sometimes called a Proposal, is submitted by prospective insureds under various types of policies, among the more common of which is the Jewelers' Block policy. The latter insures jewelers against "all" risks (except those specifically excluded) to their own merchandise and to certain classes of merchandise, belonging to others, left with

5. For an early reference to the Application for Insurance see Griswold, J., *Hand-Book of Adjustments of Loss or Damage by Fire* (3rd. Ed., New York: Insurance Monitor Office, 1894), pp. 7–8.

6. Note that "now in fire insurance the use of an application in detail is for the most part confined to certain farm properties and to exceptional instances. In the cities and towns generally the insurers have come to rely very much upon their own means of examination; and for use in the larger cities they have prepared elaborate and accurate insurance maps and surveys showing the character of the risk involved in every building." Long, Roland H., *Richards on the Law of Insurance* (4th. Ed., New York: Baker Voorhis & Co., 1932), Sec. 15.

them. The application for the Jewelers' Block policy includes designation of the dates and amounts of the two latest inventories (or the amounts of the monthly inventories for the last twelve months), the composition of the most recent one, the average daily balance of other people's goods in the possession of the insured and of the insured's goods in the custody of others, the maximum inventory value during the preceding twelve months, and the loss history of the insured. Information is also supplied concerning the insured's bookkeeping system, including indication of the frequency of detailed inventories.

The information presented in the Declarations or in the Proposal may, by incorporation of a copy or by reference, constitute part of the insurance contract. Where the statements made by the insured are held to be warranties,[7] the insured's failure to comply with the Declarations may cause repudiation of the contract by the insurer.[8] Under the recent revision of the New York Insurance Law, the force of the warranties, and representations,[9] is reduced, the Statute providing that a policy shall not be voided for breach of warranty unless the breach materially increases the risk of loss to which the warranty relates [10] and that a misrepresentation by an insured shall not void the policy unless knowledge of the fact misrepresented would have led to a refusal by the insurer to issue the policy.[11]

The insured's accountant generally assists in assembling inventory figures and consigned goods data for submission in the Proposal for

7. A warranty has been defined as "a term of the insurance contract which prescribes as a condition of the insurer's promise the existence of a fact which diminishes the probability of the occurrence of an insured event, or the non-existence of a fact which increases such probability. . . ." Patterson, Edwin W., *Cases and Materials on the Law of Insurance* (Chicago: The Foundation Press, Inc., 1947), p. 452.

8. See Crobaugh, Clyde J., *Handbook of Insurance* (New York: Prentice-Hall, Inc., 1931), pp. 389–390.

9. Huebner defines a representation as "a written or oral statement made to the insurer relating to facts essential for the latter to know in order to decide whether he will accept the risk, and at what premium. . . ." Huebner, S. S., *Property Insurance* (New York: D. Appleton-Century Co., Inc., 1938), p. 124. Representations relate to past or present facts; they are mere inducements to the insurer to write the coverage. See Patterson, Edwin W., *op. cit.*, p. 533.

10. New York, Ll. 1939, c. 882, sec. 150.

11. *Ibid.*, sec. 149. Even apart from statute, however, substantial truth of representations of fact suffices. Long, Roland H., *Richards on the Law of Insurance, op. cit.*, Sec. 81.

the Jewelers' Block policy. Understatements of the amounts of physical or book inventories, of the maximum inventory during the past twelve months, and of the total of owned or other people's goods on consignment, affect the computation of the premium on the policy and possibly also the attractiveness of the risk to the insurer. Overstatement of these items may tend to result in inflation of the amount of a subsequent claim for loss. In computing the amount of such loss the insurer's accountant generally checks the data contained in the Proposal against the books of account for the purpose of determining the truth and accuracy of the information supplied in the Proposal.

Keeping of Records and Accounts

The requirement of keeping books of account from which the amount of a loss may be computed, is found in mercantile burglary policies, and, in some states, in fire policies in what is known as the "Iron Safe Clause." [12] The mercantile burglary policies usually contain a provision in substantially the following phraseology: "The company shall not be liable . . . unless books and accounts are kept by the assured and are kept in such manner so that the exact amount of the loss can be accurately determined therefrom by the Company." [13] In some southern states fire policies contain an iron safe clause,[14] which requires that the insured have an inventory and a set of books including all purchases, sales and shipments, both for cash and credit, from the date of the inventory. These records must be kept in a fireproof safe at night and when the premises are not open for business, or in a place not exposed to a fire which would destroy the building. The clause is sometimes called the "record warranty clause," [15] and is almost ex-

12. And see 39 American Law Reports Annotated (Rochester, N.Y.: Lawyers Co-operative Publishing Co.), 1443; 62 *ibid.*, 630; 125 *ibid.*, 350.

13. Licht v. N.Y. Indemnity Co. (1928) 250 N.Y. 211, 212; Michler v. New Amsterdam Cas. Co. (1928) 104 N.J.L. 30, 139 Atl. 725, 726; affirmed 104 N.J.L. 663, 141 Atl. 920, no opinion. Also see 5 Appleman, John Alan, *Insurance Law and Practice* (Kansas City, Mo.: Vernon Law Book Co., 1942), Sec. 3024 and fn. 75. The purpose of the rule laid down is to enable the insurer to determine the amount of loss accurately and without dependence upon uncorroborated claims advanced by self-interest.

14. Long, Roland H., *Richards on the Law of Insurance*, *op. cit.*, p. 958.

15. 3 Cooley, Roger W., *Briefs on the Law of Insurance* (2nd. Ed., St. Paul, Minn.: West Publishing Co.), 2795.

clusively applied to stocks of merchandise used in trade or business.[16]

The purpose of these requirements is to permit the insurer to ascertain from the books, and aside from oral evidence, the amount of goods on hand at the time of the loss, but the necessity of assistance in explaining the system, from those who know it, is to be expected.[17] The policy terms are not complied with, however, where the loss can be computed only from memory.[18]

Comparison demonstrates that the iron safe clause in the fire policy is more exacting than the books of account clause in the mercantile burglary policy in the specification as to the details of which record must be kept. But rigid construction is not invoked by the courts:

> The "iron-safe" or "book warranty" clause does not exact any specific system or form of books to be kept by the insured, nor does it require a system of bookkeeping which will conform to the most scientific standards. The purpose of the clause is accomplished when the insured keeps his books in such a manner as to constitute a record of business transactions which a person who is of ordinary intelligence, and who is accustomed to accounts, can understand, and from which he can ascertain the amounts and value of the merchandise at the time of the loss.[19]

The requirements are often defined in language similar to the following:

> Such books do not need to be bound volumes or the modern, scientific loose leaf records utilized by banks and other business concerns where the highest degree of accuracy is required; but they must be of such a character so that by ordinary inspection the actual loss may be determined with a fair degree of accuracy. . . .[20]

16. 5 Couch, George J., *Cyclopedia of Insurance Law* (Rochester, N.Y.: Lawyers Co-operative Publishing Co.), Sec. 1023. For a copy of the Standard Forms Bureau's inventory and iron-safe clause, *see* Mowbray, Albert H., *Insurance* (3rd. Ed., New York: McGraw-Hill Book Co., Inc., 1946), p. 639.

17. N.Y. Underwriters' Fire Ins. Co. v. Malham & Co. (8 Cir. 1928) 25 Fed. (2d) 415; Mississippi Fire Ins. Co. v. Perdue (1928) 217 Ala. 292, 116 So. 142; 62 A.L.R. 628.

18. Aronson v. Maryland Casualty Co. (1926) 222 Mo. A. 490, 494, 280 S.W. 724, 726.

19. 39 A.L.R. 1443. Also see 62 *ibid.*, 630; 125 *ibid.*, 351; 3 Joyce, Joseph A., *Law of Insurance* (2nd. Ed., Rochester, N.Y.: Lawyers Co-operative Publishing Co., 1917), Secs. 2063 t–v.

20. Garten v. General Acc. F. & L. Assur. Corp. (1923) 206 App. Div. (4th. Dept) 154, 158, 200 N.Y. Supp. 546, 548; 5 Appleman, John Alan, *op. cit.*, Sec. 3025, fns. 5, 6.

Where the iron safe clause was involved, recovery was not denied for inadequacy of credit sales records which were a trivial portion of the total sales, although held required where the bulk of the sales were on credit. Where the bulk of the sales were for cash, but totalled many items of small amount, it was held not a bar to recovery, the total of each day's sales being entered in a ledger daily, that the sales slips were not put in the safe, and were destroyed by fire.[21]

The courts take into consideration that the complex systems found in large enterprises are not to be expected in modest ones. No special form of bookkeeping is required.[22] Although the "McCaskey system," described as a "register or loose-leaf system kept in drawers," has been held not a sufficient keeping of books,[23] a bookkeeping system characterized by the Court as primitive, was sanctioned,[24] the court ruling:

> The books kept by the respondent comprise a sales book, order and storage books, ledger, check book, and stubs and numerous bills, representing purchases of merchandise, and an inventory taken on January 1, 1919. On this inventory she described her merchandise by name and lot number, valuing it at cost. Her sales and order books contained entries of merchandise ordered and sold. When articles had to be manufactured, a note was made on a slip of the number of skins used, and these entries were made upon yellow cutting tickets kept by the cutter, and on completion of the garments the tickets were turned over to plaintiff and entries made in the order or sales book as the case might be. The records in the order and sales book were in duplicate, each sheet of which bore a serial number. Plaintiff's ledger contained the names of customers, the amounts charged to them and payments made. She kept no journal for the entry of purchases, but kept the bills in a file. The cutter's slips, it appears, were turned over to defendant's accountant, examined by him and plaintiff says that the accountant entered them in her book and destroyed the tickets. The records of garments left for storage or repairs were contained in a storage book, and the garment identified both by description and the name of the owner. The amounts expended for labor on garments were entered in her check book stubs. The bookkeeping system of plaintiff was rather primitive and did not commend itself to appellant's accountant, still the same accountant was able to adjust the loss sustained by two other insurers from plaintiff's records. . . .

21. Mass. F. & M. Ins. Co. v. Schneider (5 Cir. 1928) 28 Fed. (2d) 658, distinguishing Wright v. Union Ins. Co. (5 Cir. 1926) 13 Fed. (2d) 612, as involving credit sales.

22. Mississippi Fire Ins. Co. v. Perdue, *supra*.

23. See citations 5 Couch, George J., *op. cit.*, Sec. 1032, fn. 9.

24. Lenzner v. National Surety Co. (1924) 209 App. Div. (2d Dept) 464, 204 N.Y. Supp. 796.

The business, that of conducting a small retail business, consisting partly of buying and selling completed garments and partly of buying raw skins and making them up into garments, did not warrant the installation of an elaborate system of accounting. . . .

It is not a bar to recovery, it was held in Nebraska, that the records consist in part of a memorandum book listing purchases, with pencil entries of sales or consignments on approval, and returns handled at times by erasure instead of a new entry.[25] And where the insured is a bailee, for instance one who receives furs for dressing, it is not expected that he will have such records relating to the merchandise as would a dealer in the merchandise.[26]

A case in New Jersey may be regarded as an instance of extreme indulgence to the insured. The plaintiff, operating a one-man lunch room, could neither read nor write, and had no books of account and no bank account. Recovery for a hold-up loss of cash in pocket and in cash register was allowed on the grounds that the insurer was made aware that the business was not of a type where books were kept, and that books of account would not have availed to determine the amount of loss.[27]

The practical considerations recognized in overlooking bookkeeping deficiencies cease when entries are shown to be fictitious even though the purpose was only to deceive creditors or customers,[28] since "Books intended to deceive are not in any true sense books of account." [29]

Recovery will not be denied where, without fault of the insured, the records have become unavailable, as because of theft of the books by the burglars who stole the merchandise, or because of destruction by fire.[30] In a case tried in the Supreme Court of New York, Kings County, where all of the records of the insured had been completely destroyed by fire, he was permitted to prove the amount of his loss

25. T. J. Bruner Co. v. Fidelity & C. Co. (1917) 101 Neb. 825, 166 N.W. 242.

26. Mord v. N.Y. Indemnity Co. (1926) 216 App. Div. (2d Dept) 252, 214 N.Y. Supp. 693. Affirmed, no opinion, 244 N.Y. 589, 155 N.E. 908.

27. Michler v. New Amsterdam Casualty Co. (1928) 104 N.J.L. 30, 139 Atl. 725, affirmed 104 N.J.L. 663, 141 Atl. 920, no opinion.

28. Licht v. N.Y. Indemnity Co. (1928) 250 N.Y. 211.

29. *Ibid.*, at 214.

30. Leiman v. Metropolitan Surety Co. (App. Term, 1st Dept 1908), 111 N.Y. Supp. 536.

by employing the inventory figure contained in a Dun & Bradstreet report dated about a year prior to the loss, supplementing it by the testimony of suppliers of merchandise as to the purchases made by him, and by the testimony of banks as to the deposits made.[31]

In summary, in some cases the Courts have adopted liberal construction of the policy requirements; in others they have been more exacting. A prospective insured whose business or inclination does not adapt itself to maintaining a bookkeeping system is beset with the problems of the law in his jurisdiction and the hazards of litigation.

Inventory

Under the provisions of the New York Standard fire insurance policy [32] the insured is called upon to "furnish a complete inventory of the destroyed, damaged and undamaged property, showing in detail quantities, costs, actual cash value and amount of loss claimed. . . ." [33] The principal object of these provisions is to enable the company to estimate the loss.[34] In a reported case, claim was made for depreciation by reason of water and smoke from a fire across the street from plaintiff's store.[35] The inventory submitted by the insured included several items of a collective character, *viz.*, "a lot of goods in the show window," and "lot of shirt bosoms, h'dfs, fly netting, etc." The defendant claimed that the plaintiff was required to give for each article separately "its quantity and cost, and the amount claimed thereon." The Court pointed out [36] that the company should have asked the insured for further information if there seemed to be a lack of clearness or precision as to any particular lot or class of goods, and ruled that "Substantial performance is enough." But in an Oklahoma Supreme Court case re-

31. Jacoby v. United States Fire Insurance Co., *et al.*, affirmed, no opinion, 244 App. Div. (1st Dept) 781, 280 N.Y. Supp. 790 #4 (1935). Leave for further appeal denied 244 App. Div. (1st Dept) 798, 280 N.Y. Supp. 1016 #3, and 268 N.Y. 723.

32. New York, Ll. 1943, c. 671. Note that this policy, with variations in some instances, has been adopted in over 40 states. See *Fire, Casualty and Surety Bulletins* (Cincinnati, O.: National Underwriter Co., Jan. 1946), pp. Fire Csf. 1–2.

33. Lines 94–97.

34. Long, Roland H., *Richards on the Law of Insurance, op. cit.*, Sec. 286.

35. Boyle v. Hamburg-Bremen Fire Ins. Co. (1895) 169 Pa. 349.

36. *Ibid.*, at pp. 356–357.

ferred to by Sexton,[37] and involving the iron safe clause, the Court held:

An inventory, in the sense used in the insurance policy sued on, means an itemized list or enumeration of property, article by article, and is not intended merely to show the gross value of the property insured, but is for the purpose of enabling the parties to ascertain the different articles which go to make up the entire stock in order that the insurance company may test the correctness of the claim for damage in two respects: First, whether the articles composing the stock belong to the class of property covered by the policy; second, whether the valuation attached to the different items is reasonable.

Sexton reported the Court's finding that the following list of items:

Christmas good job lots Fris	$ 784.39
Clothing just received	1500.00
Racket goods by lot	900.00
Stone J.	145.00
Glass J. and silver	190.00
Enamelware	674.00
Tinware and glass	187.00
Semi-porcelain ware	387.00
Chinaware and silver	847.85

"being part of the inventory of burned stock sued on, is not an inventory such as is contracted for in the iron safe clause."

Burglary policies call for a Proof of Loss containing a complete inventory of all property stolen or damaged, reflecting original cost, actual cash value at the time of the loss, and the amount of loss. The policies also require that the insured, at the company's request, shall furnish a complete inventory of all property not stolen or damaged, indicating the original cost and the actual cash value and quantity.

Exhibition of Books, Papers and Vouchers

A requirement somewhat analogous to those of the "books of account" and "iron safe" clauses is that imposed by the New York Standard fire insurance policy. The insured must

As often as may be reasonably required . . . produce for examination, all books of account, bills, invoices and other vouchers, or certified copies

37. Sexton, William, *Fire Insurance* (San Francisco: The Coast Review, 1915), p. 45 (case citation not supplied by him).

thereof if originals be lost, at such reasonable time and place as may be designated by this Company or its representatives, and shall permit extracts and copies thereof to be made.[38]

Such provision does not make effectiveness of the policy depend upon having books or records of account. It does, however, afford the insurer an opportunity to test the bona fides of the quantity and amount of the loss claim. It also affords the insurer the possibility of a defense under the clause of the policy, if any, that recovery should be barred in the event of fraud or false swearing, if, as the result of inspection of the books, or testimony with regard thereto in an examination, fraud or false swearing be established.

The Proof of Loss

Insurance policies usually require that in the event of loss, a Proof of Loss, which is a formal, written statement of facts concerning the nature, circumstances and amount of loss, be submitted. Within sixty days after the loss, unless such time is extended by the company, the insured must

render . . . a proof of loss, signed and sworn to . . . , stating the knowledge and belief of the insured as to the following: the time and origin of the loss, the interest of the insured and of all others in the property, the actual cash value of each item thereof and the amount of loss thereto, all encumbrances thereon, all other contracts of insurance, whether valid or not, covering any of said property, any changes in the title, use, occupation, location, possession, or exposures of said property since the issuing of . . . policy. . . .[39]

A number of states have enacted legislation which precludes the predicament of untimely compliance. Thus in New York the insurer is required to make written demand that proof of loss be furnished, and to supply suitable forms.[40]

Proof of loss provisions bring about the submission of additional particulars of claims to insurance companies. Moreover, where there is a fraud clause, the requirement of proof of loss operates as a further

38. New York Standard fire insurance policy, *op. cit.*, lines 117–122. But note that in some southern states the iron safe clause is used in supplement to the records clause in the Standard fire policy.

39. See New York Standard fire insurance policy, *op. cit.*, lines 98–107.

40. New York, Ll. 1939, c. 882, sec. 172.

deterrent against unjust presentation of claim. Since it is usually required that the proof of loss be sworn to, a dishonest claimant will also be subject to forfeiture for false swearing and to penal liability. In New York State, in addition to other penal statutes there is a specific statute covering false proofs of loss.[41]

Examination under Oath

Under the terms of the Mercantile Open Stock Burglary Policy, certain all risk policies (e. g., Jewelers' Block policies) and such standard fire insurance policies as the present New York form, the insured is required, at the option of the insurer, to submit to an examination under oath relating to the loss. The requirement that the insured submit to examination as to his claim is a valid provision.[42] The object is to enable the company to ascertain the facts as to its liability, to protect itself against false claims, and to determine whether to defend or adjust the claim.[43] If the insured cannot comply through no fault on his part, he will not suffer forfeiture therefor; he is bound only so far as it lies within his power to comply.[44]

At the examination the insured must give testimony concerning the causes, circumstances, nature and amount of the loss sustained. The company is entitled to know all the circumstances of the insured's purchase of the property insured, including the price paid and the manner of payment.[45] Generally he will be asked to describe the items destroyed or lost, as well as those remaining in either damaged or undamaged form, and will be queried concerning his financial condition and the results of his business operations. Inquiry is made on the latter points for the purpose of detecting the possibility of the existence of moral hazard. Insurance lawyers find the examination useful in developing information of value in the investigation of the loss and the determination of its amount.[46]

Reed states:

41. Penal Law, sec. 1202. 42. 7 Cooley, Roger W., *op. cit.*, 5808.

43. Claflin v. Commonwealth Ins. Co. (1883) 110 U.S. 81.

44. Long, Roland H., *Richards on the Law of Insurance, op. cit.*, Sec. 291.

45. Claflin v. Commonwealth, *supra.*

46. Fox, Robert J., "The Claim—The Proof of Loss—When is Loss Payable," in Insurance Society of New York, *The Fire Insurance Contract* (Indianapolis: Rough Notes Co., 1922), p. 324.

If the loss involves the examination of a set of books, the method of keeping them and the significance of unusual entries may be inquired into. In all such cases, the answers furnish leads which can later be followed and compared with other evidence which will corroborate or contradict them. An insured who makes evasive or contradictory statements when not under oath will be compelled, when later put under examination and held to the record of his answers, to tell a consistent story or make himself ridiculous.

An examination may serve the purpose of committing the insured . . . to statements and figures bearing on the amount of loss. . . .[47]

Thus the formality of the examination under oath, as well as the consequences of wilful false testimony during the examination, tend to dissuade the insured from misstatements and inaccuracies. Wilful false swearing as to a material fact may result in the forfeiture of such claim as the insured may otherwise have had under the policy [48] as well as in the possibility of criminal charges against the insured. It has occurred, therefore, that an insured has foregone filing timely suit because it became clear during the course of the examination under oath that his claim and the testimony presented at the examination were untruthful.[49] However, the "full power" to invoke examination under oath and the related rights enumerated in examination under oath clauses is seldom exercised unless the adjuster feels the claim to be fraudulent.[50]

47. Reed, Prentiss B., *Adjustment of Fire Losses* (1st. Ed., New York: McGraw-Hill Book Co., Inc., 1929), p. 244.

48. See p. 29, *infra*.

49. Appendix A, Case 54. And see *ibid.*, Case 16, where the insured testified at the examination concerning orders received during the period immediately preceding the alleged loss, and introduced numerous invoices, bank statements, and vouchers in support of its claim. Investigation indicated the falsity of the alleged orders and of numerous invoices and vouchers.

50. Mortimer, William M., *Inland Marine Insurance* (New York: Transportation Service Co., 1934), p. 341. But see Farrar, H. M., *Fire Insurance Racket in California* (Los Angeles: 1933), wherein is presented a public adjuster's position on the point.

Chapter III

THE LOSS: PROOF AND EVALUATION FRAUDULENT CLAIMS

Methods of Proof

Having sustained a loss an insured must compute the monetary amount. In the simplest situations the insured can state from memory the quantity, nature and value of the property destroyed. This is not likely in the case of business risks, such as are discussed here, although there are instances where it is possible, such as losses of few items, or in the case of small enterprises containing a very limited variety of property.

Sometimes the circumstance is that the loss is all "in sight." Fire damage may leave all of the property in such condition, though damaged, that it may be identified as to original character and value. The task of computation of the monetary amount of the loss may be more complex when property has been consumed by fire or has been stolen, and the extent of loss can only be determined by computation based upon records of the property that had been on hand. There may be both a stock of merchandise, and equipment consisting of fixtures, machinery, and other items.

As to merchandise, the conventional and obvious process of computing the loss, in other than the simple cases noted, is to start with the total of the latest inventory preceding the loss. To this are added the accessions—net of returns—and the charges for freight and express and for production costs, where applicable. From the aggregate are subtracted the reductions brought about by sale.[1] From the balance, which represents the value of goods on hand before the loss, must be deducted the inventory figure of goods left after the loss. The remainder

1. The figure deducted would be that for cost of sales, i. e., sales minus gross profit.

represents the estimated amount of loss. This procedure is approved by the courts.[2] It is concurred in by writers on accountancy [3] and insurance adjusters.[4]

Calculation is simplified when the insured property is bought and resold, in the same form, unprocessed. However, if the insured is a manufacturer the cost is obviously not merely the purchase price of the material acquired, but, in addition, the cost of the labor of manufacture plus other factors such as rent of the space used, light, heat, power, supervisory expense and other items which enter into the cost of the finished product, ready for sale. These are details which constitute part of the entries in the bookkeeping system of a properly-managed concern. They are items which are entailed in the calculation of the value of merchandise on hand, and which may be properly claimed in a loss adjustment.

With increasing business magnitude, and consequent division of labor, the element of personal knowledge becomes increasingly difficult of supply. Accordingly, the tendency of the courts [5] and of the legislatures [6] is to admit records upon proof that they were made in the regular course of business, contemporaneously with, or at a reasonable time after, the occurrence.

2. Ingersoll v. United Surety Co. (1910) 141 App. Div. (1st Dept) 527, 528, 126 N.Y. Supp. 391, 392; Malin v. Mercantile T.M.I. Co. (1904) 105 Mo. App. 625, 642, 80 S.W. 56, 60.

3. Kester, Roy B., *Advanced Accounting* (4th. Ed., New York: Ronald Press Co., 1946), p. 325; Newlove, George Hillis, Smith, C. Aubrey, and White, John Arch, *Intermediate Accounting* (Boston: D. C. Heath & Co., 1939), pp. 445–446; Finney, H. A., *Principles of Accounting. Advanced* (3rd. Ed., New York: Prentice-Hall, Inc., 1946), pp. 101–103; Eggleston, De Witt Carl, *Auditing Procedure* (2nd. Ed., New York: John Wiley & Sons, Inc., 1935), pp. 389–390. And see Blacklock, Frank, "Suggestions to a Young Accountant on Adjusting a Fire Loss," Business, Vol. 18, No. 5 (May 1898), pp. 296–297, and Spicer, Ernest Evan and Pegler, Ernest C., *Book-Keeping and Accounts* (3rd. Ed., London: H. Foulks Lynch & Co., 1914), pp. 348–349.

4. See Hall, Thrasher, *Adjustment of Losses from the School of Experience* (Indianapolis: Rough Notes Co., 1917), pp. 27–28, and Reed, Prentiss B., *Adjustment of Fire Losses* (1st. Ed., New York: McGraw-Hill Book Co., Inc., 1929), pp. 110–111.

5. The Spica (C.C.A. 2d 1923) 289 Fed. 436, 441–445. See also Litchfield v. City of N.Y. (1926) 244 N.Y. 251, 270–272, 155 N.E. 116, 121–122.

6. 5 Wigmore, John Henry, *Evidence* (3rd. Ed., Boston: Little, Brown & Co., 1940), Sec. 1519, fn. 1, citing, among other statutes, N.Y. Civil Practice Act, § 374a.

Adjusters' Participation

The insured is generally represented in negotiations for settlement by its broker or by an independent or "public" adjuster. Small losses involving merchandise are frequently settled or adjusted by the agent of the company which wrote the business; larger losses, through company representatives, known as adjusters, who may be salaried employees, independent professional adjusters engaged on a fee or per diem basis, or adjustment organizations or bureaus, the latter controlled by the companies.[7] Where losses affect several companies, one or more adjusters are often designated to represent the entire group of companies. Thus, for example, the New York Board of Fire Underwriters, its membership made up of stock companies operating in the metropolitan New York area, has organized a Committee on Losses and Adjustments to represent the member-insurers in all cases where three or more companies are involved, and under certain circumstances where fewer companies are affected. Among the classes of losses referred to the Committee even if only one company is interested, are fraud cases, claims involving warehouses or furs, and those made by contractors on wearing apparel.[8] As losses occur, the Committee selects independent or company adjusters to act for the insurers.

The assignment of adjustment work to individuals and organizations operating independently of the insurance companies is objected to by at least one writer as tending to result in excessive adjustment costs and in unreasonable power for the adjusters.[9]

7. See Patterson, Edwin W., *Cases and Other Materials on the Law of Insurance* (New York: Commerce Clearing House, Inc., 1932), p. 586; Wolfe, F. E., *Principles of Property Insurance* (New York: Thomas Y. Crowell Co., 1930), p. 120; and Buenemann, J. P., "History of Fire Insurance Adjusting," Bulletin of the Insurance Club of Chicago, Inc., Vol. 19, No. 6 (May 1922), pp. 3–8. And note the tabulation of the characteristics of the successful adjuster in Dean, A. F., *Philosophy of Fire Insurance* (Chicago: Edward B. Hatch, 1925), Vol. 1, pp. 18–19; in Steeb, Geo. Velten, *Special Agents and Adjusters Handbook* (2nd. Ed., Chicago: The Spectator Co., 1922), pp. 60–62; and in Reed, Prentiss B., *op. cit.*, pp. 277–279. The duties and procedure of the adjuster are described on pages 5–7 and 10 of the latter work.

8. "Loss Committee of the New York Board," Eastern Underwriter, Vol. 27, No. 30 (July 23, 1926), p. 24.

9. Farrar, H. M., *Fire Insurance Racket in California* (Los Angeles: 1933), *passim*.

Evaluating Merchandise Lost or Damaged

The Standard Fire Policy adopted in New York in 1943 [10] and used, in some cases with minor statutory variations, in over forty states, the District of Columbia, Alaska and Hawaii [11] limits recovery to "actual cash value of the property at the time of loss, but not exceeding the amount which it would cost to repair or replace the property with material of like kind and quality within a reasonable time after such loss. . . ." [12]

Increase or decrease in value since acquisition, including decline through depreciation or obsolescence, is considered in arriving at loss settlements. The causes of depreciation include incomplete assortments, style changes, wear, irregularities in size, and other indications of deterioration in value.[13]

Where the merchandise lost or damaged consists of agricultural products such as grain or cotton, the valuation is set by the market quotations in the market at or nearest the scene of the loss.[14]

Relating to dealers, rather than producers, Bonbright's study revealed no case bearing directly on the point "whether a court would permit a recovery in excess of replacement cost, measured either by full selling price or by some mid-price such as net selling price, when the insured can prove that he has lost an opportunity to make a profit. . . ." As to manufacturers, it was found that in an analogous situation, i. e., where the manufacturer could not produce new goods

10. New York, Ll. 1943, c. 671.

11. *Fire, Casualty and Surety Bulletins* (Cincinnati: National Underwriter Co., Jan. 1946), pp. Fire Csf. 1–2.

12. On the valuation of property damaged or destroyed as a result of fire loss see: Bonbright, James C., *Valuation of Property* (1st. Ed., New York: McGraw-Hill Book Co., Inc., 1937), Vol. 1, Ch. XV; Nelson, Oscar S., *Fire Loss Adjustment Problems in the United States* (Chester, Pa.: 1930), Ch. V; and " 'Actual Cash Value' of Insured Property: The Normal Rules and Their Wartime Modifications," Notes, 91 University of Pennsylvania Law Review and American Law Register, pp. 59–68 (1942), (Philadelphia: University of Pennsylvania Law School).

13. Brown, D. C., "Adjustment of Stock Losses," in Insurance Society of New York, *The Fire Insurance Contract* (Indianapolis: Rough Notes Co., 1922), p. 421.

14. Dargan, J. T., Jr., "Fire Loss Settlements," in Home Insurance Co., *Insurance Adjustments*. Reprint of a series of lectures. Lecture 1 (New York: n.d.) p. 4; and see Kester, Roy B., *op. cit.*, p. 321.

in time to meet his market, the courts have sometimes allowed indemnity in excess of replacement value.[15] Accordingly, the possibility was suggested that a dealer who could demonstrate that replacement in kind did not constitute full indemnity, because he could not replace the goods in time for resale, might receive the same treatment as a manufacturer.[16] This question was squarely presented in a recent case [17] wherein profit was not allowed the insured, a dealer in textile waste who had a contract for resale of his merchandise at such profit.

Under some circumstances greater liberality has been manifested. The practice is reported of paying the insured the sales price of garments purchased at his retail shop but left there by customers as "will calls" (i. e., items paid for in full, or left under deposit) in cases where the items must be obtained from a manufacturer or distributor to replace those lost.[18] It has been suggested that under war and postwar conditions in insurance adjusting the proper indemnity for merchandise which cannot be replaced if destroyed, or which can only be acquired by purchase from a competitor, is the amount the owner would have realized had he sold it.[19]

Fire coverage may be obtained providing indemnification at selling price, reduced by trade discounts and expenses not incurred; [20] likewise, where the market value of a commodity rises because of the removal from the market of the goods destroyed or damaged, insurance is obtainable for the difference between market value at the time of the loss or damage, and actual cost to replace within a designated short period.[21]

15. Bonbright, James C., *op. cit.*, p. 374. And see Hall, Thrasher, *Hall on Insurance Adjustments* (1st. Rev. Ed., Indianapolis: Rough Notes Co., 1916), pp. 30–32; also "The Insurance Man Speaks," Haskins and Sells Bulletin, Vol. XII, No. 6 (June 1929), p. 49.

16. Bonbright, James C., *op. cit.*, pp. 374–375.

17. Crowley *et al.* v. North British & Mercantile Ins. Co., Limited (W.D.S.C., 1947) 70 Fed. Supp. 547.

18. "Insurability of Merchandise at Its Counter Cost," Dry Goods Economist, Vol. 89, No. 5 (November 1934), p. 47.

19. Reed, Prentiss B., "New Factors Enter Loss Adjusting; No Fixed Rule During Wartime." Address delivered before the Risk Research Institute, February 24. Eastern Underwriter, Vol. 44, No. 10 (March 5, 1943), p. 22.

20. Myers, Lawrence S., *Manufacturer and Insurance* (Rev. Ed., Cincinnati: National Underwriter Co., 1940), p. 9.

21. *Ibid.*, p. 23.

Unlike "ordinary fire insurance" where "recovery is limited to actual replacement cost at the time of the fire . . . ," in the inland marine field valued policies are available, the insured contracting in advance upon a fixed basis per unit, or some other type of fixed valuation, to be employed in any loss adjustment.[22] Merchandise may thus be covered in advance of a shipment, upon any reasonable method of valuation. Common methods are the value shown in the reports of shipments, or the sum of the invoice and all charges including prepaid freight, plus ten percent.[23]

Where the coverage is of other than the valued type, it the insured has reduced the inventory valuations of items in the periodic physical inventory sheets to reflect anticipated declines in prices, such reason, as well as the extent of reduction, should be reflected in the inventory sheets. Otherwise, should a loss occur, the reason for the downward revaluation might not be determinable by the insurer and the figures in the inventory sheets might be used as the basis for the loss adjustment.[24]

New problems in valuation arise under the unusual war and post-war business conditions, for example:

> About ten percent of a stock of merchandise was destroyed or badly damaged. The loss involved an item for which insured had pair 25c per pound which when fire occurred could not be replaced for less than 75c per pound.
>
> Insured's loss on that item was the replacement cost of 75c per pound but his insurance was based upon his merchandise account in which it was included at 25c per pound. Adjusters said, "O.K., we will include the item in the loss at 75c per pound but it will be necessary to value your entire stock at present prices to determine the actual value upon which contribution is based and will be applied." [25]

Also requiring consideration are the following: the effect of government limitations of output upon replacement prices; the problem of

22. "Du Bois Urges Assureds to Take Advantage of Inland Marine Forms," Eastern Underwriter, Vol. 36. No. 15 (April 12, 1935), p. 34.

23. Myers, *op. cit.*, p. 153.

24. See Hall, Thrasher, "Adjustment of Fire Losses." Address before 71st Meeting of Central Supply Association, Chicago, June 22, 1916 (n.d.) pp. 2 and 13–16. Also see his *Adjustment of Losses from the School of Experience*, *op. cit.*, pp. 32–33, and see *infra*, p. 64.

25. Erion, Frank L., "War and Defense Measures Raise Adjustment Problems," Journal of American Insurance, Vol. 18, No. 10 (October 1941), p. 22.

valuation where imported articles cannot be replaced; the situation where a large premium above prices quoted for delayed deliveries is required to obtain immediate delivery.[26]

Despite all the difficulties in valuation, which constitute but one phase of the problem of loss adjustment, amicable settlements are generally effected.[27]

The Fraudulent Claim

Insurance policies often contain provision barring any recovery in the event of fraud in the presentation of the claim. The New York Standard fire insurance policy reads:

> This entire policy shall be void if, whether before or after a loss, the insured has wilfully concealed or misrepresented any material fact or circumstance concerning this insurance or the subject thereof, or the interest of the insured therein, or in case of any fraud or false swearing by the insured relating thereto.[28]

Jewelers' Block policies contain a similar clause.

In the absence of such provision, despite exaggeration of claim or indulgence in falsification to improve the plausibility of claim, recovery may be had to the extent of actual damage.[29]

Insurers are so much dependent upon the good faith of their insured that they deem a "fraud clause" essential as a deterrent to dishonesty:

> By the very nature of things, the company is obliged in a marked degree to look to the assured, and to depend very largely upon his statements and representations for the ascertainment of the actual loss sustained; and hence it is required of him, and he has accordingly agreed, under the penalty of a forfeiture of his right to the enforcement of the contract, that he will answer faithfully and truly touching the amount of such loss. . . .[30]

26. *Ibid.*, p. 23, and see Reed, Prentiss B., "War Increases Adjuster's Problems," Weekly Underwriter, Vol. 144, No. 1 (Jan. 4, 1941), p. 38.

27. "Litigation for the purpose of fixing value or loss is a last resort and rarely indulged in." Reed, Prentiss B., "Adjusting and Paying Losses." Chapter II of Fire and Marine Insurance—Course No. 1, Weekly Underwriter, Vol. 148, No. 1 (January 2, 1943), p. 65.

28. New York Standard fire insurance policy, *op. cit.*, lines 1–7. But note that the insurer would be required to prove intentional falsity.

29. ". . . the ordinary rule that fraud occurring after the fixing of liability will not affect the rights of the parties. . . ." 7 Cooley, Roger W., *Briefs on the Law of Insurance* (2nd. Ed., St. Paul, Minn.: West Publishing Co.), 5834.

30. Fowler v. Phoenix Ins. Co. (1899) 35 Ore. 559, 563–564.

Such provision is unnecessary to defeat claim upon the ground that the casualty did not occur, for example, where a burglary is a mere concoction. In fire insurance it is less conceivable but does at times arise. Thus in one claim, a merchant's heating apparatus was defective, the pipes fitting insecurely so that much smoke escaped at times, passing through the store above. A passerby, thinking there was a fire, made report to the authorities. There was no fire, and no water was applied, yet the insured, availing of the fortuity, made claim for soiled obsolete merchandise, and for other stock which he asserted was damaged by smoke accompanying the "fire." He magnified the values, and claimed as well for never-existent property the "remains" of which was a heap of accumulated empty bottles and rubbish. The firemen were ready to testify that there had been no fire. The insured discontinued his suit.

The policy provisions apply alike to written or oral fraudulent statements. As a practical matter it is the written statements, namely, proofs of loss, inventories, examinations provided for by the policies, books, bills, vouchers and other records submitted by the insured which are made the basis of defense.

The various possible frauds are infinite. The most common form in property insurance is a claim of larger loss than occurred, both in physical units and in monetary value. False bills may be presented to evidence purported acquisition of property or higher than actual cost. Records of sales, and consequent diminution of stock on hand, may be suppressed and monetary proceeds may be diverted from disclosed depositaries. Books may be altered for all of these purposes. Inventories used as a starting point, to which are added subsequent acquisitions and from which are deducted subsequent depletions, may be purely fictitious, with magnified quantities and values.

Apart from deception as to actual amount of loss, of which the foregoing is an outline, there may be a false show of opulence. Existence of pecuniary stress evidences possible motive for creating a claim, or padding a fortuitous claim. Proof of financial adversity is admissible [31]

31. Sternfeld v. Park F.I. Co. (1888) 50 Hun 262, 265. See also Demarest v. Westchester F.I. Co. (1932) 234 App. Div. (1st Dept.) 556, 255 N.Y. Supp. 325. There recovery was denied upon finding that the claim was fraudulently made. The Court also commented that the evidence showed that the business had been unsuccessful for a period of years.

and so there is temptation to create an appearance of affluence, to dispel suspicion of wrongful motive.

If fraud be practiced recovery is barred notwithstanding that the loss actually exceeds the amount of insurance. This result is justified by the consideration that the exaggeration is calculated to avoid close scrutiny or investigation.[32] The consequence is the same whether there be a fraud effected, or a fraud attempted,[33] though the insurance company has not actually been deceived or misled to its detriment [34] and though it knew or had opportunity to know, the truth, and therefore could not have been deceived.[35] The general construction is that fraud as to a part of the claim vitiates the whole.[36]

While knowingly making false statements precludes recovery,[37] the courts recognize that a misstatement of loss may be an honest expression of opinion and as such would not prevent recovery.[38]

32. Vaughan v. Virginia F. & M. Ins. Co. (1904) 102 Va. 541, 545, 46 S.E. 692.

33. Claflin v. Commonwealth Ins. Co. (1883) 110 U.S. 81.

34. Fowler v. Phoenix Ins. Co., *op. cit.*, 559.

35. Columbian Ins. Co. v. Modern Laundry (8 Cir. 1921) 277 Fed. 355.

36. Long, Roland H., *Richards on the Law of Insurance* (4th. Ed., New York: Baker Voorhis & Co., 1932), Sec. 233, p. 367; 7 Cooley, Roger W., *op. cit.*, 5858; 1 Clement, George A., *Fire Insurance* (New York: Baker Voorhis & Co., 1905), 285.

37. Orenstein v. Star Ins. Co. of America (4 Cir. 1926) 10 Fed. (2d) 754, 757.

38. 7 Cooley, Roger W., *op. cit.*, 5852.

Chapter IV

MORAL HAZARD: MOTIVE FOR FRAUDULENT CLAIM

Introduction; Definition of Moral Hazard

The newspapers have frequently carried headlines like "Faces Court as Arsonist. Officer of Shirt Company Accused of Setting Fire in Factory."[1] and "Bares Arson Racket at $3,000 a Blaze. Originator of Idea Confesses to Tuttle His $500,000 'Jobs of Complete Destruction.' "[2]

In reviewing books of account in loss claims, the possible existence of moral hazard, which might tend to induce the making of fraudulent claim, must be considered. Moral hazard relating to insurance may be defined as "the chance that the insured will secretly and designedly cause or enhance the loss";[3] it exists whenever he is in position to secure economic or other gain through the destruction or loss of his property,[4] and conversely, where the insurance coverage is less than the value of the property at risk, the presumption is that the insured will exercise unusual care to prevent the occurrence of a loss.[5] Where the financial condition of the insured is very poor, or operating results have been unsatisfactory over a long period of time, or the inventory is obsolete, or a long-term lease is held in a vicinity which has become undesirable, the temptation may exist to plan a fraudulent loss

1. *New York Times*, January 12, 1932, 13:2.
2. *Ibid.*, March 17, 1930, 1:5.
3. Patterson, Edwin W., *Essentials of Insurance Law* (1st. Ed., New York: McGraw-Hill Book Co., Inc., 1935), p. 291.
4. Steinmetz, Richard C., "What about the Moral Hazard?" Weekly Underwriter, Vol. 141, No. 23 (December 2, 1939), p. 1161.
5. Gibson, J. D., "Excessive Insurance Brings High Loss Ratio and Is Unfair to Companies and Policyholders," Insurance Field, Fire-Casualty Edition, Vol. 61, No. 28 (April 7, 1932), p. 6.

and make claim against the insurer. Where a loss has actually occurred, inflated claim might be made.[6]

Proportion of Losses Attributable to Moral Hazard

Estimates of the proportion of losses attributable to moral hazard vary widely. For fires, for example, Rodda [7] puts the figure at between five and ten percent, the latter for depression years, and Hardy [8] estimates the proportion of incendiary fires at ten percent. But other writers set the figure much higher, Wolfe [9] pointing out that the estimates have ranged from ten to thirty-five percent, and, again, Cabot [10] reporting estimates of from ten to fifty percent of the fire loss total.

Exaggeration of Loss

Although few insureds would initiate the casualty against whose occurrence they are covered, some who have sustained losses are not unwilling to exaggerate the extent of loss.[11] But exaggeration may be inadvertent:

Many times an assured, because of his lack of knowledge, will be accused of attempting fraud because he includes some items in a loss about which he is in doubt. Rather than display his shortcomings and particularly if there

6. See Magee, John H., *General Insurance* (Rev. Ed., Chicago: Richard D. Irwin, Inc., 1942), pp. 94–95: "Because it simplifies the work for the underwriter, the method of objective analysis, which carries with it the assumption that moral hazard increases with the advent of motive, is widely accepted. Even those underwriters who know that normal hazard does not of necessity make its appearance with the development of a situation that makes fraud profitable, nevertheless, so far as the insured is concerned, arrive at the same position by cancelling on the ground of taking no chances."

7. Rodda, William H., "Bad Business Conditions and Incendiarism," Weekly Underwriter, Vol. 127, No. 14 (October 1, 1932), p. 648.

8. Hardy, Charles O., *Risk and Risk Bearing* (Rev. Ed., Chicago: University of Chicago Press, 1931), p. 301, fn. 1.

9. Wolfe, F. E., *Principles of Property Insurance* (New York: Thomas Y. Crowell Co., 1930), p. 92.

10. Cabot, Edgar V., "Two Eras of Arson for Insurance," Journal of American Insurance, Vol. 14, No. 4 (April 1937), p. 20.

11. Huebner, S. S., *Property Insurance* (New York: D. Appleton-Century Co., Inc., 1938), p. 155, and Dominge, Charles C. and Lincoln, Walter O., *Fire Insurance Inspection and Underwriting* (5th. Ed., Philadelphia: The Spectator, 1939), pp. 614–615.

is a serious doubt in his mind, he may try to camouflage the item. and if it is discovered it casts suspicion on the entire loss.[12]

Over-Insurance

"Over-insurance leads to fraud, full insurance to carelessness, and even partial insurance to some diminution of watchfulness . . ."; [13] underwriters' efforts at limiting coverage to the maximum value of the merchandise likely to be at risk are therefore understandable.[14]

Valued policies, i. e., those which contain agreements, made in advance, on the amounts to be paid in case of loss or destruction of the objects at risk, have been said to violate the principle of indemnity since settlement is based on the value at the time of placing the insurance, rather than at the time of loss. Objection is made that such policies thus tend to foster over-insurance. However, in cases where a high degree of skill in appraisal is required, e. g., in placing a value upon art objects, manuscripts, and collections of rare postage stamps or coins, there is general agreement upon the desirability of this type of coverage. The more common type of merchandise, or stock in trade, are not covered under such policies.

Arson

"Arson is the wilful, felonious, and malicious burning of property with the intent of destruction." [15] Briefly stated, the underlying motives may be to collect fire insurance; conceal a previous crime; destroy books, records or other incriminating evidence; for revenge, intimidation, racketeering, extortion and business rivalry.[16]

12. Sullivan, W. A., "Settlement of Losses Without Controversy." Paper before American Management Association, Insurance Conference, New York, May 15, 1933. *American Management Series, Insurance 15* (New York: The Association, 1933), p. 34.

13. Willett, Allan H., *Economic Theory of Risk and Insurance,* Columbia University, Faculty of Political Science. Studies in History, Economics and Public Law, Vol. 14, No. 2 (New York: Columbia University Press, 1901), p. 114.

14. But note Manes's comment: "Many insurance contracts make it relatively easy to obtain unjust profits. Often it is difficult to avoid over insurance, that is, insurance on amounts higher than the real value of the property covered. . . ." Manes, Alfred, "Insurance Crimes," Journal of Criminal Law and Criminology, Vol. XXXV, No. 1 (May–June 1944), p. 34.

15. Crobaugh, Clyde J., *Handbook of Insurance* (New York: Prentice-Hall, Inc., 1931), p. 92.

16. New York City Fire Department. Wall Exhibit, New York City Building, World's Fair of 1939, Flushing, New York.

At common law, arson was the wilful or malicious burning of the property of another. Modern statutes tend to extend the definition to the burning of one's own property, and to create a related crime, that of burning with the intent to defraud an insurer.[17] The discussion which follows relates mainly to the latter class. The temptation to burn a stock of merchandise is great in cases where the character of the insured is weak and financial pressure strong.

The most common cause of arson is over-insurance: there seems to be no more likely cause of fire than "the friction between a two-thousand-dollar stock of goods and a five-thousand-dollar policy of insurance!" [18]

Steinmetz tabulates in detail possible causes of commission of arson to defraud:

(a) Owner no longer wants property and is unable to dispose of it otherwise.
(b) Liquidate a business enterprise.
(c) Overstock inventory.
(d) Obsolete merchandise.
(e) Seasonable business at an end.
(f) Failure to receive expected orders.
(g) Cancellation of orders.
(h) Poor business conditions in general.
(i) Unable to collect accounts receivable.
(j) Urgent need for ready cash.
(k) Settle an estate.
(l) Sale of land with buildings to be removed before a certain date.
(m) Desire to move from a certain locality.
(n) Business quarters outgrown.
(o) Dissolve a partnership.

17. See Michael, Jerome and Wechsler, Herbert, *Criminal Law and Its Administration* (Chicago: The Foundation Press, Inc., 1940), pp. 351–361.

18. Campbell, Alexander Colin, *Insurance and Crime* (New York and London: G. P. Putnam's Sons, 1902), p. 121. To the same effect: Kent, George, "Trail of the Torch," *Collier's,* Vol. 105, No. 10 (March 9, 1940), p. 46; Hall, Norman, *Elements of Fire Insurance Practice* (Manchester: "Policy-Holder" Journal Co., Ltd., 1928), pp. 40–41; and Hall, Thrasher, *Hall on Insurance Adjustments* (1st. Rev. Ed., Indianapolis: Rough Notes Co., 1916), p. 210. But note the novel reason for attempting arson cited in a recent annual report to the National Board of Fire Underwriters by its Committee on Incendiarism and Arson. The insured was ". . . having trouble making out his returns for sales taxes, income taxes, social security and the many other taxes imposed upon him." *Proceedings of 73rd Annual Meeting of the National Board of Fire Underwriters* (New York: 1939), p. 142.

(p) Assured has been able to obtain too much insurance.
(q) Unable to meet financial obligations.
  (1) Employees' wages.
  (2) Mortgage interest.
  (3) Taxes.
  (4) Rent.
  (5) Debts—Accounts past due.
  (6) Unable to pay fire insurance premium.
(r) Fire started by a professional arsonist. The assured receives direct benefit and the "torch" burns for a livelihood.
(s) Where there is doubt as to the value of [sic] the productivity of the property.
(t) Where the building has been condemned or [is] apt to be because of unsanitary conditions.
(u) New business ventures which have not demonstrated their earning power.[19]

Fraudulent fire claims are more common on contents losses than building losses[20] because fires affecting the former are much less likely to leave traces of damaged goods from which original values may be determined.

Fires have been set to conceal thefts, dishonest disposal of goods or other causes of merchandise shortages, in the hope that it would be impossible to discover the loss attributable to them.[21] But the arsonists are rarely as skillful in concealing the motive for the fire as in setting it; frequently the plot is revealed once the motive is uncovered.[22]

Where the intent is to defraud the insurer the records may display a more satisfactory financial condition at the date of the loss than is revealed by reconstruction of condition based upon the debris remaining after the fire.[23]

Discovery of claim inflation through inclusion of merchandise shipped from the insured's premises before the loss, but not so re-

19. Steinmetz, Richard C., *op. cit.*, p. 1163.

20. See Daly, C. L., "Loss Adjustments." Lecture before Insurance Institute of Winnipeg. Fire Course, I. March 3, 1937 (unpublished), p. 13.

21. See Reed, Prentiss B., "Moral Hazard of Custodians," Ounce of Prevention, Vol. 2, No. 7 (April 1924), pp. 1 and 3; and see Hall, Norman, *op. cit.*, p. 41.

22. Cabot, Edgar V., "Arson—An Ancient Art—Ever New," Journal of American Insurance, Vol. 13, No. 11 (November 1936), p. 13.

23. See Duncan, John C., "Property Accounting for Fire Losses," Journal of Accountancy, Vol. 5, No. 6 (April 1908), p. 446.

corded in the books of account, might cast suspicion on the honesty of the entire claim, the omissions indicating possible planning of the loss. Chief Fire Marshal Brophy of New York City cites the case of a bonded warehouse which was set afire after the surreptitious removal of merchandise on which duty had not as yet been paid, claim being thereafter made that the goods had been consumed in the fire.[24] Claim inflation might also result from the situation where the insured's lease provides for increased rentals as the volume of business increases, incentive existing to omit sales from the records for the purpose of reducing the rent. In the event of loss, claim—if taken from the records—would include merchandise sold but omitted from the books.

Insurance annals are replete with cases where poor financial condition or the desire to conceal evidence of the occurrence of theft have created moral hazard. In fraudulent losses it is generally difficult to verify the amount of the loss claim from the records. For example, a fire occurred at the premises of a flour and feed merchant who also sold consigned merchandise on a commission basis. An inventory, taken after the fire, revealed considerable disparity between the quantity of goods in sight after the loss and what should have been there, based on the books. No fictitious entries were found on the records. The adjuster settled the loss; later it appeared that the insured had probably sold much of the consigned merchandise without making record of the sales, and, expecting a visit from a representative of the consignor, had decided to destroy the means of discovery of the dishonesty.[25]

Confessions by members of an arson ring reveal a similarity of pattern in the plans to defraud insurers, the procedure being

> the purchasing of goods on credit, their subsequent removal from the insured premises, the concealment of moneys realized on such surreptitious sales, and then setting on fire of the premises after they had been denuded of all valuable merchandise and where nothing but worthless junk was left in the premises, the identity of which it was hoped to destroy by means of a fire, that was supposed to be . . . a "total destruction job." [26]

24. Brophy, Thomas P., "The Arson Racket." Lecture at 43d Annual Convention of International Association of Chiefs of Police, Police Journal, Vol. 13, No. 2 (April–June 1940), pp. 225–226.

25. Case reported in Reed, Prentiss B., *op. cit.*, p. 1.

26. "Firebug's Arrest Hits Arson Racket," Eastern Underwriter, Vol. 31, No. 12 (March 21, 1930), p. 32.

Business Depression as a Factor

Authorities differ upon the relation between periods of business depression and increases in fire losses. Hardy [27] finds little to support the theory that losses rise as a result of the decline in property value and the increase in financial pressure; and Goble [28] cites Patterson to the effect that fraudulent fires are responsible for only a small part of the annual fire loss in the United States. However, a study of business conditions and fire losses in Boston covering a period of thirty years resulted in the conclusion that "Boston's fire losses are high [relatively] when business is depressed, and *vice versa* . . .";[29] and Bradstreet's Pacific coast superintendent offered the opinion that the moral hazard in fire insurance "advances or recedes with the record of commercial failures. . . ." [30] The experience of Phillips, now Un-

27. Hardy, Charles O., *op. cit.*, p. 301.

28. Goble, George W., "Proposed Revision of the Standard Fire Insurance Policy with Special Reference to Hazard Clauses," Journal of American Association of University Teachers of Insurance, Vol. 4, No. 1 (March 1937), p. 49.

29. Boston. Mayor's Committee on Fire Insurance Rates, *Report on the Problem of Fire Waste and Insurance Rates in the City of Boston* (Boston: 1929), p. 127.

30. Stanton, John C., "Moral Hazard," *Proceedings of the Fiftieth Annual Meeting of the Fire Underwriters' Association of the Pacific* (1926) p. 92. And note the announcement by an insurance publication of a prospective "guide to possible moral hazard conditions," which was to be a tabulation prepared by a credit information bureau, showing style changes in specific industries, business declines, shifts in consumer demand and employment opportunities, and similar conditions likely to produce moral hazard. "Current Conditions That Tend to Create Moral Hazard Fires," American Insurance Digest and Insurance Monitor, Vol. 72, No. 1 (January 5, 1924), p. 9. Note also: "The moral hazard which the fire insurance people feared at the outset of 1942 failed to develop among small business men to any appreciable extent, W. C. Perry, manager of the Chicago office of the Retail Credit Co. said at a meeting of the Association of Fire Insurance Examiners of Chicago. . . .

"Quite a number of small businesses were forced out in 1942, including some auto dealers and approximately 33,000 food stores. However, many of the food stores and other businesses closed because the merchants went into defense plants, because of a shortage of merchandise, and because of entering armed service. The significant point here is the individuals involved were not forced to liquidate in the usual sense. They have been able to replace the income that previously came to them through their businesses. This is true also of filling station operators, many of whom were mechanically trained and could engage in war work. They have replaced previous income, perhaps have done better. Consequently there has been little moral hazard." "Moral Hazard Not Serious Fire Insurance Factor Now," National Underwriter, Vol. 47, No. 4 (January 28, 1943), p. 3.

derwriting Credit Manager of the Committee on Losses and Adjustments of the New York Board of Fire Underwriters, in earlier work as credit manager of a textile mill, was somewhat similar: "We soon became accustomed to accept a fire as the logical outcome in situations where the debtor's assets were frozen. . . ." [31]

Observations to substantially the same effect are common in the popular periodicals, for example, in an article about Thomas P. Brophy, Chief Fire Marshal of the City of New York, in the *New Yorker:*

If there has been a suspicious-looking fire in the garment district, Brophy is extremely likely to know whether the firm whose stock was destroyed had been doing well, or whether it was in such bad shape that its proprietors were desperate. He knows a good deal about business conditions in general—how things are going with manufacturers of women's hats, for instance, and which of the warehouses down on the waterfront are packed with perishable goods that owners will never be able to sell. . . .[32]

Following a study of commodity prices and the ratio of net fire, lightning, marine and inland marine losses incurred to net premiums written for the period 1913 to 1917, as well as a study of the corresponding relationship for fire and lightning premiums for the period 1918 to 1932, one expert found that "with an astounding degree of fidelity the loss ratio has gone up as commodity prices decreased, and has gone down as commodity prices rose. . . ." [33]

31. Phillips, George H., "Underwriting from a Credit Standpoint." Insurance Society of New York. Howe Readings in Insurance No. 14. Three Special Lectures. (New York: The Society, 1932), p. 33.

32. McKelway, St. Clair, "Profiles. Firebug-Catcher—1," New Yorker, Vol. XI, No. 49 (January 18, 1936), pp. 20–21.

33. "Shallcross Comments as to Sixty-Day Loss Payment Rule," National Underwriter, Vol. 37, No. 35 (August 31, 1933), p. 9. Note also: ". . . The abnormally high losses of the depression years have usually been attributed to the so-called 'moral hazard,' or, to use a harsher and franker word, arson. . . ." Van Deusen, E. A., "Bank and Insurance Stocks. This Week—Insurance Stocks," Commercial and Financial Chronicle, Vol. 160, No. 4328 (October 26, 1944), p. 1804. And note the National Board of Fire Underwriters' observation, in commenting that the end of the war did not bring about any perceptible reduction in the demand for commodities nor for practically all types of buildings: "Prices of personal property and of buildings have continued . . . upward. Consequently, such fires as have had profit for a motive have been confined to cases where the circumstances were very unusual and have been very few in number." Report of Committee on Incendiarism and Arson. *Proceedings of Eightieth Annual Meeting of National Board of Fire Underwriters* (New York: 1946), p. 138.

Case Studies

The case studies presented in Exhibit A include numerous specific situations where moral hazard existed and where the loss claims were either fraudulent or overstated, or attempt was made to establish a false impression of financial stability or successful operating results. For illustrations, note the denial by alleged customers of an insured that they had placed large orders; [34] the obvious alteration of purchase bills [35] including one bearing an alleged date which was about a year after the supplier had gone out of business, [36] the claims for loss of goods stolen on an earlier occasion [37] and for damage to merchandise manufactured during the preceding season for an unsuccessful, speculative venture, but represented, after the loss, as new merchandise; [38] the uncommon circumstance that expensive merchandise, in stock for several years, had been sold on the day before the hold-up of the insured's store, the proceeds of the sales being lost in the hold-up; [39] the coincidence of poor financial condition and false and missing entries; [40] the unusually large alleged purchases of material by a customer despite the latter's own low business volume [41] and, in the same case, the unusual haste of the seller, the insured, in arranging to effect delivery of a large order as a single shipment; the report to the insurer of large net profits and a large net worth when in actuality losses had been sustained and the net worth was much lower; [42] excessive claims as to the amount of the inventory on hand at the time of the loss; [43] and the glaring falsification of an inventory listing.[44]

Insureds' adjusters observe that a business which has been in existence for a long period, particularly at a single address, has generally achieved such excellent reputation as to render improbable exaggeration of claim. However, this is not always true.[45]

Investigation of Insured's Background, Financial Condition and Operating Results

Careful investigation by the insurer, at the time of application for insurance, of the value of the property to be covered and the back-

34. Appendix A, Case 16.
35. *Ibid.*, Cases 7 and 16.
36. *Ibid.*, Case 45.
37. *Ibid.*, Case 32.
38. *Ibid.*, Case 54.
39. *Ibid.*, Case 22.
40. *Ibid.*, Case 1.
41. *Ibid.*, Case 8.
42. *Ibid.*, Case 12.
43. *Ibid.*, Cases 4 and 14.
44. *Ibid.*, Case 20.
45. See *ibid.*, Cases 27 and 43 where claims were made by such firms for greater quantities and values than were proper.

ground, business history and financial condition of the insured, as well as painstaking attention to the details of adjustment following the occurrence of the loss and the making of the claim, are likely to result in a reduction in the number of inflated and otherwise fraudulent claims.[46]

Where there is doubt about the moral hazard of a risk offered for coverage, and insufficient data concerning the prospective insured are available through the insurance company's representatives, mercantile credit agencies can generally be counted on to supply information about financial condition, as well as material such as this: resources, antecedents and reputation; business experience; merchandising ability; buying facilities; prospects; insurance claim collection history; other matter related to character and reputation.[47] Among the better-known agencies are Dun and Bradstreet, Inc., the Hooper Holmes Bureau, Inc., and the Retail Credit Company.[48]

Estimate of the moral hazard risk may on occasion be facilitated by inspection of the insured's financial statements. Foulke, of Dun and Bradstreet, Inc., reports on the fire loss sustained by a wholesale and retail plumbing supply house.[49] Analysis of the company's financial statements was made after the loss. The balance sheet, dated several weeks before the fire, indicated current assets of $76,100.00, including accounts and notes receivable of $41,900.00 and inventory of $32,-400.00. Current liabilities totalled $39,600.00, and tangible net worth,

46. And see Campbell, Alexander Colin, *op. cit.*, p. 151, citing an article in the Insurance Monitor, dated 1876. Also note the situation where a firm made claim for the loss of diamonds and jewelry stolen from its salesman. A mercantile agency report, obtained during the review of the claim, disclosed that the history of one of the principals included a conviction for arson.

47. See Rupprecht, Charles F., *Modern Fire Underwriter* (Philadelphia: The Spectator, 1940), p. 11A. Also see Thistle, Edward B., "Underwriting Burglary and Theft Risks," in *Lectures on Insurance. Intermediate Course. Casualty and Surety* (New York: Underwriter Printing and Publishing Co., 1923), p. 74. Likewise of interest is "Stewart Gives Tips on Moral Hazard Risks," Eastern Underwriter, Vol. 31, No. 43 (October 10, 1930), p. 29.

48. The scope of the Retail Credit Company examinations is discussed in several of its publications, *viz., Inspector's Handbook. Fire Insurance Underwriting and Reporting* (Atlanta: Retail Credit Co., 1941), Chapter II; *Inspector's Handbook. Burglary Insurance Underwriting and Reporting* (Rev. Ed., Atlanta: Retail Credit Co., 1934), Chapter V; *Character Inspection Services for Fire Insurance Companies* (Atlanta: Retail Credit Co., undated), pp. 20–23.

49. Foulke, Roy A., *Relativity of the Moral Hazard* (New York: Dun & Bradstreet, Inc., 1940), pp. 11–13.

$54,000.00. The gross income for the year was $84,000.00, made up of merchandise billed at $44,000.00 and services at $40,000.00. The inventory, Foulke observes, was too large, considering the total sales, and probably included much outmoded or otherwise unsalable merchandise. The receivables, representing about one-half the gross income for the year, doubtless included a large proportion of uncollectible items.

In recent years the Information Bureau of the Committee on Losses and Adjustments of the New York Board of Fire Underwriters has obtained from the specialized credit reporting bureaus for the principal industries in the metropolitan New York area, copies of reports issued by the agencies on individual business enterprises in the district.[50] The Bureau reviews and summarizes the information for the purpose of apprizing the underwriters of the undesirable factors reported in the trade concerning the firms. When insurance companies inquire about prospective insureds at the Bureau, but credit reports are either unavailable or incomplete, the Bureau submits directly to the prospective insureds a questionnaire concerning financial condition, business history, and the books and records maintained. The data received are analyzed in fashion similar to those obtained from the trade credit associations. A specimen questionnaire is presented as Appendix E of this volume.[51]

Inspection

Companies insuring merchandise against burglary generally inspect the place where the goods are to be kept. The efficiency and economy of a central burglary inspection service has been suggested.[52] But some companies find their own inspection facilities adequate and others prefer to use independent credit or survey bureaus. Fire companies

50. See Phillips, George H., *op. cit.*, pp. 43–44.

51. On the work of the Board also see "W. A. Riordan Describes Vital Work of New York Board Loss Committee," Eastern Underwriter, Vol. 31, No. 48 (November 7, 1930), p. 32, and "Benefit Is Seen in Credit Work," National Underwriter, Vol. 38, No. 16 (April 19, 1934), pp. 5 and 40. In the latter reference is also made to the departments maintained by individual companies or groups of companies to study the moral hazard risk on business submitted.

52. See "Central Burglary Bureau Now Being Advocated," National Underwriter, Vol. 35, No. 48 (November 26, 1931), p. 35.

are reluctant to inspect the property of all prospective policy-holders because of the cost.[53]

A Committee on Fire Prevention and Insurance of the Merchants Association of New York has opposed the imposition of a requirement that all property be inspected before fire insurance coverage is issued, on the grounds that it would be inconvenient to merchants, manufacturers, bankers and others, and that it would not tend to prevent incendiary fires nor to insure the existence at the time of the loss, of the values on hand when the inspection took place.[54]

The Committee has also disapproved a recommendation by the Fire Department of New York City that inspection of the books of suspected (*sic*) firms and individuals who are applying for insurance be made by the Department to ascertain the applicant's financial condition.[55]

Insured's Ability to Comply with Policy Conditions

It is important that the insurer determine, before writing the coverage, whether the insured will be able to comply with the provision in the policy—where such provision exists, e. g., in the mercantile burglary policy—requiring the keeping of records from which the amount of the loss may be accurately determined.[56] However, "especially in the case of movable property, all reliance upon estimates of

53. McKelway, St. Clair, *op. cit.*, p. 22.

54. Merchants Association of New York, *Report of Committee on Fire Prevention and Insurance on Incendiarism* (New York: The Association, 1913), p. 8. And to the same effect, see Moore, Francis C., *Fire Insurance and How to Build* (New York: Baker & Taylor Co., 1903), pp. 50–53. Where inspection of the physical hazard is undertaken, however, it has been suggested that it be expanded to include consideration of the quantity, quality and pricing of merchandise on hand, to reduce the risk of moral hazard attributable to the accumulation of excessive or over-priced inventories. "Inspection Basis Changing," Weekly Underwriter, Vol. 106, No. 19 (May 13, 1922), pp. 968–969. Note also the comment by the head of an independent inspection company: "The first thing we teach our inspectors . . . is . . . to inspect the assured first. It is . . . important to know that he understands his business, that he has been successful, has met his obligations and is dependable. . . ." "Vlachos Views Fire Underwriting Problems in N.Y. City after War," Eastern Underwriter, Vol. 45, No. 16 (April 21, 1944), p. 22.

55. Merchants Association of New York, *op. cit.*, pp. 10–11.

56. See "Underwriting Mercantile Open Stock Insurance," Eastern Underwriter, Vol. 31, No. 10 (March 7, 1930), p. 44. And see *supra*, p. 14.

value, and attempts to restrict insurance to a safe figure, count for little as compared with intelligent estimates of the character of the assured. . . ."[57]

Apparel Manufacturers' Losses

Because of the frequency of occurrence of fire losses at the premises of contractors engaged in manufacturing men's, women's and children's apparel, and "the way in which the relations between contractor and manufacturer ramify and the almost endless ways in which fraud may be perpetrated upon various insurers . . . by collusion . . ." since 1923 such losses occurring in the New York metropolitan area, insured by any company which is a member of the New York Board of Fire Underwriters, have been adjusted under the supervision of the Committee on Losses and Adjustments of the Board, the Committee designating the adjuster to represent all the member-companies involved.[58]

Goods of High Value; Off-Season Losses

Where a loss involves merchandise of high unit value and small bulk, for example, diamonds or diamond rings, and there is a suspicion of fraud, the adjuster and accountant will generally find it useful to consider factors—including a number referred to above—which may affect the bona fides of the loss but which are not directly related to it, for example, the financial position of the insured, the results of business operations, and the loss history and police record, if any. Some of this information is obtainable readily from the reports of mercantile credit agencies.[59]

As would be expected, fires (and burglaries) which take place during the off-season periods of a business are more likely to be investigated at length than those which occur during the busy season. Losses which

57. Moore, Francis C., *op. cit.*, p. 50.

58. "Apparel Contractors' Committee Reports," Eastern Underwriter, Vol. 24, No. 17 (April 27, 1923), p. 17; "New York Board's New Way to Handle Apparel Losses," *ibid.*, pp. 1 and 18.

59. See Faulkner, J. M., "Adjustment of Inland Marine Losses Referring Chiefly to Personal Property and the Transportation Classes," in Scott, L. J., and Faulkner, J. M., *Lectures on Insurance* (New York: Insurance Institute of America, Inc., 1936), pp. 43–44.

follow extreme changes in fashion in an industry, for example, in the millinery business, are looked upon with suspicion.[60]

Investigation of Losses

Beard has suggested that in investigating questionable fires and total fires: "The first step . . . should be to determine the financial condition of the insured and the value of the property, utility value. The fire may not appear suspicious unless and until this phase of the loss has been investigated." [61] This is likewise true of mercantile burglary [62] and other merchandise losses. Thus where the loss appears to have taken place under questionable circumstances, examination should be made of the insured's balance sheet as of the date of the loss, and of his profit and loss or operating statements covering a period of several years preceding the loss, including the interval between the end of the previous fiscal period and the date of the loss. The conditions displayed by these statements may assist the adjuster in deciding upon the likelihood that the casualty was planned.[63]

The questions to be addressed the insured during the adjustment of a loss vary from case to case, but in the main are designed to bring out information which will assist the adjuster in deciding upon the validity of the claim. Over half a century ago Griswold presented this list of questions for a fire loss adjuster:

First: At what hour of the day or night did it [the fire] occur? When first discovered? By whom? In what part of the premises? Accessible or remote? Under what circumstances?

60. See Underwriter, "The Moral Hazard," Spectator, Vol. CXXVI, No. 10, (March 5, 1931), pp. 10–11. A series of incidents concerning fraudulent fires in the apparel industry is found in Vlachos, William, *Moral Hazard* (2nd. Ed., Philadelphia: Vlachos & Co., 1929).

61. Beard, Roy C., *"Investigation and Adjustment of Questionable Fires," Proceedings and Papers of Thirty-sixth Annual Convention of the National Association of Mutual Insurance Companies* (Chicago: 1931), p. 82.

62. See Rees, Fred H., *Investigators and Adjusters Handbook* (2nd. Ed., Chicago: The Spectator Co., 1926), pp. 242–243.

63. See Mayer, F. J. Alex, "Scientific Bookkeeping and the Adjustment of Book Losses, With and Without Books," *Proceedings of Twenty-ninth Annual Meeting of the Fire Underwriters' Association of the Pacific* (1905), p. 73, where the extreme position is taken that the statement of financial condition of the insured at the time of the loss should be as important an item to be submitted to the companies as the statement of the loss claim itself.

Second: As to the insured and his possible agency in the fire. His moral character, standing, and business circumstances should be weighed; his antecedents should be inquired into. Was he at home or absent at the time of the fire? Has he been burned out before? Was he insured? Did he recover the insurance? Any suspicious circumstances attending such fire? Did he lose anything above the insurance? Is he now involved, or over-loaded with unsalable stock on a falling market? Is he owner of the property, or is it leased—in litigation or unproductive? Has he made any attempts to sell? *Is he over-insured?* In fine, do circumstances indicate, in any way, that it would be an object for him to sell to the underwriters?

Third: Attendant circumstances: Do they indicate anything suspicious? Is incendiarism apparent? Are there grounds for any suspicion against personal enemies? Any cause for spontaneous combustion or explosion about the premises? Had the premises been regarded as a nuisance from any cause by the neighborhood? Are there indications of carelessness or design on the part of anyone? Any threats? Opportunity for theft by employees, or to cover up defalcations? [64]

Sixty-Day Rule

It has been suggested that delay in the payment of insurance loss claims is likely to reduce the number of fraudulent claims. The theory is that an arsonist, or one who submitted a fraudulent claim, would be deterred from the commission of such crime by the knowledge that the anticipated reward for his pains would be delayed, hence the rule requiring delay in the payment of claims until the expiration of a given number of days after they were filed. A rule deferring payment for sixty days was adopted in New York and other states in 1933 during the bank emergency, and was subsequently continued for the purpose of discouraging prospective claimants in the "moral hazard" group. Later the period was shortened to thirty days, and finally this time limitation was dropped except in cases suspected to be fraudulent.[65] Patterson notes that insurance commissioners have criticized

64. Griswold, J., *Fire Underwriters' Text-Book* (2nd. Ed., Montreal: Insurance and Finance Chronicle Office, R. Wilson Smith, 1889), p. 582.

65. For indication of the comments made upon the shortening of the period to 30 days, see "Modified 30-Day Rule Satisfactory," National Underwriter, Vol. 38, No. 6 (February 8, 1934), p. 5. For comment when the time limitation was abolished, except for suspicious claims, see "National Board Eases Loss Payment Rule," Eastern Underwriter, Vol. 36, No. 48 (November 8, 1935), p. 18.

the companies for encouraging fraudulent and over-valued claims through promptness in settlement.[66]

Community Attitude

Unquestionably the community's attitude concerning claims made by insureds against the companies, i. e., the possibility that the "moral climate" may condone fraudulent or inflated claims, will affect the incidence of insurance claims. Thus, from time to time, prudence may dictate that an insurer withdraw from conducting business in specific territories as the best method of avoiding the unusually great moral hazard encountered in covering risks there.[67]

66. Patterson, Edwin W., *op. cit.*, p. 32.

67. See "Psychology of Community Is Important in Underwriting," National Underwriter, Vol. 38, No. 12 (March 22, 1934), pp. 2, 7.

Chapter V

THE RECORDS: REVIEW AND CHECK

Introduction

When the insurance company's adjuster is in doubt about some particularly important bookkeeping or accounting features of a merchandise loss claim, or when he considers intensive analysis of the claimant's accounts desirable, he engages an accountant to check the insured's books and related records. The "tedious and methodical examination of records and accounts" is often necessary to compute the amount of loss properly and to eliminate the possibility of claim inflation.[1] In almost every insurance adjustment the element of estimate enters into the computation of the amount of loss; estimating the loss from the accounts is "often a difficult matter, involving expert accounting and considerable calculation. . . ." [2] More than half a century ago a well-known adjuster suggested that every young adjuster "undergo critical examination in double entry bookkeeping" before being entrusted with book losses.[3] In the same vein, a recent writer commented as to reporting, or provisional cover:

> We have had experience with many bookkeeping systems, but we have yet to find one where data could be taken directly from the books and used—without alterations—to make a true report of value under a provisional form. . . .[4]

1. See Brown, D. C., "Adjustment of Stock Losses," in Insurance Society of New York, *The Fire Insurance Contract* (Indianapolis: Rough Notes Co., 1922), pp. 418–419.
2. Riegel, Robert, and Loman, H. J., *Insurance Principles and Practices* (Rev. Ed., New York: Prentice-Hall, Inc., 1929), p. 410.
3. Lowden, William H., "Losses and Adjustments," *Proceedings of the Eleventh Annual Meeting of the Fire Underwriters' Association of the Pacific* (San Francisco: 1887), p. 100.
4. Davis, Gordon, "Provisional Insurance Loss Adjustments," Journal of American Insurance, Vol. 22, No. 4 (April 1945), p. 24.

However, the accountant's problems relate more to the proof of the amount of loss than to the mechanics of bookkeeping.[5]

Preliminary Steps

In preparation for his work the accountant should always obtain this information: general nature of the loss; surrounding circumstances; type of coverage in effect; loss limitations at given locations; summaries of comments by the insured concerning such matters as the types and quantities of merchandise traded in, the sizes of periodic inventories, the manner of doing business, and the cost of sales. The accountant's working papers should include a schedule listing and describing the contents of the books and related records available for examination.[6]

The latest balance sheet and operating statement preceding the loss are often employed as starting points, or points of reference. Difficulties may arise because of incomplete records: "Many problems are encountered in adjusting total losses since proper records, inventories, invoices, accurate descriptions of property, plans and specifications are in many cases destroyed by the fire itself or misplaced in years gone by. . . ."[7] Obviously, in proportion as the records are more complete, the adjustment is expedited.

The accounting and auditing procedures generally employed by accountants are likewise used in determining or verifying the amounts of insurance claims for lost or damaged merchandise. Common problems in manufacturing cost accounting, for example, the method to be employed in allocating items of overhead, such as indirect labor, maintenance, repairs and plant depreciation, are frequently met.

Sometimes routine investigation by a company's loss adjuster of the circumstances of the claim brings to light evidence that it is fraudulent, subsequent audit of the books of account revealing poor financial condition or operating results which may have constituted the motive for making fraudulent claim. On the other hand, audit of the records,

5. Cox, Henry C., *Advanced and Analytical Accounting* [Greeley, H. D., *Business Accounting*, 5 Vols., Vol. 4], (New York: Ronald Press Co., 1920), p. 265.

6. Such schedule is illustrated in Reed, Prentiss B., *Adjustment of Fire Losses* (1st. Ed., New York: McGraw-Hill Book Co., Inc., 1929), pp. 324–326.

7. "Insurable Values Discussed," National Underwriter, Vol. 45, No. 44 (October 30, 1941), p. 4.

undertaken following an adjuster's brief investigation of the loss—which disclosed no unusual circumstances—may reveal unstable financial condition or poor business, making desirable scrutiny of the items comprising the claim and more extended review of the circumstances under which it arose. Usually this aspect of loss claim accounting is given little or no attention by the insured's accountant.

There are innumerable classes of record-distortion, ranging from the accidental to the ingeniously-planned, which may result in improper claims. Sometimes errors cause understatement of the claim; more often, not. One of the country's prominent adjusters has observed:

> The confusion of the times has been responsible for an unusual number of errors in even the best accounting departments. In one recent loss, a high grade concern doing a nation-wide business lost track of a $12,000 invoice and presented a claim which was therefore $12,000 short of the true figure. Another one . . . duplicated a $7,000 entry which they later discovered and reported . . . with great embarrassment.[8]

The principal types of distortion encountered by accountants in loss claim work are analyzed in the following discussion.

Incomplete Purchase and Sales Records

Occasionally an insured engages in barter, exchanging his own merchandise for other items. More commonly, particularly in small retail establishments, he buys merchandise for cash, making incomplete record, and reduces the receipts for sales, likewise not recorded formally, by the amounts disbursed for purchases.[9] Periodically, but not necessarily daily, the accumulation of net receipts from business, reduced by the disbursements for personal needs, is deposited. The accountant's difficulties in determining the amount of loss under such circumstances are easily seen.

The purchases figure must be rebuilt by investigation and inquiry among suppliers whose names are furnished by the insured and obtained from his records. The total sales of merchandise must be esti-

8. Reed, Prentiss B., "New Factors Enter Loss Adjusting; No Fixed Rule During Wartime." Address delivered before the Risk Research Institute, February 24, Eastern Underwriter, Vol. 44, No. 10 (March 5, 1943), p. 22.

9. See Hall, Thrasher, *Adjustment of Losses from the School of Experience* (Indianapolis: Rough Notes Co., 1917), p. 29.

mated. Provision must be made for goods unaccounted for through shortages—including those caused by shoplifting, thefts by employees, inaccurate weight or measurement, wastage and spoilage—revealed by physical inventory.[10] It may develop that no consideration has been given to such shortages in the insured's records; often major differences remain undiscovered until inventory-taking or until inspection of receiving and shipping records by the insurer after claim has been made.

Inventory

When the loss is less than complete or total, inventory is taken of the goods remaining. The object is to avoid later controversy about the quantity of merchandise lost or damaged. In fire losses, particularly where the debris has salvage value, the task of inventorying the damaged and undamaged merchandise is often assigned to an organization like the Underwriters Salvage Company, which is owned by a large group of insurance companies.[11]

In case of loss at the premises of a clothing contractor [12] inventory is taken and checked against the records of the contractor's principal, the "manufacturer." Based upon the contractor's payroll, production and shipping records, estimate is made of the value of the labor performed upon the merchandise delivered to the contractor for completion. It is trade practice for the manufacturer to bill cloth and trimmings to the contractor at a price in excess of actual cost. When the completed garments are returned the contractor is credited with the amount originally billed, supplemented by compensation for the labor performed. Therefore, the accountant must review the manu-

10. And see McLoughlin, Stephen, "Mercantile Safe and Mercantile Open Stock Burglary Insurance." Address to Second Year Casualty Students of Insurance Society of New York (Unpublished: February 3, 1932), p. 22. Also note the reference to shortages in the discussion of the computation of gross profit, *infra*, p. 62.

11. For a description of the functioning of the company, see Stratton, G. F., "Underwriters Salvage Company and Its Relation to the Adjustment of Fire Losses," *Proceedings of the Fifty-fourth Annual Meeting of the Fire Underwriters' Association of the Pacific* (1930), pp. 124–131.

12. The business of such contractor is the manufacture of apparel from material and trimmings sent to it by a "manufacturer." The latter is more correctly, but less commonly, referred to as a jobber or wholesaler.

facturer's purchase invoices and other cost records to determine the true cost of the merchandise shipped to the contractor.[13]

Sometimes ludicrous claims are made as to the size of the stock of merchandise on hand prior to the casualty. The reasonableness of such claims should be reviewed in the light of general business conditions.[14] Occasionally an insured rationalizes his dishonesty in making inflated claim following a loss, itself honest as to origin, on the ground that the overpayment will merely compensate him for the trouble and expense to which he was put.[15] Among the inflationary devices employed are the alteration of earlier inventory figures and the addition of inventory sheets.[16] For example, an insured submitted sheets listing the actual amount of merchandise on hand, but also presented, as constituting part of the inventory, copies of these sheets, the copies reflecting doubled or trebled quantities and total values.[17]

Inventory entries in books of account should be tested for probable veracity. Occasionally alterations in general ledger account balances are hidden because of the passage of a long period of time since they

13. And see Mortimer, William M., "Inland Marine Insurance Losses—Why Careful Investigation Is Always Necessary—Transportation, Rules and Regulations." Address before National Association of Independent Adjusters, at Washington, D.C., Weekly Underwriter, Vol. 141, No. 1 (July 1, 1939), p. 22. Also note the discussion of work sheets and questionnaires to be used in connection with both fixed amount and reporting covers, in "P. B. Reed Suggests How to Fix Insurable Values," National Underwriter, Vol. 43, No. 50 (December 14, 1939), pp. 9 and 32.

14. For illustration of excessive claims and the circumstances surrounding their discovery, see "Sixteen Defendants Guilty in Great Arson Trial in London," Eastern Underwriter, Vol. 34, No. 35 (September 1, 1933), p. 19.

15. Persson, A. T., "Fire Insurance Adjusting," Journal of American Insurance, Vol. 5, No. 12 (December 1928), pp. 6–7.

16. See Nelson, Oscar S., *Fire Loss Adjustment Problems in the United States* (Chester, Pa.: 1930), p. 148.

17. See Appendix A, Case 20. Reproductions of these inventory sheets, presented in Appendix C, reveal that except for a few items, sheet 3 is a copy of sheet 1 and sheet 4 a copy of sheet 8, the quantities and total prices being doubled on sheets 3 and 4. Likewise, sheet 6 is a copy of sheet 2, except that practically all the quantities and total prices on sheet 6 are either double or treble those on sheet 2. Scrutiny of the computations on the inventory sheets indicates that sheets 1, 8 and 2 were prepared first, and sheets 3, 4 and 6 thereafter; the reasoning underlying this conclusion is presented in the summary of the case as presented in Appendix A. The inflation in value approximated $9,000.00, or almost 50% of the total inventory reported.

were made. For example, in a case reported by McKenna,[18] a company inflated its inventory by an even $100,000.00 six years before the loss and carried this inflation forward from year to year. Discovery of the condition came about upon search for explanation of the low inventory turnover. The overstatement might also have been detected by careful examination of the inventory sheets and year-to-year comparison of the quantities of the various items listed therein.

Occasionally it is found that one or more pages of a detailed inventory bear a date a year later than the alleged date of inventory-taking. This generally indicates that the inventory sheets have been re-written, since errors in dates are often made in the first few days of a new year, when one inadvertently writes the date of the year just ended; almost never is the error committed of writing, towards a year's end, the date of the year not yet begun.

Much of the work of the accountant will center about verifying the correctness of the sheets representing the latest inventory preceding the loss. Where it is practical to do so, for example, when sales invoices contain descriptions of the items sold, the accountant will test the possibility of the existence at the date of the loss of given items included in the claim. This is done by adding to the quantity of specific items found in the inventory sheets, the quantities purchased since the inventory-taking, and subtracting from these totals the quantities sold to the date of the loss. Further verification may take the form of checking or test-checking periodic inventories in similar fashion, by beginning with a set of inventory sheets dated a number of months or accounting periods prior to the loss, adding thereto, by months or periods, the purchases of specific items and subtracting sales of such items. The resulting balances at the end of each month or period are compared with the quantities shown in the inventory sheets. Occasionally such tests will indicate that the alleged physical inventory is not a true one.

For example, in the burglary loss claim made by a millinery manufacturer, the alleged physical inventory at November 30, a between-seasons date in the industry, included quantities of merchandise

18. McKenna, James A., "Ascertainment of Value and Profit from Books of Account," in Insurance Society of New York, *The Fire Insurance Contract, op. cit.*, pp. 433–434.

constituting full, i. e., complete or unbroken, invoices of goods received in November. Examination of the records revealed, however, that during November sales had been made of sample hats manufactured from goods bought that month.[19] Similarly, successive inventories of a retail dealer in diamonds and jewelry included items which, according to the sales books, had been sold between the dates of these inventories.[20]

An unexplained decrease in inventory turnover for the year preceding the loss tends to result in an increase in the quantity of goods on hand at the date of the loss. Thus decreases in turnover have at times indicated "padding," or inflation, of merchandise inventory figures reported as of the end of the accounting period, and a resultant excessive gross profit percentage for the period under review. The use of the excessive figure in estimating the cost of goods sold during the period from the date of the latest physical inventory to the date of the loss results in a higher claim for loss.

In taking inventory in situations where the loss is of suspicious origin, it is desirable to obtain complete descriptions of the items recorded, including name of manufacturer, style, size, color and any other marks of identification, for the purpose of tracing the items to suppliers' bills, and determining the degree of obsolescence brought about through the passage of time.[21]

Some efforts at claim inflation are scotched readily. Errors in addition of inventory sheets are often discovered by re-adding or by test-checking the additions, instead of accepting the insured's adding machine tapes and totals as correct. This is a common audit precaution, since on certain types of adding machines the totals of the tapes may be forced through the inclusion of figures not imprinted on the tapes themselves.

In preparing or reviewing figures for claims arising under Jewelers' Block policies the auditor should note the clause in the policy which provides that the payment to the insured shall "in no event exceed the lowest figure put upon such property [i. e., upon the items lost] in the Assured's inventories, stock books, stock papers or lists *existing at the*

19. Appendix A, Case 52.

20. *Ibid.*, Case 32.

21. Reed, Prentiss B., *Adjustment of Fire Losses, op. cit.*, pp. 96–97, and see Appendix A, Case 29.

time the loss occurred." [22] This condition imposes upon the accountant the duty of examining the major records relating to the merchandise, including inventory lists, purchase invoices, appraisals, instructions to conductors of private sales, and similar records. For illustration, one claimant, a jeweler, put up part of his stock for sale at auction. The legitimate bids being considered too low, a representative of the insured bid on the merchandise, and "bought" it, in order to prevent purchase by outsiders. The insured apparently overlooked the possible effect of the transaction as setting a low value upon the merchandise in the event of a subsequent loss claim.[23]

Another insured, making claim after a fire, maintained that "the inventories as shown at the beginning and end of the preceding year were exactly fifty percent of the actual inventory if taken at cost. . . ." [24] The books had been closed, and the tax returns prepared on this basis. Recomputation of the loss after doubling the opening and closing inventories produced a greater loss figure, principally because of the doubling of the inventory at the beginning of the year in which the loss occurred. Though he expressed the opinion that "some adjustment should be allowed for inventories due to the fact that many firms do set up inventories on their books at the close of their period at what they consider a conservative valuation . . . ," the reporter of the claim believed "Fifty percent . . . entirely too much in many instances." He observed further that "the adjuster should . . . first calculate the inventory loss on the basis of the actual book figures. . . . He can then compare this . . . with the statement submitted . . . and . . . , in many instances, save his company money." [25] In this case no consideration appears to have been given to the moral hazard existing where the insured submits different inventory figures for different purposes, selecting the figures for each on the basis of the economic advantage yielded. Nor was the possible disallowance of the claim on the ground of fraud considered.

22. Italics and material in brackets added. And see "Jeweler's Block Is a Cover of Importance," Weekly Underwriter, Vol. 132, No. 17 (April 27, 1935), p. 834.

23. See Appendix A, Case 35.

24. Greene, H. H., "Doubled Inventory Method Advanced as Means of Saving Money on Fire Loss Adjustments," Weekly Underwriter, Vol. 126, No. 2 (January 9, 1932), p. 133.

25. *Ibid.*, p. 134.

It is foolhardy for the insured to place upon his books at inventory time any figure other than his best estimate of the value of the merchandise on hand. The consequences of improper entries are not predictable. For example, an insured, for the purpose of understating income, recorded the inventory, without details, at $12,000.00, rather than at the correct figure, later estimated by the adjuster to be $20,000.00. A fire occurred before the close of the next accounting period. The amount of the loss being computed on the basis of the book inventory, the insured suffered considerable loss because the opening inventory was understated.[26] The converse of such situation is found where a business house carries inflated inventory figures on its books to deceive creditors as to financial position.

The books of account of large retail stores are generally kept on the retail inventory system, the inventories computed from the records being tested periodically by comparison with physical inventories. If kept properly, such records furnish a basis for reliable estimate of the inventory value at the date of the loss.[27]

The adjustment of a retail hardware loss claim in Nogales, Arizona, on the Mexican border, revealed an unusual incident in recordkeeping. Review of the books indicated that while all the entries were made in dollars, the purchases were in American currency and the sales in Mexican. Mexican dollars were then worth approximately fifty cents in American money.[28]

Perpetual Inventory System

Duncan discusses "inventory and record schemes for keeping track of all the materials that are in a plant, raw, finished, and partly manufactured," the "schemes" being the perpetual inventory and cost accounts of the manufacturing concern.[29] Perpetual inventories are fre-

26. Incident cited in Maltbie, Armstrong, "Loss Adjustments from a Public Adjuster's View" (Unpublished; probably a lecture, April 16, 1930), pp. 2–3.

27. For a discussion of the retail inventory method consult Kleinhaus, H. I., *Retail Inventory Method in Practical Operation* (Rev. Ed., New York: Controllers' Congress, National Retail Dry Goods Association, 1941).

28. Meade, Calvert, "Fire Loss Settlements," in Fire Underwriters' Association of the Pacific, *Lectures Delivered to the Associate Members* (San Francisco: The Association), 5 vols., Vol. 3 (1916–1917), pp. 95–96.

29. Duncan, John C., "Property Accounting for Fire Losses," Journal of Accountancy, Vol. 6, No. 3 (July 1908), pp. 166–173 and Vol. 7, No. 2 (December 1908), pp. 122–132.

quently maintained by manufacturing or trading enterprises. Periodic comparison between physical and perpetual inventories by individual items or classes of items is desirable.[30]

Where the individual units in a stock of merchandise are of low value, or where the number of different items carried is large, unless perpetual inventory records are required to help insure the availability of items for sale or for use in succeeding processes, such records are often found to be impractical, and are consequently uncommon. Failure to keep a perpetual inventory was noted in claims by a retail dry goods shop, a stationer, a druggist, a tobacco and candy wholesaler and a manufacturer of glazed fruits.[31] Often, however, perpetual inventories are not maintained although they would be simple [32] or at least, not too difficult [33] of operation.

Perpetual inventory records must be checked as to mathematical accuracy and as to manner of maintenance. The following types of errors are frequently encountered: incorrect recording of prices or quantities of goods purchased; duplication of purchase entries; failure to identify sales; [34] carrying obsolete or outmoded merchandise at the acquisition price. Occasionally direct shipments from suppliers of the insured to the latter's customers are entered by the insured as acquisitions of merchandise, presumably still on hand. Shipments by suppliers directly to dyers designated by the insured, and therefore never actually on the insured's premises prior to the loss, have also on occasion been included in claims for loss at the insured's premises.

Faulty records may result in inclusion in the claim of merchandise in transit at the date of loss, out on consignment, stored elsewhere or already shipped to customers. The insured's goods may be located at public storage warehouses, private storage rooms and stockhouses, and, in some cases, temporary stockrooms in distant cities, the latter being maintained to facilitate deliveries in those cities in the normal course of business. When a loss takes place at one of the storage places, the problem is to establish the amount of merchandise delivered for storage and the amount removed. Another matter to be considered is the possible substitution, without proper record, of inexpensive merchandise for valuable items which had been in storage.

30. *Cf.* Appendix A, Case 9.
31. *Ibid.*, Cases 11, 27, 31, 48 and 55.
32. *Ibid.*, Cases 40, 49 and 56.
33. *Ibid.*, Case 21.
34. *Ibid.*, Case 32.

It is understandable that where claim was made against an insurance company for a shortage of dresses on a specific date, the acceptability of the records was questioned when it developed that there were numerous differences between the daily balances in the perpetual inventory book and in the record of daily physical inventory-takings.[35]

Many manufacturers who produce finished items in various sizes maintain inadequate records of the quantity in each size. The accuracy of any estimate of the quantity of material consumed in production depends upon the correctness of estimate of the relative proportions of the total output represented by the various sizes. Where the proportions are in dispute, the computations made by the accountant should be fair and reasonable. In litigation the courts might resolve all doubts in favor of the claimant under the insurance policy.[36]

In a burglary loss case tried in the Supreme Court in Kings County, New York,[37] insured and insurer took opposite positions about the need for maintenance of a perpetual inventory record. The insured, a retailer of coats and dresses, employed the customary general books of account, but did not keep a perpetual inventory record.

The loss took place on February 27. The claimant arrived at the number of dresses stolen by starting with the quantity shown by a physical inventory list dated February 1, adding the number of dresses purchased between then and the date of the loss, and subtracting from this total the number sold or returned to manufacturers and the number on hand after the loss. Using this method of computation, the insured estimated the loss as 767 dresses. The items constituting the inventory at February 1 had been classified under two price divisions, namely, "Under $10.00" and "Over $10.00," but no style numbers or other descriptions were furnished.

Then, there being no perpetual inventory record, to arrive at the value of the missing dresses the insured prepared a series of sheets, each headed by the name of a manufacturer from whom one or more

35. *Ibid.*, Case 9.

36. *Cf.*, Olney, Peter B., "Accountant's Role as a Fact Finder and as a Witness," New York Certified Public Accountant, Vol. 11, No. 6 (March 1941), pp. 366–367.

37. Golub v. Fidelity & Casualty Co. of New York. Judgment for plaintiff. Affirmed, no opinion, 246 App. Div. (2d Dept) 537 (1935), 283 N.Y. Supp. 987 #1. Leave to appeal further denied. 246 App. Div. (2d Dept) 616, 284 N.Y. Supp. 377 and 269 N.Y. 679. The discussion of this case is based upon the Record on Appeal.

purchases had been made during the six-month period preceding the loss. There were 115 such manufacturers. On each sheet the insured listed, showing style number and quantity, the purchases made during the six-month period, the sales during the same period, and the inventories remaining. The sales and inventories of specific style numbers were offset against the purchases, and the remaining items, totalling 751 in number and $7,016.00 in amount, were presented as representing the details of the loss claim.

The insurance company pleaded no liability, citing, among other grounds, the clause in the policy which read: "The Company shall not be liable for any loss or damage . . . unless books and accounts are regularly kept by the assured and the loss can be accurately determined therefrom by the company." Judgment for the insured was granted by a jury in the Supreme Court. Thereupon the insurer pleaded before the Appellate Division: [38]

> The crowning feature of the haphazard and wholly unforgivable method of computing this claim was found in the evidence that the accountant and plaintiff's son (who was also an accountant) first ascertained by what was called a computation that there were 767 garments supposed to be missing.
>
> Then they had to manipulate a computation that would show a loss of that number of garments, so what did they do?
>
> They took the most recent purchase bills, those most recent to the date of the alleged loss, and they worked backward, month by month, with the purchases and with the sales, until they exhausted the amount of purchases that they needed, i. e., until they had compiled a number of garments that they put in the proof of loss as having been stolen. . . .
>
> If that wasn't putting up the brickwork first and then afterward slipping in the kind of foundation that would fit, we do not know what was.
>
> What reliance could be placed upon any such method? How could *anyone* be sure that the garments for which the plaintiffs were making claim were actually involved in the alleged loss?
>
> Plaintiff's accountant admitted that if the computation by that method was carried still further back, to a date prior to August 1933, that "if he worked back further still the amount in his proof of loss would be greater." . . .

The insured responded as follows, outlining and defending his method of computing the loss: [39]

38. Appellant's Brief, pp. 15–16. Citations of folio numbers from the record of the trial are omitted.

39. Respondent's Brief, pp. 12–15. Citations of folio numbers from the record of the trial are omitted.

Computing the value of these dresses at the lowest figure of each price class indicated a loss amounting to $6,623.50. . . . While accurate as to quantity, this method did not enable each dress to be identified and accurately priced. It was, however, a close approximation. . . .

To procure the exact price of each dress stolen, the following procedure was adopted which, it is suggested, would have been impossible in a business where records were not kept as thoroughly and completely as plaintiff's.

It was determined that there was little likelihood that any dresses were on the racks which had been purchased more than four or five months earlier. As above indicated, older styles were usually placed upon the bargain rack and closed out at reduced prices. . . . The accountant recommended, nevertheless, that an analysis and tabulation be made of every dress purchased and sold during the six months preceding the loss in order to be sure that it covered the whole ground. . . . The only effect of failure to work back far enough (if it should happen that there were a few scattered dresses of earlier vintage) would be that these dresses would not be included in the claim and hence could not prejudice the defendant. . . .

An examination of the accounts payable ledger showed purchases from 115 manufacturers during the six months period and a separate memorandum sheet was prepared for each manufacturer. . . . The 115 sheets are in evidence . . . , a typical sheet being printed in the record. . . . Each sheet is numbered to correspond with the number assigned to the particular manufacturer by the plaintiff. . . . These slips constitute a complete record of every purchase and sale during the preceding six months. Taking each bill of each of the 115 manufacturers, a notation was made on the sheet bearing his name and number of the quantity, cost, price and date of purchase of every dress purchased during the period, identified by style number. . . . Since it was likely that the stock on hand comprised mostly the more recent purchases, the invoices were tabulated in the reverse of chronological order, beginning with February, 1934, and running back to September, 1933. . . . These entries were verified against the purchase book. . . .

After recording all purchases, the sales book was used to check off on each memorandum sheet every dress sold as identified by the manufacturer's number and the style number, and adjustment was made for every dress returned as shown on the purchase return book. . . . When completed these sheets constituted an accurate inventory of every dress on hand immediately preceding the burglary with the possible exception (not detrimental to the defendant) that the few dresses which might have been purchased before the fall of 1933 would not be included. This process is practically a reconstruction of what would have been a perpetual inventory such as was described by . . . defendant's accountant, with the single difference that a perpetual inventory is made up daily from similar records whereas here the purchases and sales over six months were tabulated at one time.

The net result of this method was that instead of 767 dresses stolen, as found on the basis of February 1st inventory, the check-up showed a total of 751 dresses stolen, identified by the name of the manufacturer, the style number, the date of purchase and the purchase price. The difference of sixteen dresses doubtless represents the relatively insignificant quantity purchased prior to September, 1933, and hence not embraced in the tabulation.

The proof of loss . . . contains a transcript of these figures, each dress being identified as above indicated. In addition to the cost price, it indicates the fair market value as of the date of loss, an allowance being made for depreciation in value of the older dresses. . . .

A perpetual inventory was unnecessary, said the insured,[40] because of the

unusual completeness of the plaintiff's bookkeeping system—unusual, certainly for a retail store of this type . . . defendant's own accountant characterized the books as being complete, accurate and up to date, with the single exception that they might have been improved upon only by a perpetual inventory system, a wholly unnecessary extravagance in the face of the detailed purchase and sales records so carefully kept by the plaintiff.

The adequacy of the plaintiff's records was summarized with the observation: [41]

The completeness and accuracy of plaintiff's books may . . . be pointed out as an example of how the records of such a retail store should be kept. By a wide margin they exceeded the requirements of the policy.[42]

The Appellate Division upheld, without opinion, the Supreme Court's judgment for the insured.[43]

Gross Profit Percentage

When perpetual inventory records are maintained the quantities involved in a loss may frequently be determined from such records almost exactly and the existence of a good cost accounting system may permit the evaluation of the inventory on hand at the time of the loss without undue difficulty. If there is no perpetual inventory, but the specific items or classes of items are identifiable in the sales records, and the costs are obtainable from purchase bills, manufacturing cost accounts or a stock book, the value of inventory on hand at the date

40. *Ibid.*, p. 23. 41. *Ibid.*, p. 38.

42. Citing Mord v. New York Indemnity Co. 216 App. Div. 252 (Affirmed 244 N.Y. 589) and Licht v. New York Indemnity Co. 250 N.Y. 211.

43. See citations at fn. 37.

of the loss may likewise be estimated readily. The computation may be shortened by the use of tests employing selected months or items considered typical of the entire period.[44] Of course, the possibility of shortages resulting from pilferage of merchandise, over-generosity in weight or measurement on sales, or from similar causes, should be considered.[45]

When a perpetual inventory is not maintained, or when sales records are not kept in such fashion as to facilitate identification—for costing purposes—of the items sold, it is generally necessary to estimate the value of the inventory on hand by using the gross profit percentage method. An estimate is made of the average gross profit percentage for a number of accounting periods preceding the loss. This figure is then subtracted from the figure 100%, and the difference, representing the percentage relationship of cost of sales to sales, is applied against the sales figures for the period between the end of the latest fiscal year preceding the loss and the date of the loss, to yield the estimated cost of sales—in dollars—for that period. The cost of sales is then subtracted from the total of inventory, purchases, freight-in, acquisition cost, etc., from the close of the preceding accounting period to the date of the loss, to produce the estimated inventory at the time of loss. The further deduction of the inventory on hand after the loss (including the salvage value of the damaged merchandise) yields the amount of the insurance loss.

As to the method of arriving at the percentage of gross profit, Kester writes:

> The record of all purchases, purchase returns, sales, and sales returns from then [the close of the previous fiscal period] until the time of the fire, and the records of previous years, should also be available in order to determine the average rate of gross profit. If such rate of gross profit is not available, there must be a rate agreed upon by the insured and the company as the basis for settlement.[46]

44. For an early reference see Mayer, F. J. Alex, "Scientific Bookkeeping and the Adjustment of Book Losses, With and Without Books," *Proceedings of Twenty-ninth Annual Meeting of the Fire Underwriters' Association of the Pacific* (1905), p. 86.

45. See Williams, T. H., *Fire Insurance Contract, with Legal Decisions* (2nd. Ed., San Francisco: Underwriters' Report, 1930), p. 188.

46. Kester, Roy B., *Advanced Accounting* (4th. Ed., New York: Ronald Press Co., 1946), p. 325. Also see Bell, Ernest W., "Adjustment of Fire Losses," Public Accountant, Vol. 23, No. 1 (July 30, 1923), p. 21.

Often there is considerable variation from period to period in the percentage of gross profit earned, rendering difficult decision upon the number of years, or accounting periods, to be used in computing the average gross profit percentage. Once a decision has been reached a weighted arithmetic average of the gross profit percentages for the periods selected is commonly employed, greater weight generally being given to the figures for the most recent periods. Of course, consideration must be given to the extent to which abnormal circumstances may have occurred in certain or all of the periods [47] and to the variation in rate of gross profit from season to season.[48] Likewise, it must be considered that there are frequently variations in the rates of gross profit earned on the diverse classes of merchandise traded in. For example, in a retail shop dealing in women's wear the percentage of profit on the sale of millinery varies from that on the sale of dresses or coats.[49]

Some merchants incorrectly employ as the gross profit percentage, applied in reduction of sales to arrive at the cost of goods sold, the percentage of profit computed on cost price.[50]

At least one writer on accounting apparently considered the determination of the average gross profit percentage used in estimating the inventory on hand at the date of the loss a battle of wits between insured and insurer. Soulé refers to a case in which it was "to the interest of . . . [the insureds] to show a large gain . . . on sales; and . . . the Insurance Companies [,] . . . a small gain. . . ." [51] He observes that if agreement cannot be arrived at by using the general books of account, the average percentage of gross profit must be com-

47. Grant, H. M., "Upon the Element of Estimate in Loss Adjustments," *Proceedings of the Fifteenth Annual Meeting of the Fire Underwriters' Association of the Pacific* (1891), pp. 118–125. Also see Hall, Thrasher, *Hall on Insurance Adjustments* (1st. Rev. Ed., Indianapolis: Rough Notes Co., 1916), p. 197.

48. Thus one may accept with reservation the comment, "The gross profit method can be used only when there has been a virtually constant relation for several years between the cost of goods and the sales. . . ." Students' Department, Journal of Accountancy, Vol. 28, No. 5 (November 1919), p. 395.

49. The effect of the failure to consider such variations in the percentage of gross profit is demonstrated in illustrations supplied in Castenholz, William B., *Auditing Procedure* (Chicago: La Salle Extension University, 1931), pp. 348–351.

50. Grant, H. M., *op. cit.*, p. 120.

51. Soulé, George, *Soulé's New Science and Practice of Accounts* (7th. Ed., New Orleans: 1903), p. 600.

puted based upon the tabulation of the cost and sales figures for the major classes of merchandise. But, he notes, the principal difficulty centers about the selection of items, the insurance companies "insisting on items upon which a small gain was realized, and . . . [the insureds,] items upon which a large gain was realized. . . ."[52]

Finney discusses the effect upon the computation of the estimated value of merchandise at the date of the loss, if the inventory value at the last closing of the books preceding the loss has been marked down to give consideration to a decline in market value, or to depreciation or obsolescence.[53] Illustrative figures, shown below, are presented by him, and he suggests the possibility that all, or a large part, of the merchandise on hand at the last closing of the books may have been sold prior to the date of the loss. Under such circumstances, Finney concludes, the estimate of total merchandise on hand at the date of loss would be too low, and the insured would suffer an "unwarranted loss" ($5,000.00 in the illustration furnished) in the estimated value of merchandise then on hand. The following table shows, in summary, the figures cited:

	Case I: Where inventory at date of last closing was not written down		*Case II: Where inventory at date of last closing was written down*	
Inventory at date of last closing		$30,000.00		$25,000.00
Add purchases		60,000.00		60,000.00
Total		$90,000.00		$85,000.00
Less estimated cost of sales:				
Sales	$75,000.00		$75,000.00	
Less gross profit—33⅓%	25,000.00	50,000.00	25,000.00	50,000.00
Estimated inventory at date of fire		40,000.00		35,000.00

The illustration appears to be based upon the assumption that sales prices would remain unchanged although market prices of the mer-

52. *Idem.*

53. Finney, H. A., *Principles of Accounting. Advanced* (3rd. Ed., New York: Prentice-Hall, Inc., 1946), pp. 101–102.

chandise had fallen or the merchandise had been marked down because of deterioration or obsolescence. As a general rule such decline in inventory value would be accompanied or followed shortly by a proportionate decline in sales prices. Thus, approximately the same gross profit percentage (33⅓% in the instant case) might conceivably be maintained although the opening inventory was valued at a figure lower than cost, and market prices had fallen. Injustice would not necessarily result to the insured through a reduction in the book value of the inventory at the beginning of the accounting period in which the loss occurred. It is true, however, that if an unwarranted write-down of the opening inventory had been made, an unwarranted loss might ensue to the insured through the computation of the loss by the gross profit method.

Approval is accorded [54] the suggestions made in H. C. Bentley's series of articles in the *Journal of Accountancy*, that inventories of shop-worn or other damaged merchandise, or goods whose value has fallen because of changes in style or season, be taken at both cost and depreciated value. This would tend to reduce controversy between insured and insurer on the point whether inventory totals shown in the books of account reflected provision for market decline, depreciation and obsolescence. However, accountants do not generally concur with Caldwell [55] that where the market value of merchandise is well above the book inventory figure adjustments should be made to the latter to bring it to market value. If the merchandise lost or damaged can be identified, it should not be difficult to establish the replacement price.

54. In "Correspondence," Journal of Accountancy, Vol. 14, No. 2 (August 1912), pp. 144–145 (Letter from Prentiss B. Reed).

55. Caldwell, Eugene, "What Executives Should Know about Fire Insurance. Part II," American Business, Vol. 7, No. 11 (November 1937), p. 57.

Chapter VI

THE RECORDS: REVIEW AND CHECK
(*Continued*)

Expense in Buying and Receiving

The cost of acquisition is properly added to purchase price in determining the value of merchandise lost or damaged. In the loss adjustment following a fire at a large Providence, R.I., department store the list of items accepted as constituting acquisition cost included buying expense, transportation and cartage-in, transportation office expenses, the cost of receiving and marking, and certain clerical and statistical work. The insured, located near the New York City buying market, found that the total of the items enumerated averaged 4¾% of the purchase price of merchandise.[1] In a Dayton, Ohio, loss five percent was added to cost for buying, receiving and marking, and warehousing expenses.[2] When special buying trips are required in replacing the destroyed or stolen goods the cost of such trips is includible in the claim for loss.[3]

Freight-in; Discounts

Freight-in on purchases is also to be included in reaching the figure for inventory at the time of loss. In deducting the cost of goods sold, from the estimated value of merchandise available for sale, freight-in on merchandise sold must be included as part of the cost of goods sold. Otherwise the figure for merchandise on hand before the loss will be

1. See National Retail Dry Goods Association, Controllers' Congress, "The Shepard Co. Fire," Insurance Bulletin, Vol. 8, No. 3 (November 1924), p. 11.
2. Stokes, H. E., "Fire Loss Adjustment," Best's Insurance News. Fire and Casualty Edition, Vol. 44, No. 8 (December 1943), p. 73.
3. "Insurability of Merchandise at Its Counter Cost," Dry Goods Economist, Vol. 89, No. 5 (November 1934), p. 14.

inflated.[4] Using an alternative method of computation, freight and expenses in buying and receiving may be omitted from both inventory and cost of sales figures. Then, when the amount of loss, exclusive of freight, buying and receiving costs and related charges, has been determined, appropriate proportion of the total freight and other charges under discussion may be added to the figure for the estimated loss.[5]

In the writings on insurance adjustments, the treatment of discounts in computing the amount of loss is considered at length.[6] Although Grant [7] and others prefer the elimination of discounts from the total of merchandise purchased and from the inventory figure, before computing the amount of the loss (and presumably likewise with respect to sales), the bookkeeping treatment of discounts varies from firm to firm. Most concerns reduce both sales income and purchases cost by the amount of trade discounts, many also eliminating cash discounts; the gross profit percentage will naturally be affected by the method employed.

In the adjustment of the Providence department store fire claim referred to above, although the insurance policy was clear on the point that the insurer was not liable "beyond the actual cash value of the property," the question arose whether the gross amount of the purchase invoices covering merchandise destroyed, or this sum reduced by the cash discounts allowed, was the amount for which the insurers were liable.[8] The referee found the language of the insurance policies decisive, and ruled that cash discounts were to be deducted from the invoice price of the goods. Experience indicates that in loss

4. See Sexton, William, *Fire Insurance* (San Francisco: The Coast Review, 1915), pp. 53–58; also, Sexton, William, "Adjusting," *Proceedings of Twenty-first Annual Meeting of the Fire Underwriters' Association of the Pacific* (1897), pp. 56–63. These writings also contain illustrations of fire loss computation schedules showing the treatment of freight, depreciation and discount.

5. See Griswold, J., *Hand-Book of Adjustments of Loss or Damage by Fire* (3rd. Ed., New York: Insurance Monitor Office, 1894), p. 31.

6. See *The Forum* (Indianapolis: Rough Notes Co., 1914), pp. 21–23, wherein are presented three different opinions as to the amount of a given fire loss computed on a cash basis, all three opinions being based on the same set of figures. And see Reed, Prentiss B., *Adjustment of Fire Losses* (1st. Ed., New York: McGraw-Hill Book Co., Inc., 1929), pp. 111–121.

7. Grant, H. M., "Upon the Element of Estimate in Loss Adjustments," *Proceedings of Fifteenth Annual Meeting of the Fire Underwriters' Association of the Pacific* (1891), p. 124.

8. See National Retail Dry Goods Association, *op. cit.*, pp. 7–9.

adjustments cash discounts available to the insured are deducted whether or not taken. Trade discounts, also, are always deducted.

Where the determination of the amount of loss centers about the gross profit percentage method, and under the bookkeeping system in use cash and trade discounts are shown separately, the simplest procedure in computing the gross profit percentage would be to reduce the purchases by the trade discounts. Then, upon reaching the estimate of the amount of merchandise on hand prior to the loss, and reducing that figure by the total for merchandise remaining on hand after the loss, the balance, representing the merchandise lost, may be reduced by the average percentage of cash discount available.

Cost of Manufacture

Verification of the total charge for labor entering into the computation of the cost of merchandise produced has been simplified in recent years by federal and state regulations requiring the keeping of somewhat detailed payroll records. More difficult, and frequently requiring extended review, is the question of the propriety of the methods employed by an insured in allocating expenditures to manufacturing cost, general administrative, and selling expense. It may develop that in a claim involving manufactured products, a most liberal view, e. g., one where the entire total of cost and expense is considered to constitute manufacturing cost, may nevertheless not yield a pre-loss inventory figure as high as that cited by the insured. Thus, in one claim decision was necessary on the proportion of "expenses" of $9,600.00, including the principal officer's salary of $5,400.00, properly classifiable as manufacturing overhead. The total of opening inventory, materials purchased, direct labor, and manufacturing costs (excluding both the officer's salary cited and all other items designated as "expenses"), amounted to $12,300.00 for the period of approximately one year under review; by co-incidence the entire sales volume was also $12,300.00. Whatever part of the "expenses" was properly treated as manufacturing overhead was also to be considered in evaluating the inventory at the time of loss.[9]

Manufacturing records are frequently inadequate. Note the cases where: a dentist stated that he did not retain dental laboratory bills

9. See Appendix A, Case 4.

nor maintain records as to the patients for whom laboratory work was required; [10] where the identity of items could not be followed readily throughout the period of processing; [11] where there was no manufacturing record whatever; [12] where the cost calculation records were erroneous, as well as incomplete.[13]

When various grades of a product all go through the same process of manufacture or preparation for market, e. g., the lumber produced by a saw mill, the "average" cost of production per unit, arrived at by dividing total cost by output, may prove to be higher than the sales price per unit of the poorer grades. In such cases the most common practice is to allocate the cost of production to the various grades produced, on the basis of total sales volume. A somewhat different, and less common, method is outlined by Sexton in his discussion of a lumber loss adjustment. The sales price of the cheaper grades of lumber, selling below average production cost, was considered to be the "value" of those grades. The difference between (1) the product of the average production cost per unit and the number of units of the cheaper grades sold, and (2) the total income from sales of the cheaper grades, was treated as an element of cost of the higher grades.[14]

Inter-company, -department and -store Transactions

Consideration must be given to inter-company transactions and to those between departments of a business or branches of a chain of stores. Illustrating a failure to do so is the somewhat uncommon situation, cited by Hall from a textbook for underwriters, dealing with what is now an infrequently-encountered product. The insured was a jobber of merchandise who also operated a lantern factory. The sales figure used in the adjustment erroneously included part of the total price at which completed lanterns had been transferred from the factory to the jobber, as well as the total representing sales of such merchandise to outsiders. Likewise, the purchases figure was inflated since it included not only actual purchases from outsiders for the jobbing

10. *Ibid.*, Case 10. 11. *Ibid.*, Case 6. 12. *Ibid.*, Case 3.

13. *Ibid.*, Case 52. And see *Ibid.*, Case 35, where components of cost were duplicated in the value attributed to one of the items in the claim.

14. Sexton, William, "Adjusting Lumber Losses," *Proceedings of Thirty-second Annual Meeting of the Fire Underwriters' Association of the Pacific* (1908), pp. 81–86.

and factory divisions, but also, in duplicate, material transferred from the jobbing department to the factory.[15]

Often, for example in the diamond and jewelry or the clothing business, quantities of merchandise for sale, or samples for solicitation of orders, are in the custody of traveling salesmen. Care must be taken to insure the elimination of the items from claims for merchandise lost at the insured's place of business.[16] Particularly difficult to discover are such situations as that where a furniture store in a small town opened an apparently unrelated, competing radio store a short distance away, transferring to it radio sets later claimed to have been included in a fire loss at the furniture shop.[17]

Component Parts

Precaution is always exercised in checking the sum of the values assigned to various parts of a product, against the value assigned to the completed item, and against the sales price. This will prevent the approval of claims like that of a manufacturer of metal beds, consisting of a head, foot, and two side rails, who valued the unassembled, individual parts at sums whose total exceeded the sales price of the completely-assembled bed. Likewise, indication that certain items in a company's inventory are worth little more than the scrap or disposal value will be furnished where the items in question constitute finished parts of objects not usually traded in, or where these parts represent so large a quantity as to preclude the possibility of purchase or manufacture of the remaining parts required to make the completed product. Occasionally the insured's inventory will include outmoded items carried at excessive values. Where these goods were obtained from recognized dealers, or are standard, branded merchandise, the age of the

15. See Hall, Thrasher, *Adjustment of Losses from the School of Experience* (Indianapolis: Rough Notes Co., 1917), pp. 68–69. And note Aaronson's suggestions that business firms keep receiving and shipping records at every location where business is conducted, and that accountants' statements of operating results and financial condition be prepared monthly. Aaronson, Benjamin, "Collecting Fire Losses," Pace Student, Vol. VI, No. 10 (September 1921), p. 157.

16. See the reference to the questions concerning the contents of the merchandise account in Griswold, J., *op. cit.*, pp. 101–102.

17. Reported in Retail Credit Co., *Inspector's Handbook. Reporting Financial Information* (Atlanta: Retail Credit Co., 1941), pp. 38–39, based upon material assembled by the Atlanta Association of Credit Men.

products may be confirmed readily by reference to the suppliers or by examination of catalogues.[18]

Occasionally the suspected inflation of a fire claim may be detected by examining the damaged merchandise remaining. In one claim, assembling damaged heels of shoes in pairs indicated the existence of an inventory before the loss worth less than half that claimed to have been on hand.[19]

Lot or Style Numbers

Where the merchandise handled can be identified by lot or style number from the time of acquisition through the time of sale, a month by month study of opening inventory, purchases and sales, analyzed by styles, may indicate the age, and possible deterioration and consequent decline in value, of the merchandise.[20] Tests may shed light on the correctness of inventory figures or the difficulty of sale of merchandise.[21] Such tests include tracing the sales and cost prices of selected items to determine whether the normal gross profit has been maintained. In the absence of recent invoices covering purchases of specific items, the appearance of the items in successive inventories in substantially unchanged quantities may indicate that the goods are unsalable. Frequently, the improbability of the insured's possession of certain types and quantities of merchandise at the time of loss is indicated, though not beyond contradiction, by the absence of such items from the records of purchases and sales made in the period preceding the loss.

Audit Check-lists; Cross-checks

Lowden [22] suggests an affidavit which might be prepared by a small

18. See Appendix A, Case 29, where the insured's stock of radio sets and refrigerators included numerous types long outmoded; also see Case 24, where old-fashioned, tarnished and broken hat, dress and purse ornaments remained in stock, in anticipation of possible return to fashion.

19. Clarke, Arthur A., "Adjustment of Losses Under Pacific and Atlantic Coast Conditions," *Proceedings of Forty-sixth Annual Meeting of the Fire Underwriters' Association of the Pacific* (1922), p. 68.

20. See Appendix A, Case 43.

21. See Reed, Prentiss B., *op. cit.*, pp. 106–108.

22. Lowden, William H., "What to Do When the Books Are Burned," *Proceedings of Fourteenth Annual Meeting of the Fire Underwriters' Association of the Pacific* (1890), pp. 81–84.

merchant if his books burned and it became necessary for him to narrate to an insurer the circumstances of the loss and the details of operation of his business; and Sexton [23] outlines a series of inquiries, designed to elicit similar information, to be asked at the examination under oath.[24] The affidavit and outline have been considered in the preparation of the following check-list of points to be covered by an accountant in determining the amount of a merchandise loss: [25]

1. Business organization: Date of commencement of business, type of organization, changes in structure of business with dates and details including estimates of financial position at times of changes.
2. Capital: Form, amount, sources and disposition.
3. Purchases: Sources, types and amounts, form and amount of payments on account, balances due creditors, percentages of purchase discount allowed and taken, freight or express charges, receiving expense and depreciation, obsolescence or spoilage.
4. Sales: Estimates—by months if possible (or indication of annual volume and slow or active periods), balance due from customers, percentage of sales discount allowed.
5. Expenses: Types and amounts, payments on account (form and amounts), balances due to creditors.
6. Gross profit percentages: Estimates, for recent years, by major classes of merchandise.
7. Financial statistics: Details of condition at time of loss, details of operating results for current fiscal period.
8. Inventories: Dates and estimated amounts.
9. General: History of insurance losses, unusual business transactions undertaken at various times during business history (e. g., purchase, sale or leasing of buildings), personal financial transactions likely to affect or be affected by results of business operations (e. g., purchase of residences, automobiles or securities by officers or principals), borrowing or lending of funds or withdrawals of merchandise by officers or principals, amounts and details of cash received from sources other than sales.

Particular attention should be paid to the figures for the period between the date of the last inventory-taking and the loss.

A useful check-list of questions concerning the business history and

23. Sexton, William, *Fire Insurance, op. cit.*, p. 61.

24. For a comparable list of points to be covered in the examination under oath, see Williams, T. H., *Fire Insurance Contract, With Legal Decisions* (2nd. Ed., San Francisco: Underwriters' Report, 1930), pp. 190–191.

25. On this subject also see Eggleston, De Witt Carl, *Auditing Procedure* (2nd. Ed., New York: John Wiley & Sons, Inc., 1935), pp. 381–382 and 388–389.

financial affairs of individuals or organizations is available in Form No. 3. Statement of Affairs (For Bankrupt or Debtor Engaged in Business), of the Official Forms provided under the General Orders in Bankruptcy.[26] The questions cover these points: nature, location and name of business; books and records; financial statements; inventories; income other than from operation of business; income tax returns; bank accounts and safe deposit boxes; property held in trust; prior bankruptcy proceedings and assignments for benefit of creditors; loans repaid; transfer of property; accounts receivable; losses; withdrawals; names and addresses of partners, or of officers, directors, managers and principal stockholders of corporation.

Even where the records are kept properly, as in the cases of most large business enterprises, the task of determining the amount of merchandise on hand at the date of the loss may be a burdensome one. In the case of a fire at a large department store, it took about two months to arrive at this figure, principally because a large number of invoices had been lost in the receiving room during the fire.[27] However, tracing merchandise shipments to determine whether they had been received prior to the fire was expedited by the receiving room record. In reporting to the Controllers' Congress, the insured's financial secretary pointed out the need for keeping office records up to date. A number of the supporting records had been lost in the fire at the store, and under some circumstances such destruction would have rendered almost impossible arriving at the exact amount of the merchandise loss.

An excellent summary of the procedure to be followed by an accountant in determining the amount of loss in cases where all the books, records and correspondence of a company have been destroyed as a result of a fire is attributable to a Canadian chartered accountant:

Procure from the bankers the last statement of affairs lodged with them; ascertain from the travelers the names of all their customers and communicate with the latter asking the fullest detail available as to dealings since the date of the statement of affairs; communicate with all supply houses asking similar assistance. The information in the former case would be incomplete, of necessity, to the extent that your customers were dishonest or

26. Official Forms in Bankruptcy. Form No. 3. 11 U.S. Code Annotated (St. Paul, Minn.: West Publishing Co.) 155.

27. National Retail Dry Goods Association, *op. cit.*, pp. 10–11.

indifferent, but it is all you have to go on; in the latter case you would get at facts. In the circumstances . . . the banks . . . [would go] to great trouble to supply every information within their power as to bills, etc.

Work along these lines . . . [would give] a foundation on which to build, and it being the best that could be done, the results . . . [would be] accepted by insurance companies in their adjustments if bone fides were apparent.[28]

In situations where the books are incomplete or are said to have been lost or destroyed, the insured's memory is often excellent as to the precise quantities and the specific items lost. In such cases the claims require particular scrutiny, since often the assertion that the records are gone is fraudulent.[29]

Inquiry of employees as to the volume of business done, the number of transactions undertaken and similar matters may shed light on the probability of the existence at the time of the loss, of the quantities claimed to have been on hand. Where the amount of the loss claim appears to be unusually high in the light of the extent of the fire, or the circumstances of the burglary or other casualty, and the records are lost or damaged, the insurer's auditor should supplement his review of the imperfect records by inquiry of creditors, banks, mercantile agencies, credit bureaus and others. If possible, copies of financial statements issued to these groups should be obtained. The insured's bank statements and copies of its bank deposit tickets should be examined. In some cases, published material, such as corporate financial manuals, e. g., Standard and Poor's, or Moody's, may be available; in others, bankruptcy and other court records may be accessible.

Numerous cross-checks of information supplied by the insured are suggested by Lowden.[30] Where the estimated debt to merchandise creditors is too high, the figures for purchases, and for inventory at the date of the loss, will likewise be excessive. Efforts at verification of the liabilities to creditors will help establish the correctness of the in-

28. Students' Department, Journal of Accountancy, Vol. 19, No. 6 (June 1915), p. 479 (Letter from Geo. U. Stiff). And on the same point see Morpeth, C. D., "Fire Loss Adjustments," Accounting, Commerce and Insurance, Vol. 10, No. 6 (September 29, 1923), p. 170.

29. Griswold, J., *op. cit.*, pp. 88–89. "In numerous instances," Griswold adds, "new books of account have been fabricated, or old ones made up for the occasion." *Ibid.*, p. 89.

30. Lowden, William H., *op. cit.*, pp. 92–93.

sured's figures. Unduly low estimates by the claimant of cash on hand or accounts receivable balances will tend to result in too high a total of merchandise on hand, since the latter figure will not have been reduced sufficiently by the deduction of sales, reflected in cash on hand or in outstanding accounts receivable. Lowden confirms that "a thorough knowledge of accounts is more necessary to the proper adjustment of a loss when the books are destroyed than when they are saved. . . ."[31]

Where the claimant receives most of his merchandise by freight from a common shipping point, Hall suggests a rough check on the total purchases made during a given period by dividing the total paid for freight, by the estimated percentage relationship between freight cost and cost of merchandise purchased.[32]

Procedures followed by payroll auditors may be used as cross-checks in merchandise claims, for example:

1. Comparison of wages recorded with the total cost of the finished product.
2. Comparison of total payroll recorded with the product obtained by multiplying the number of employees by the union scale of wages.
3. Reconciliation of book payroll figures with those shown in payroll reports and summaries made to the government.
4. Extension, where fraud is suspected, beyond the usual channels of information. This might entail, among other procedures:
    a. Consideration of possibilities for distortion of records and concealment of information, and effort at nullifying such possibilities.
    b. Obtaining credit agency report.
    c. Inquiry among competitors as to insured's volume of business, number of employees, and other relevant points.[33]

In a stockyards fire loss claim the physical remains of the loss were used successfully in checking both the insured's and independent shipping and receiving records. The insured prepared "book statements" based upon records at the shipping point, St. Louis, and the receiving point, Atlanta. These statements were reconciled with each other, and compared with the railroad's receiving and shipping records for the

31. *Ibid.*, p. 93.

32. Hall, Thrasher, *Hall on Insurance Adjustments* (1st. Rev. Ed., Indianapolis: Rough Notes Co., 1916), pp. 208–209.

33. See Hebard, C. F., "Audits of Exposure," in Michelbacher, G. F., *Casualty Insurance Principles* (2nd. Ed., New York: McGraw-Hill Book Co., Inc., 1942), pp. 337–344 and 349–351.

week preceding the loss. The stockyards foremen reported upon the number of animals in their care immediately before the fire, and a count was made of the carcasses found in the ruins of the stockyards, the count confirming the foremen's report.[34]

Concerning fire losses involving cotton, an audit procedure has been suggested tending to minimize the possibility of claim for merchandise not actually in possession of the cotton dealer at the time of the fire, and to show the number of bales in his possession at various times before the loss.[35] The cotton is covered under reporting policies. Periodic indication of the value of cotton in the insured's possession, on which figures the premium is based, is required. From time to time insureds supply reports understating these figures.[36] Under the suggested audit procedure, verification would be undertaken at compresses, warehouses, banks, merchants' premises and railroads, and the data obtained from each source would be checked against those assembled at the others. The accountant's work would help reveal whether the insured owned, or was legally responsible for damage to, the specific bales of cotton for which claim was made.

Fraudulent and Excessive Loss Claims

Generally, extended review of an insured's accounts is not feasible. It is practical only when the claim is large, or when the surrounding circumstances are so suspicious that the insurer is impelled to undertake the work. The task may well become laborious, requiring the lengthy, continued co-operation of accountant and investigator, each furnishing suggestions for inquiry to the other. The accountant must undertake a painstaking examination of books of account, sales and purchases bills, creditors' statements, bank statements, bank vouchers and deposit slips, correspondence files, warehouse and factor's records, tax reports, stock records, inventory sheets and many other records.

34. Case reported in Reed, Prentiss B., "Loss Adjustments." Lecture before Examining Underwriters Association of New York, The Examiner, Vol. 2, No. 5 (April 1925), pp. 10–11.

35. See Windle, Joseph J., "Adjustment of Cotton Losses and Cotton Salvage Handling," in Insurance Society of New York, *The Fire Insurance Contract* (Indianapolis: Rough Notes Co., 1922), pp. 511–512 and 516–522.

36. Records showing property valuation at various locations are desirable. Finney, H. A., *Principles of Accounting. Advanced* (3rd. Ed., New York: Prentice-Hall, Inc., 1946), p. 100.

But often the labor and expense are more than justified by the outcome.

For example, in a lumber claim it was estimated that if the figures claimed were correct, every square inch of the lumber yard was covered with lumber to a height of eighty feet.[37] Although the bills submitted in support of the claim bore the names of wholesale lumber dealers in various parts of the country, they were discovered to have been printed in the same shop and to bear the same watermark.

In another claim which proved to be fraudulent the insured presented a single invoice for $76,000.00 on a long billhead, in support of a fire loss claim for approximately that sum. The merchandise was said to have been shipped to the insured, in Alabama, from the supplier in Indiana. Suspicion about the authenticity of the invoice and the legitimacy of the claim was aroused because the invoice was not folded despite its length, and because the amounts of invoice and claim were almost equal. The insured had apparently obtained a blank billhead and had filled in fictitious quantities, prices and totals.[38]

Consummate skill went into plans to defraud insurers through a group of warehouse fire claims amounting to $150,000.00. The merchandise destroyed consisted of rags and waste of low value, but the books of account, invoices and other records indicated the presence—before the loss—of merchandise greater in quantity and higher in quality than was actually the case. The plan required three years. New companies were organized, a warehouse acquired, and books, invoices and other records and documents falsified. Spurious bills were received from a confederate whose net worth was so low as to render extremely unlikely the availability of such large quantities of merchandise for shipment to the insureds. One item of wool waste costing about $300.00 was recorded at over $16,000.00. Items were removed from storage without record. Some books of original entry were rewritten so that false entries might be recorded; the posting source folios in the general ledger did not correspond with the relevant page numbers in the rewritten books of original entry. A fictitious opening inventory was recorded, and bank deposits were entered as representing the proceeds

37. Claim reported in Vlachos, William, *Moral Hazard* (2nd. Ed., Philadelphia: Vlachos & Co., 1929), p. 19.

38. "Adjusters' Work Provides Background of Proof to Decide Attalla Arson Case," *Insurance Field*. Fire-Casualty Edition, Vol. LXII, No. 17 (March 2, 1933), p. 6.

of sales of merchandise when, in reality, the moneys were drawn from the account of the insured ostensibly in payment of purchase invoices (which were fictitious), and re-deposited.[39]

In a British claim,[40] it developed that the insured had sold merchandise to prominent firms at prices which would result in substantial loss, the receipt of repeat orders giving the impression that the seller was conducting a profitable business. To indicate the acquisition of large quantities of goods, purchase invoices were forged. In this case it was reported that the books of account [41] had been stolen from the insured's automobile.

Planning a fraudulent claim frequently involves an elaborate system for building a large, though false, total of goods at risk. In a fur fire loss claim [42] the insured entered purchase bills reflecting overstated quantities and values. He also removed merchandise, and omitted sales from the records. A reputable firm of accountants had opened the books about seven months before the loss, the initial figures being those submitted by the insured and his bookkeeper.[43] A financial statement was then presented to a fur dealers' association as the basis for the granting of credit by its members. Subsequently many entries were made recording transactions which appeared to be legitimate. Later, claim was made based upon the books, which had been audited monthly. Following the exposure of the fraudulent claim the insured's accountants remarked that the records had been accepted as correct, but that the conclusions drawn by the accountants from the records would have been different if it had been known that the transactions reported were fictitious.

39. See Kaplan, Abraham and Berger, Samuel A., *The Wilson Warehouse Case* (New York: 1930), *passim*. And compare the numerous similar devices described in Appendix A, Case 16.

40. See Ball, A. J. Lougborough, *Trial and Error* (London: Faber & Faber, Ltd., 1936), *passim*.

41. "Singularly unattractive booty . . . ," *ibid.*, p. 219.

42. See Kaplan, Abraham, and Berger, Samuel A., *The Dachis Case* (New York: Davidson Press, 1930), *passim*.

43. Compare this situation with that described in Exhibit A, Case 16, where the insured engaged an accountant to prepare a trial balance from the general ledger presented to him. This trial balance, submitted on the accountant's letterhead, was used by the insured as the starting point for the computation of the claim. It was subsequently established that the purchases figure was greatly overstated.

In another British claim inflammable merchandise, damaged in an earlier fire, was bought at bargain prices and placed on the books at inflated values, based upon false purchase bills.[44] The discovery of a swatch book kept by one of the principals of the insured, showing the sources and prices of the materials bought, helped reveal the deception. In a silk shop claim the insured "was able to dispense entirely with the tedious routine of book-keeping."[45]

One of the most unusual documents encountered in loss claim work is a Settlement Sheet prepared by insureds following the adjustment effected with the insurer after a planned, fraudulent loss. The Sheet,[46] which fell into the hands of investigators of the fire, is reproduced as Appendix D of this volume. It reflects the receipt of £2533/6/6 (designated "Insurance Cheque") from the insurance company. From this sum were deducted expenses totalling £1414/12/4, including a "fee" of £650 (designated "Westwood's fee") to the individual who went through the motions of conducting a shop where the fire started. The balance of £1118/14/2 is marked as representing "Profit" on the fire, and its disposition, including both payments on account and a sum "Held in hand for other Settlement," is indicated.

In an American claim, a company operating as importer and wholesaler of embroidery and laces had recently changed its name, the proceeds of numerous sales made thereafter being deposited in an account maintained in the former name. Thus no indication of the sale of this merchandise appeared on the books, and the claim for merchandise lost was inflated. The proceeds of other sales were deposited in bank accounts of individuals related to the principals of the insured, or were credited on the insured's books to an account called "Exchange," as though the items were temporary loans to the company. Subsequent checks drawn to the order of "Cash" effected the diversion of these funds from the business bank account to the personal use of the principal. Merchandise paid for by a customer was recorded fraudulently as having been returned. The customer's account was credited, and a check in offset drawn to "Cash" was deposited in the principal's

44. Dearden, Harold, *The Fire Raisers* (London: William Heinemann, Ltd., 1934), pp. 8–15. And see Neuner, John J. W., "Insurance Claims Racketeers," Journal of American Insurance, Vol. 12, No. 3 (March 1935), p. 26 for a similar incident.

45. Dearden, Harold, *op. cit.*, p. 53.

46. *Ibid.*, p. 203.

personal bank account. The insurance claim amounted to $131,000.00; suppressed sales totalled $70,000.00.[47]

In one case the entire merchandise account was re-written at one sitting, the manipulation amounting to $10,000.00; [48] in another claim, false purchase invoices were prepared and checks drawn in apparent settlement. The checks were cashed over the counter of the insureds' bank, presumably by the makers, since the alleged creditors stated that they had never issued the bills nor received the checks.[49]

Numerous claims have been made based on fraudulent mercantile burglary losses. Firms on the verge of bankruptcy have bought large quantities of merchandise on credit, and secreted the goods, maintaining their records in such fashion as to support the insurance claims made. It has been suggested that no cash settlement be made with the insured in such suspected, but unproved, cases, settlement being effected, instead, through replacement of the goods claimed to have been stolen.[50]

In a necktie manufacturer's claim the dates of an unusually large number of old invoices, representing merchandise received several years before the loss, were altered so that the bills would appear to be current, evidencing purchases in the period immediately preceding the loss.[51] Verification of purchase invoices is generally best effected by visit to, or confirmation with, the suppliers; in a number of claims suspicion that the dates and amounts of bills were altered was confirmed upon examination of the records of the alleged suppliers.[52] On rare occasions it develops that the supplier, through the desire to befriend a customer, has attempted to assist in deceiving the insurer. For example, a wholesaler might furnish the insured with statements showing purchases exceeding those actually made.[53] Where collusion

47. Claim reported in Fox, Robert J., "The Claim—The Proof of Loss—When Is Loss Payable," in Insurance Society of New York, *The Fire Insurance Contract, op. cit.*, pp. 306–312.

48. "Few Loss Crooks Can Beat Game, Say Pitcher and Tate, Adjusters," Eastern Underwriter, Vol. 32, No. 6 (February 6, 1931), p. 22.

49. Appendix A, Case 16.

50. See Rees, Fred H., *Investigators and Adjusters Handbook* (2nd. Ed., Chicago: The Spectator Co., 1926), pp. 159–160.

51. Appendix A, Case 16.

52. For example, see Appendix A, Cases 7, 16 and 30. Also see Appendix B-1 relating to Case 7 and Appendices B-3, B-4 and B-5, relating to Case 16.

53. Appendix A, Case 19.

between claimant and alleged supplier is suspected, the latter might be asked to show bills of lading, express or delivery receipts, inventory records, purchase bills, and related documents and records. If the insured has presented altered bills without the supplier's knowledge, which is generally the case where bills are altered, the supplier is usually incensed at his customer and is most co-operative with the insurer; [54] if the supplier has been apprised of the proposed deception, or has participated in it actively, resistance is usually encountered by the insurance company's accountant.

Where fraudulent bills have been discovered, this usually develops from work done by the insurer's investigator, although leads for investigation are often supplied by the accountant, frequently because he has found in the records indication of unusually large purchases of goods of certain types, styles or sizes, or has noted inconsistent entries.

A number of banks have adopted the practice of photographing on microfilm the face, and, under some circumstances, the reverse, of checks drawn by their depositors. In one case such photographs revealed that checks issued currently, apparently in payment of invoices, were imprinted with a bank rubber stamp showing that the checks were cashed over the bank's counter, despite the fact that the payees were business firms of considerable size.[55] It developed that the invoices were actually re-entered by the insured after alteration of the dates and often the amounts, of old bills, the object being to inflate the claim.

Loss claims have been exaggerated by charging the Purchases account with items properly recorded elsewhere. For example, officers' salaries, recorded as purchases, have been included in computing the claim for merchandise lost; [56] the object of the improper charge was to avoid disclosure of the full salaries paid to stockholder-officers.

Where the records under review bear evidence of alteration, it may be possible to restore the original text through photography. Clark [57] discusses the subject of documentary photography, presenting pictures of documents before and after photography, or restoration, by infrared, and describing the photographic method employed by the Bureau of

54. See *ibid.*, Cases 30 and 45.

55. *Ibid.*, Case 16; and see Appendices B-3 to B-5.

56. Appendix A, Case 12.

57. Clark, Walter, *Photography by Infrared* (2nd. Ed., New York: John Wiley & Sons, Inc., 1946), pp. 200–209.

Standards to decipher charred records. He also notes that the various methods usable by the examiner of documents include

> chemical methods of identification of inks . . . ; photographic and photomicrographic methods, including the use of filters in photography by visible light; photography by reflected ultraviolet or of the fluorescence induced by it; and infrared photography.[58]

The verification of fine arts floater losses at commercial enterprises involves substantially the same type of accounting examination as do other classes of merchandise claims. The principal distinguishing feature of the fine arts loss, from the point of view of the accountant, is the higher unit value of the items at risk. As with other types of losses, the paucity of records may reduce the accountant's contribution to the adjustment.[59]

Clearly, audit of the books and records of an insured will be somewhat more extended for claims suspected to be fraudulent than for those believed to be honest. On this point note the incident of the British adjuster, who, convicted of inducing an insurance company to pay a loss claim when he knew it to be fraudulent, wrote a book protesting his innocence.[60] He described some of the procedures undertaken in the adjustment and indicated the deceptions claimed to have been practiced upon him by the insured. The adjuster's position was that following a fire loss if merchandise were indentifiable and could be checked physically, in contrast with the situation where it was destroyed beyond recognition, examination of a purchase invoice describing the merchandise constituted adequate verification of its acquisition, recourse to the books of account being unnecessary. The adjuster had spent considerable time in a physical check of the quantity and quality of goods remaining after the loss and these details agreed closely with the claim, the invoices submitted covering every item in the claim. It developed that the invoices had been forged cleverly, but the adjuster pointed out that falsifying the books of account would have been no more difficult. He considered it of no importance

58. *Ibid.*, p. 200.

59. See Hubbard, Clarence T., "Flying Arts and Flames," Weekly Underwriter, Vol. 126, No. 10 (March 5, 1932), p. 581, involving an art shop where the fire coverage in effect totalled $90,000.00 although the stock at the time of the fire set by the insureds was worth but $1,500.00.

60. See Ball, A. J. Lougborough, *op. cit.*, Chapters 2 and 3.

whether the stock had been paid for, although he conceded that suspicion would have been aroused had there been many old accounts.

Evidence was introduced at the trial of the adjuster that he had asked no questions about the books, nor, as far as the insured knew, had he examined them, nor made any inquiries concerning the insured's ability to pay for the stock of merchandise. The accountant engaged later to review the insured's books expressed the opinion that no "serious check" of the claim or the insured's books had been made by the adjuster. There were numerous items in the claim which were not in the stock book. There were also many indications that the claim had not been checked against the invoices and documents which the accountant examined.

The adjuster had reported that the insured's accounts showed the business to be in good condition; the investigating accountant considered the condition most unsatisfactory. It should be noted, however, that the accountant had begun his investigation two and a half years after the fire, knowing that the claim was fraudulent; this would naturally affect the thoroughness of examination of the books and records. Further, the adjuster could not be expected to possess the same degree of skill in the examination of accounts as did the accountant. Finally, it may have been that invoices and documents made available in the prosecution of the adjuster were not shown to the latter during his visits to the insured's premises.

Suppression of sales entries is a common method of inflating loss claims. Naturally, such suppression is more easily effected when undertaken prior to a loss, than after. In the latter case, cash register tapes, sales books, cash receipt book entries, and similar evidence are often found to have been destroyed or altered, or to have disappeared. Most businessmen, realizing the value of these important personal documents and papers, place such records in safety deposit boxes, safes or vaults. If corresponding precautions were taken for such documents as the physical inventory sheets and annual financial statements, the adjustment of losses, rendered difficult because the books of account had disappeared or had been destroyed, would be a good deal simpler.

It has been said of the honest claimant:

In loss on stock of merchandise, [he] produces his books of account, especially the most frequently missing—the cash book; does not claim 35 or 40 per cent. profit, when his books shows [sic] it did not exceed 20 per cent., and every one knew he had been selling at cost. He . . . gives the cost of each article from an honest trademark although invoices may be burned. . . .[61]

In contrast, consider the loss of the cash book, purchase book and creditors ledger in a fire claim.[62]

In view of all these illustrations of record-distortion, somewhat optimistic were the authors of a manual for appraisers, who observed: "Books of account are generally true in all matters except the plant account. . . ." [63]

Accounting for the Loss

The customary practice in recording the loss is to open an account under such title as Fire Loss, Burglary Loss or Insurance Loss. To this account are charged the estimated value of merchandise lost, destroyed or damaged, as well as expenses incurred in the adjustment, and such part of the unexpired insurance premium as relates to the settlement received from the insurer. The credits to the account are the proceeds of the insurance settlement and any sum, received as salvage on the sale of damaged merchandise, in excess of the estimated salvage value agreed upon during the adjustment negotiations. The excess of estimated salvage value over actual salvage would be charged to the Insurance Loss account.[64]

Until relatively recently it had been the practice to transfer the balance in the Insurance Loss account to Surplus or Capital, rather than to Profit and Loss, on the principle that a fire, burglary or similar loss was an extraordinary or non-recurring item, and should therefore be excluded from the operating statement, to avoid distorting the presentation of the results of the normal business operations. The current practice, however, is to show even the non-recurring items in the operating statement. Consequently insurance losses or gains (the lat-

61. Thomas, W. P., "Losses and Adjustments," *Proceedings of Tenth Annual Meeting of the Fire Underwriters' Association of the Pacific* (1886), p. 67.

62. Appendix A, Case 16. Also see McKenna, James A., "Ascertainment of Value and Profit from Books of Account," in Insurance Society of New York, *The Fire Insurance Contract, op. cit.*, p. 437, on the subject of missing records.

63. Cleminshaw, J. M., Co., *Appraisers Manual* (Cleveland: 1937), p. 204.

64. For comprehensive discussions of the fire loss account *see* Finney, H. A., *op. cit.*, pp. 101 and 103, and Kester, Roy B., *Advanced Accounting* (4th. Ed., New York: Ronald Press Co., 1946), pp. 324–325.

ter generally being only "book" gains) are reflected in the Non-Operating, or Other Income and Deductions, section of the Profit and Loss statement.

Co-insurance

Accountants are familiar with the co-insurance clause found in fire insurance policies. The clause provides that as a condition for the payment of the full amount of the loss, up to the face amount of the policy, the insured shall maintain his insurance coverage at not less than a stated percentage of the value of the property at the time of loss. Under the terms of an insurance policy containing a co-insurance clause, the maximum amount payable to the insured in the event of a fire would be determined by multiplying the amount of the loss by a fraction the numerator of which was the amount of insurance under the particular policy, and the denominator, the minimum amount required to be carried to avoid a contribution to the loss by the insured. In no event could the amount payable exceed the face of the policy or the amount of the loss.[65]

Non-concurrency

In the adjustment of fire losses, difficulties frequently arise as a result of overlapping coverage or variations in policy clauses or endorsements. These difficulties would not occur were policies covering the same property identical as to subject matter of the insurance and terms and conditions, or, as the expression is, "concurrent"; non-concurrency is "A condition existing when a number of fire insurance policies intended to cover the same property are not identical as to the extent of their coverage. . . ." [66] Non-concurrency gives rise to the problem of risk-allocation among the insurers, or "apportionment" of the amount of insurance. To reduce the litigation arising from divergent decisions in various states in cases involving adjustments of non-concurrent apportionments, in 1934 the National Board recommended

65. See Finney, H. A., *op. cit.*, pp. 98–100; Kester, Roy B., *op. cit.*, pp. 321–323; Newlove, George Hillis, Smith, C. Aubrey, and White, John Arch, *Intermediate Accounting* (Boston: D. C. Heath & Co., 1939), pp. 442–444; Streightoff, Frank Hatch, *Advanced Accounting* (New York & London: Harper & Bros., 1932), pp. 508–509.

66. Piver, Jack, *So You're New in Fire Insurance* (San Francisco: Pacific Insurance Magazine, 1946), p. 43.

that its members and others follow a number of suggested rules of procedure in such cases, since generally the problems represented ". . . a controversy between the companies, the assured having ample insurance in the aggregate to be paid his full loss."[67] The rules—not reproduced here because their application is a company, rather than an accountant's, problem—are gaining wide acceptance.[68]

67. National Board of Fire Underwriters. *Non-Concurrent Apportionments. Recommendations of the National Board of Fire Underwriters* (New York: The Board, January 1934), unpaged, first page. Based upon experience gained in applying the rules they were revised in 1942, and published in: National Board of Fire Underwriters. *Non-Concurrent Apportionments. Recommendations of the National Board of Fire Underwriters* (New York: The Board, 1942), pp. 2-7.

68. See also Ehrenzweig, Albert, "Apportionment of Losses under 'Non-Concurrent' Fire Policies," Best's Insurance News. Fire and Casualty Edition, Vol. 42, No. 9 (January 1942), p. 67.

Chapter VII

CONTROVERSY AND LITIGATION

Role of the Accountant

It has been shown that the accountant's procedure when he is assembling claim figures on behalf of the insured, and his procedure when checking such figures as representative of the insurer, differ. On occasion a claimant objects to the company's accountant that the figures sought or the audit methods employed go beyond the claimant's concept of the steps necessary to determine the amount of loss. Occasionally, the insured complains to his broker or adjuster, and through him to the insurance company. The objection is voiced that the auditor's visit is unduly long and consequently is disruptive of business routine. These are not, perhaps, unnatural reactions, but the reviewing accountant's reluctance to discontinue his work before completion is equally understandable. The position of the claimant was commented upon over half a century ago:

> The best *adjusters,* in the honest discharge of their duties, cannot always fail to give offense. Even among *business men* he is not infrequently called exacting, when he simply insists upon the same vouchers for his company, before paying a claim for loss, that would naturally and without question pass between merchants in an ordinary settlement of business affairs—there being this difference, however, against the adjuster: he must depend largely upon the honesty of the claimant, the subject of the settlement *being in ashes,* and not producible in evidence.[1]

The personal characteristics desirable in accountants engaged in loss claim work—as indeed of other professional workers—are integrity, imagination and tact. Basic accounting training and business background are needed in the work of adjusting. Supplementary experience in public accounting and auditing are desirable.

1. Griswold, J., *Fire Underwriters' Text Book* (2nd. Ed., Montreal: Insurance and Finance Chronicle Office, R. Wilson Smith, 1889), p. 576.

The independent accountant's report to his claimant-client generally begins with a brief narration of the scope of the engagement and the audit procedure undertaken. This is followed by indication of the estimated amount of loss, supported by a summary of the figures on which the estimate is based. The insurer's accountant renders a somewhat similar report. Quite often a copy of the accountant's report to the claimant is given to the insurance company; almost never are the entire contents of the company's accountant's report disclosed to the insured.

An insurer anticipating litigation concerning a claim would expect its accountant to include in his working papers such data, abstracts, transcripts and reproductions from the insured's records as would be needed in litigating the claim. These would include material similar to that presented in Appendices B-1 and B-3 to B-5.

Claimant's Reaction to Settlement

Although it is one of the most common contracts, the insurance policy is doubtless one of those least commonly read, and perhaps least understood. Consequently much of the dissatisfaction expressed by policyholders who are discontented with their insurance adjustments is attributable to the inadequate consideration given the policies at the time the insurance is written.[2] The insured's disappointment should the amount of the settlement be lower than he anticipated is understandable. But one writer on Accounting has commented—mistakenly, it is felt—that

> Fire insurance adjusters often take advantage of the business man whose records are poorly kept. Consequently he is usually forced to settle his insurance claim upon a basis satisfactory to the adjuster. If, however, the business man's last inventory has been certified to, he can refuse to compromise and insist upon the full amount of his claim. . . .[3]

2. See Wright, James R., *Fire Insurance* (Toronto: Sir Isaac Pitman & Sons, Ltd., 1932), pp. v–vi. Also note: "With the policy correctly written, and the assured thoroughly familiar with his obligations under the contract and properly fulfilled during the policy term, the loss is practically adjusted before it occurs. . . ." "Check Points for Agents on Adjusting Losses," National Underwriter, Vol. 45, No. 34 (August 21, 1941), p. 21.

3. Castenholz, William B., *Auditing Procedure* (Chicago: La Salle Extension University, 1931), p. 349. Note the reference to the inventory as being "certified to"; what was meant is doubtless the checking or testing of quantities and values by an accountant, or, less likely, an appraiser.

The responsibility of the adjuster, lawyer or accountant who represents an insurer becomes clear when it is considered that the policyholder's lasting evaluation of the desirability of doing business with a given insurance company is made at the time of loss settlement, rather than when the coverage is placed:

> "Loss adjusting is the stock in trade of the insurance business." . . . The public is not impressed . . . by the policy itself nor . . . any other incidents to indemnity; but . . . can and does form its whole impression of insurance from the . . . adjustment. . . .[4]

The claimant who believes that he has been dealt with unfairly has recourse to litigation, but seldom resorts to it.[5] It may be, however, that unsatisfied claimants are deterred from litigation by the expense and delay entailed.

Insured's Books, Records and Abstracts as Legal Evidence: Admissibility

The simplest situation as to proof of amount of loss is personal knowledge and recollection. A household loss may be thus proved. Likewise a mercantile loss in the case where few units are involved, or where the remains are sufficiently "in sight" for identification, and the quantities and values involved may be determined by observation. Mercantile stocks generally present a more complicated case, however. There have been an in-come and an out-go; there has been a combination of raw products, in processing; labor and various other items of cost and expense have entered into the calculation of the pre-loss inventory; merchandise has become unrecognizable, or has been consumed, stolen or the like. Under such circumstances, recourse must be had to records.

Ordinarily "the person whose statement is received as testimony should speak from personal observation or knowledge. . . ."[6] The

4. Bachman, Roy G., "Adjustment of Losses." Chapter I of Fire and Marine Insurance—Course No. 1, Weekly Underwriter, Vol. 147, No. 19 (November 7, 1942), p. 1070.

5. "Only a fraction of 1 percent of the total claims on fire insurance policies result in litigation or even in resort to arbitration. . . ." Bowen, Leroy, "Few Fire Claims Are Litigated," National Underwriter, Vol. 43, No. 46 (November 16, 1939), p. 8.

6. 5 Wigmore, John Henry, *Evidence* (3rd. Ed., Boston: Little, Brown & Co., 1940), Sec. 1530, p. 376.

fact that he may have forgotten, or be unable to carry in mind, all of the details but can refresh his recollection by recourse to memoranda of any kind, presents no problem of departure from restrictions against heresay testimony. It is definitely established that recourse may be taken to such aid to recollection.[7] The privilege of cross-examination is available.[8]

But we must also deal with cases where records may be the combined work of several- even many- individuals or, in whole or in part, of individuals who are unavailable. An unavailable witness may be dispensed with upon proof that the entries were made in the regular course of business.[9] Likewise courts have admitted verified, regularly-made entries without requiring all the links of proof which would otherwise be necessary where there have been a number of participants in the chain of acquisition or depletion, and entry.[10] A number of statutes have been enacted, among them a Federal Statute, admitting records in evidence upon proof that they were made in the regular course of business. Uniform Statutes have been proposed, and the subject is under consideration by legislatures.[11]

Accountant as Expert Witness

The accountant who is called upon to testify in court concerning his examination of the insured's records, should present his testimony in impartial, objective fashion. His answers should be direct and responsive. Information sought should not be withheld; on the other hand, overzealousness, which might be reflected in volunteering information or conclusions, is to be avoided.[12] Working papers built up during the accounting engagement should be arranged in such fashion as to expedite rapid reference if the necessity for consulting the papers during the testimony develops. Tabular statements presented to the Court should be simple. Technical accounting terminology, including such words as *debit* and *credit*, is best avoided, as being unfamiliar to

7. "Any writing may be used to stimulate and revive a recollection." 3 *Ibid.*, Sec. 758, p. 100.

8. *Ibid.*, Sec. 762, p. 108.

9. 5 *Ibid.*, p. 378.

10. *Ibid.*, p. 379.

11. *Ibid.*, Sec. 1520, p. 365.

12. See "Legal Notes," Journal of Accountancy, Vol. 64, No. 1 (July 1937), pp. 65–66.

those who are not accountants. Other simplifications and clarifications are beneficial.[13]

Admissibility of Accountant's Testimony

As the magnitude of the business process increases, the complexity of the records increases. It becomes impractical to resort to these records placed in evidence en masse: "The convenience of trials demands that other evidence be allowed . . . , in the shape of the testimony of a competent witness who has perused the entire mass and will state summarily the net result. Such practice is well established. . . ."[14] Most courts require that the records so summarized be available to the opposing party, for testing of correctness and for cross examination.[15] And, of course, whether it be by an individual who made the entry based on personal knowledge, or under the relaxation of a "regular course of business" rule, some preliminary authentication of the records is necessary.[16]

The law has also been summarized, however, that "an audit made by, or the testimony of, a private auditor, is inadmissible in evidence as proof of original records, books of accounts, reports, or the like"[17] and, to the contrary, upon support of other decisions: "where records . . . have been lost, or . . . are voluminous, or where for other reasons it is impracticable or impossible to produce them in court for examination, an accountant who has examined them may testify as to the contents thereof.[18]

In U.S. v Mortimer the Court stated:

There are numerous cases holding admissible on the testimony of a supervising agent statements compiled from voluminous records according to

13. See Cutforth, A. E., "The Accountant as Expert Witness." Lecture delivered to the London Members of the Institute of Chartered Accountants, October 22, 1931, The Accountant, Vol. LXXXV, No. 2972 (November 21, 1931), pp. 678–679.

14. 4 Wigmore, John Henry, *op. cit.*, Sec. 1230, p. 434.

15. *Ibid.*, pp. 434–435.

16. Rich, Wiley D., *Legal Responsibilities and Rights of Public Accountants* (New York: American Institute Publishing Co., Inc., 1935), pp. 168–170.

17. 52 *American Law Reports Annotated* (Rochester, N.Y.: Lawyers Co-operative Publishing Co.) 1266 shows the objections.

18. *Ibid.*, 1268.

a method at once practicable and offering reasonable guaranty of accuracy, even though the supervisor had not examined each record himself. (Citations.) [19]

Summarizing, the tendency is to accept records in evidence on proof that they were made in the course of business. The effect of accepting the records in evidence is to dispense with proof of actual observation of the acts reflected by the entries, acts in which a number of individuals participated and proof of which, by testimony of the participants, often could not be supplied. And accountants are permitted to summarize the contents of voluminous records.[20] In the last analysis, each case must be considered from the standpoint of the precedents in the jurisdiction involved.

19. (2 Cir. 1941) 118 Fed. (2d) 266, 269 (holding this principle applicable as well where the compilations were made for exclusive use as evidence in the case, *ibid.*, 270).

20. Rich, Wiley D., *op. cit.*, p. 154.

Chapter VIII

SUMMARY AND CONCLUSIONS

THIS STUDY OF the accounting problems and procedures involved in the adjustment of insurance loss claims on merchandise directs particular attention to the methods employed in estimating the amount of loss and in detecting inflated claims. The nature of the insurance company's undertaking pursuant to the insurance contract was reviewed (Chapter I). It was noted that certain clauses or conditions in the insurance policies facilitate the work of the accountant (Chapter II). Methods of proof and evaluation of the loss were discussed (Chapter III). Consideration was given to the possible existence of moral hazard, constituting motive for fraudulent or excessive claim (Chapter IV). The consequent necessity for critical review of financial condition and operating results, and for scrutiny of the various items compromising the claim, was next taken up. The major accounting problems and the techniques employed in solving them were discussed, manifold reference being made to actual claims (Chapters V and VI). This was followed by consideration of controversy and litigation arising from the loss claim. The attitude and characteristics of the accountant, transcripts of records, the accountant's report, and court testimony in loss claims, were then reviewed (Chapter VII).

This study deals with certain loss adjustment problems affecting the insured, the insurer and the community. It is a descriptive analysis of accounting theory and method in the adjustment of claims. Any mechanism which facilitates the proper adjustment of claims helps bring about equitable results to insured and insurer. Studies might be undertaken from the standpoint of the particular problems of the insured or of the insurer. Such studies would consider the divergent interests of these parties.

The conclusions flowing from the present study represent an accountant's thoughts on procedures which would better enable insurers to estimate risks and adjust losses. The conclusions may be summarized as follows:

I. *Uniformity of Books and Records Clauses*

The difficulties encountered by the accountant in book loss examinations are attributable in large measure to faulty record-keeping.[1] Writers on insurance have expressed themselves strongly on the subject of inadequate records. For example, note Moore's observation:

> Where a merchant does not keep satisfactory books of account in a safe depository at night, taking an inventory at least once a year, and keeping copies of it, it is best to let him insure himself. . . .[2]

Thistle's comment:

> no risk should be accepted unless it is determined in advance that the assured will be able to prove the amount of his loss by his books, as required by the policy.[3]

and Sexton's terse summation:

> A merchant who does not keep books of account should not be insured.[4]

Such strong position is obviously unlikely of whole-hearted approval by brokers and agents, not to speak of prospective insureds.

Most manufacturing or trading businesses take inventory only once a year. Even where inventory is taken as often as monthly it is rare that the purchase and sales records are maintained in such fashion as to reveal, following an insurance loss, the quantity and description of specific items, or classes of items, lost or destroyed. In small businesses, when loss claims occur the insured frequently relies upon rough computations, supplemented by his memory as to specific missing items.[5]

1. See the tabulation of significant points in the case studies presented in Appendix A, and the illustrations in Chapters V and VI.

2. Moore, Francis C., *Fire Insurance and How to Build* (New York: Baker & Taylor Co., 1903), pp. 48–49.

3. Thistle, Edward B., "Underwriting Burglary and Theft Risks," in *Lectures on Insurance. Intermediate Course. Casualty and Surety* (New York: Underwriter Printing and Publishing Co., 1923), p. 75.

4. Sexton, William, *Fire Insurance* (San Francisco: The Coast Review, 1915), p. 30.

5. See Appendix A, Case 27 for illustration of the difficulties which arose in a loss claim at a retail stationery, book and toy shop. The policy requirement

Controversies resulting where bookkeeping records are insufficient are seldom settled satisfactorily to either insured or insurer.[6]

Comparable to the record-keeping requirement in the burglary policy[7] is the insured's obligation under the iron safe, or record warranty, clause in certain fire policies, to keep books showing a complete record of business transacted.[8] The New York Standard fire insurance policy provides merely that following a loss the insured "shall produce for examination all books of account, bills, invoices, and other vouchers. . . ."[9] Where the insured maintained only haphazard records, the phrase "all books of account" might conceivably mean almost no books of account.

The problems of loss determination in burglary cases are similar to those in fire losses where little, or no, damaged merchandise remains after the loss. The disappearance of goods through burglary, or complete destruction by fire, makes necessary the use of records for determination of the amount of loss. The difficulties such situations present could be alleviated by an endorsement, to be attached to policies on risks for which the underwriters would consider the keeping of records essential. The phraseology of the endorsement could be somewhat similar to that of the record warranty clause. The latter is more specific than the books of account clause in the mercantile burglary policy and more exacting than the records clause in the Standard fire policy. From the point of view of an accountant, there would seem to be little reason for variation of record-keeping requirements among the various types of policies insuring merchandise.

The probable objections that considerable additional work would be required of the insured, and that the suggested record-keeping requirements are uncommon, are without substance. The record-keeping requirements already imposed upon the insured as a taxpayer are that he "shall . . . keep such permanent books of account or records, including inventories, as are sufficient to establish the amount of the

that the insured keep records in such manner that the Company can accurately determine the amount of loss from the records, is clearly impossible in businesses like the one in question.

6. See Fritz, George C., "Mercantile Open Stock Burglary Insurance," in *Budget Supplement* (Baltimore: Maryland Casualty Co., December 1927), p. 6.

7. *Supra*, p. 14.

8. *Supra*, p. 14.

9. Lines 118–119. And see *supra*, p. 19.

gross income and the deductions, credits, and other matters required to be shown in any return. . . ." [10]

It is also noted that many foreign countries require all individuals or companies engaged in business to maintain specific books of account, such as the Journal or Day Book, and the Ledger. In some countries the individual pages of these books must be stamped by a designated official before use, and the records must be reviewed and stamped (or "rubricated") annually after the completion of entries for the year, including the recording of the annual balance sheet and detailed inventory.[11]

II. *Availability of Specific Records for Inspection When Claim Is Made*

Records clauses in fire policies generally require that the insured make available all "books of account, bills, invoices and other vouchers." Extended discussion frequently takes place between the insured and the company's representative concerning what is embraced in those terms. Copies of income, payroll and other tax reports often help substantiate the claimed loss figures; financial statements issued to banks and other sources of credit are likewise useful. An accountant would desire that all of the insured's records which shed light on the accuracy of the claim be obtainable. The task of determining the amount of loss would be expedited if it were specifically stipulated that there be made available for review by the insurance company after a loss the insured's income tax returns, financial statements, public accountants' reports, and similar records. The insured often regards such request as an invasion of its financial privacy and frequently resists presenting such data or refuses outright.

Canada offers a somewhat unusual suggestion concerning requirements for the availability of specific records. An insurance investigating

10. U.S. Treasury Department, Bureau of Internal Revenue, Supplement to Regulations 111, Relating to the Income Tax Under the Internal Revenue Code (Washington, D.C.: U.S. Government Printing Office, 1946), Section 29.54-1. But note that such Regulations do not always have the effect of inducing small businesses to maintain satisfactory sets of books.

11. For example, for the bookkeeping requirements in Mexico, see U.S. Department of Commerce, Bureau of Foreign and Domestic Commerce. Trade Promotion Series No. 152 (Revised December 1, 1934), Ramirez, Mariano H., *Trading Under the Laws of Mexico* (Washington, D.C.: U.S. Government Printing Office, 1935), pp. 14–15.

commission, reporting to the Legislative Assembly of Ontario, recommended that in mercantile risks insureds be required to take inventory annually, depositing a copy of the inventory sheets with a bank for retention until the next succeeding annual stocktaking occurs, and the inventory sheets therefor are delivered to the bank.[12] The writer is not in accord with such an extreme position.

III. *Inspection of Risk as Pre-requisite to Writing Coverage*

Moral hazard may be attributed, in part, to over-insurance. Insufficient investigation, at the time of application for coverage, of the business history of the insured, the value of items at risk, the financial condition of the insured's business and the results of operations, may result in placing on the insurance company's books business of greater-than-average possibility of loss. Some insurance companies have demurred at undertaking more exhaustive investigation of the affairs of the insured than is now the practice, because of the cost; others, in their desire for increased premium volume, it is said, accept accommodation lines without adequate inquiry into the insured's business affairs. Both these factors tend to create additional physical or moral hazard.

To be sure, inspection of the merchandise at risk before coverage does not guarantee the existence at the time of the casualty, of the quantities claimed to have been lost or damaged, since in normal course the form or quantity of the merchandise, or both, would change soon after inspection. Where inspection preceded coverage, however, the tendency would be to reduce the likelihood of fraud through overstatement of quantities or values of merchandise in the loss claim.

IV. *Financial Statements to be Submitted on Applying for Coverage*

Another suggestion is that the prospective insured be asked to submit a balance sheet and an operating statement upon applying for coverage on merchandise. Since practically every business periodically prepares balance sheets, and every one prepares operating state-

12. Ontario Insurance Commission, "Report on [sic] Insurance Commission." The Hon. Mr. Justice Masten, Commissioner. Printed by order of The Legislative Assembly of Ontario (Toronto: A. T. Wilgress, Printer to the King's Most Excellent Majesty, 1919), p. 38. Presumably the sheets would be available to the insurer in the event of a loss.

ments—even if the latter be only those presented in income tax returns—as a general rule the insured would not be inconvenienced by a requirement to supply copies to the prospective insurer. The insurance company would be in better position to appraise the credit and moral hazard risks in writing the insurance, and in the event of a loss claim there would be available data concerning merchandise inventory and other accounts, of use in checking the loss claim.[13]

V. *Application for Insurance*

It has been observed by insurance men that little practical purpose would be served by requiring the filing of a written application for insurance on merchandise. Their contention is that many of the conditions reported upon in the application, e. g., financial position and operating results, might change considerably during the period of the policy. Similar reasoning could be employed in opposing the universally-accepted practice of making written application for a life insurance policy. However, insurers find it necessary, in deciding whether to accept an applicant for life insurance, to consider his history, shown in the application, as well as the present habits, financial condition and prospects of the insured. The latter are revealed by agencies which make supplementary inquiry on behalf of the insurance company.

In addition to information now submitted orally in applying for coverage on merchandise, *viz.*, identification of property at risk, location, amount and type of coverage, and similar matter, the insured might be required to include in a written application itemization of the books and records maintained, indication of the frequency of inventory-taking, names of banks and accountants, insurance loss history, bankruptcy or insolvency history of the company, its principals and predecessor companies, and similar information. In brief, such material as would be of use to the insurer in deciding whether to accept the risk and to its accountants in connection with the checking of loss claims should be submitted.

It is noted that where formal application is at present required in insuring merchandise, e. g., for Jewelers' Block policies, the insured

13. Note the reference (*supra*, p. 42) to the Statement form of the New York Board of Fire Underwriters, reproduced as Appendix E.

accepts as a matter of course the necessity for responding to the list of questions contained in the Proposal or Application.

Independent of all other reasons, written application would be justified if it should result in decreased moral hazard because the insurer is put in possession of financial data which could be checked against the loss claim.

VI. *Central Claim Files*

Extension of central insurance claim record bureaus to embrace all merchandise claims, by whatever insured risk, should tend to reduce the possibility of fraud through the detection of repetitious claimants. Another effect would be to make unavailable, or to curtail, coverage to applicants with bad loss records.

VII. *Independence of Loss Department from Underwriting Department*

Successful insurance companies probably tend to be more liberal in settling claims than companies which have been losing money. However, some insurers allow what appear to be overpayments on claims, on the theory that it is good business to do so. The adjustment policy of the claim department unquestionably affects the insurer's underwriting income. Liberality tends to result in a higher loss ratio. Although a severe adjustment policy may bring about a lower loss ratio, the company's reputation for strict adjustments may result in reduced premium income.

Some insurers are opposed to claims litigation as being poor business policy; others frequently litigate even though it be indiscreet, business-wise, to do so. Most companies consider, before undertaking to contest specific claims, the possibility of unfavorable publicity and the resultant harmful reaction on business, as well as the chance that adverse legal precedents may be set. Expediency may thus occasion the insurer's apparent disregard of its independent accountant's computation of the amount of loss.

From time to time the underwriting department may be confronted by the situation in which a broker threatens to remove all the "lines" he has placed with the company unless a satisfactory adjustment is effected on a given claim. Thus "soft," or liberal, adjustments are at times made because of their value in obtaining or retaining other profitable items or "lines" of insurance coverage.[14] Such practice is to be discouraged as tending to increase the ratio of loss payments to premium income and to result ultimately in increased premium rates.

VIII. *Independence of Accountants*

It is suggested that when an insurance company considers the examination of a claimant's books necessary, and also anticipates possible litigation, it is desirable that an independent public accountant be engaged for the work rather than that a company employee be assigned to it. The findings of a company employee are frequently attacked by the claimant as being biased. Such charge is less likely to be levied against the independent accountant.

14. See Russ, Harry D., "Claim Adjustments," Insurance Age, Vol. LIII, No. 7 (February 15, 1924), p. 12; Barnard, Chester F., "Loss Management," *Proceedings of the Fifty-fourth Annual Meeting of the Fire Underwriters' Association of the Pacific* (1930), pp. 48-50; Wisconsin. Report of the Wisconsin Legislative Fire Insurance Investigating Committee of the Senate and Assembly, Made to the Governor Pursuant to Joint Resolution 130, A., and Chapter 512 of the Laws of 1911 (Madison, Wis.: Democrat Printing Co., State Printer, 1913), p. 61; "Report of Committee on Adjustments," *Proceedings of the Seventy-first Annual Meeting of National Board of Fire Underwriters* (New York, 1937), p. 88; and Scammell, E. J., "Standard Claims Manual Urged as Aid to Holding Fire and Motor Business," Weekly Underwriter, Vol. 128, No. 18 (May 6, 1933), pp. 857 and 864.

APPENDIX A

Case Studies

Case #	*Type of Business*	*Type of Loss*
1	Diamond Importer	Hold-up
2	None (Household Furniture Loss) *	Fire
3	Fur Garment Manufacturer	Disappearance
4	Picture Frame Manufacturer	Fire
5	Coat Lining Manufacturer	Fire
6	Diamond Importer	Hold-up
7	Dress Shop	Fire
8	Scrap Metal Dealer	Theft
9	Dress Manufacturer	Disappearance
10	Dentist	Burglary
11	Retail Dry Goods	Fire
12	Pocketbook & Glove Retailer	Fire
13	Fur Storage Vault	Burglary
14	Spaghetti & Macaroni Manufacturer	Fire
15	Retail Dry Goods	Fire
16	Necktie Manufacturer	Fire
17	Women's Coat Jobber	Burglary
18	Retailer of Groceries, Spices & Spiced Meats	Fire
19	Fruit & Vegetable Retailers	Fire
20	Upholstered Furniture Manufacturer	Fire
21	Fur Dealer	Fire
22	Retail Luggage & Leather Goods	Hold-up
23	Wholesale Automobile Tires	Hold-up
24	Ladies' Handbag Manufacturer & Novelty Jewelry & Ornament Jobber	Fire
25	Diamond & Jewelry Importer & Wholesaler	Hold-up
26	Furriers & Fur Storage Vault Operators	Burglary
27	Stationery & Toy Shop	Burglary

Case Studies

Case #	*Type of Business*	*Type of Loss*
28	Manufacturer of Model Airplanes & Airplane Parts	Fire
29	Retailer of Radio Sets, Refrigerators & Electrical Appliances	Fire
30	Men's Clothing Shop	Fire
31	Retail Druggist	Fire
32	Retail Diamonds & Jewelry	Burglary
33	Wholesale Rings, Mountings & Mounted Diamonds	Disappearance
34	Wholesale Cultured Pearls	Burglary
35	Retail Jewelry	Hold-up
36	Sales Agent for Manufacturer of Unleavened Bread & Related Products	Fire
37	Night Club Operator *	Fire
38	Women's Underwear Manufacturer	Fire
39	Pocketbook Manufacturer	Fire
40	Diamond Dealer	Burglary
41	Hardware & House Furnishings Retailer	Fire
42	Necktie Manufacturers	Fire
43	Converter & Jobber of Cotton & Rayon Yarn	Fire
44	Spaghetti & Macaroni Manufacturer	Fire
45	Dealer in Inexpensive Furs	Disappearance
46	None (Fur Coat Loss) *	Burglary
47	Women's & Children's Hat Jobber	Fire
48	Tobacco & Candy Wholesaler	Hold-up of Truck
49	Jewelry Wholesalers	Hold-up
50	Hat & Cap Retailer	Fire
51	Resident Buyer of Dresses	Fire
52	Women's Hat Manufacturer	Burglary
53	Retail Men's & Boys' Clothing	Fire
54	Necktie Manufacturer	Water Damage
55	Glazed Fruit Manufacturer	Fire
56	Women's Knitted Sportswear Manufacturer	Fire

* Although not merchandise losses, these cases are presented because the principles of record-checking involved are similar to those employed in merchandise losses.

TABULATION OF SIGNIFICAN

CASE

	1	2	3	4	5	6	7	8	9	10	11	12	13	14	15	16	17	18
EXCESSIVE CLAIMS MADE		X		X	X			X			X	X		X		X		
RECORDS																		
PERPETUAL INVENTORY OR STOCK RECORD																		
MAINTAINED	X								X									
FALSE:																		
GENERAL LEDGER	X				X							X				X		
GENERAL JOURNAL	X											X						
ENTRIES (FOR REASONS UNRELATED TO CLAIM)												X						
PURCHASE BILLS OR OTHER PURCHASE RECORDS	X						X					X				X		
STOCK RECORDS	X																	
MANUFACTURING RECORDS																		
APPLICATION FOR INSURANCE	X																	
INVENTORY FIGURES														X				
ACCOUNTS RECEIVABLE																		
CUSTOMERS' ORDERS													X			X		
INCOMPLETE:																		
STOCK BOOK ENTRIES	X							X										
IDENTIFICATION OF ITEMS TRADED IN											X							
MANUFACTURING RECORDS				X		X				X								
DESTROYED OR LOST														X		X		
ERRORS:																		
STYLE NUMBERS INCORRECT																		
IN APPLICATION FOR INSURANCE						X												
STOCK NUMBERS DUPLICATED																		
INCONSISTENCIES CONCERNING ITEMS IN																		
CLAIM LIST:																		
SOLD BEFORE LOSS																		
NOT IN PRECEDING INVENTORY NOR BOUGHT																		
SINCE																		
DIFFERENT DESCRIPTIONS & VALUES IN																		
INVENTORIES			X															
LISTED IN POST-LOSS INVENTORY																		
UNUSUAL ITEMS																		
METHOD OF LOSS DETERMINATION																		
SALES FEW IN NUMBER																		
MOST EXPENSIVE CLASSES OF GOODS TRADED IN																		
INCLUDED IN CLAIM																		
PROCEEDS OF SALE THEREOF IN CASH																		
REGISTER AT TIME OF HOLD-UP																		
TERMS OF CONTRACT FOR SALE OF LOST																		
MERCHANDISE								X										
GROSS PROFIT PERCENTAGE:																		
METHOD USED IN AUDITING CLAIM				X	X			X				X						
EXCESSIVE RATE CLAIMED												X		X				
FINANCIAL CONDITION*																		
GENERAL FINANCIAL CONDITION	P			P				P				P		P			P	
LIQUID OR CURRENT POSITION				P		G						P						
EXCESSIVE PRE-LOSS INVENTORY																		
FORMER SEASON MERCHANDISE INCLUDED																		
IN CLAIM												X						
RESULTS OF BUSINESS OPERATIONS*				P		P			P	G		P		P				
NET WORTH (O=OVERSTATED, D=DECLINING)			D	O								O						
*G=GOOD; F=FAIR; P=POOR																		

'OINTS IN CASE STUDIES

ERS

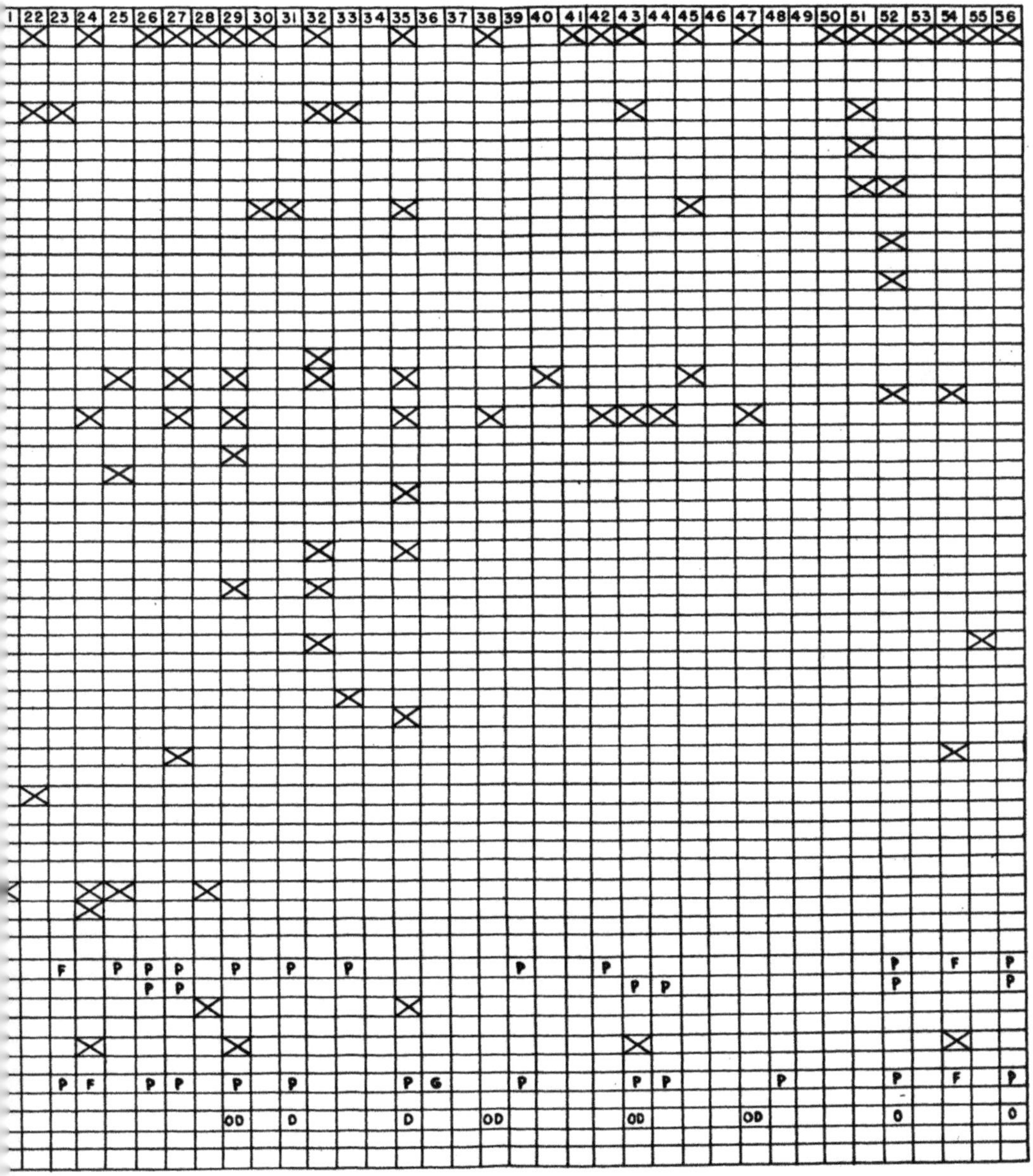

Case 1

Diamond Importer: Hold-up

A loss of over $100,000.00 was reported. The records maintained included the customary journals, ledgers, memorandum and stock books. For reasons not revealed by the insured, prices shown on invoices entered in the purchase and stock books represented undervaluations, and some purchases of merchandise were not entered in either of the books. The entries required to place on the records the remainder of the sums actually paid for merchandise appeared to have been made in general ledger accounts designated as loans receivable from various associates and relatives of the principals of the insured. One purchase invoice bore a notation in a foreign tongue, presumably written by the supplier, to the effect that the bill was not a true one, the true bill being forthcoming.

The insured's financial condition was poor. To avoid revealing a top-heavy inventory condition, merchandise figures were falsified in financial statements issued to the banks and false entries were made in the books to record purported sales of merchandise. Customers' notes amounting to several hundred thousand dollars were under discount with banks at all times. Few of these notes were met at maturity. Generally, the customers made small payments on account and gave new notes to offset the balances due. The new notes were discounted at banks other than those at which the maturing notes were held, and the proceeds of the new discounts, supplemented by the necessary additional cash, were applied to meet the maturing notes. Many notes purporting to represent the proceeds of sales were received from alleged customers; actually the notes were given as accommodations to assist the insured in financing itself through the discounting of these notes.

Considerable disparity existed between, on one hand, figures cited in the application or Proposal for insurance, and, on the other, figures in the books and in financial statements issued to the banks. The inventory figures in the Proposal represented the balance before giving effect to the false sales entries recorded in the books. The totals for other items in the Proposal also differed from corresponding figures in the general ledger.

CASE 2

Household Furniture: Fire

The prices of individual items in the Proof of Loss were much higher than corresponding figures in the statements received by the insurer from the shops where the furniture was bought.

CASE 3

Fur Garment Manufacturer: Disappearance

The insured reported the disappearance of fur pieces and fur coats from the premises of a consignee. Upon investigation it developed that the disappearance took place while the claimant's representative was negotiating a loan secured by the merchandise rather than while the consignee was preparing to show the furs to a prospective customer.

The records were incomplete and were kept poorly. Since there was no manufacturing record, it was impossible to verify the number of skins and the value of labor applied in manufacturing the lost furs. As to some of the items included in the claim, discrepancies were found between the descriptions and valuations reported and those shown in the last inventory taken before the loss.

At the date of the loss the net worth of the insured was $18,000.00, reflecting a decline of $9,000.00 from the close of the preceding year, $12,000.00 from the second year preceding and $28,000.00 from the third. The volume of business for the four months preceding the loss was $19,000.00; the volume had been $73,000.00 for the year preceding the loss, $40,000.00 for the second year preceding and $117,000.00 for the third. The merchandise inventory reported to be on hand at the date of the loss represented approximately 90% of the net worth.

CASE 4

Picture Frame Manufacturer: Fire

The customary ledgers and journals were maintained, but no records were kept of the labor consumed in manufacturing specific items. The insured stated that its inventory at the date of the fire amounted to $15,500.00. This was 125% of the gross sales made during the period of eleven and one-half months since the end of the preceding fiscal year.

An important point in arriving at the estimated value of this inventory was the treatment of overhead expenses. It could not be determined from the insured's records what proportion of the "expenses" of $9,600.00 (including the principal officer's salary of $5,400.00) represented manufacturing expense. Part of the item was unquestionably general administrative expense.

It was noted that although the annual volumes of production and sales were falling, the total of the "expenses" was rising.

The insurer's accountant compiled the following figures:

% of "Expenses" Considered to be M'f'g Expenses in Computing Cost of Merchandise Produced	*Estimated Maximum Value of Inventory Available at Time of Loss (after Deducting Cost of Sales, Computed on Basis of Average Gross Profit %)*
25	$6,500.00
50	7,500.00
100	9,400.00

The highest of these estimated inventory figures is far below the inventory figure of $15,500.00 submitted by the insured.

The rejection of an excessive percentage of overhead expense in computing the value of merchandise on hand at the date of loss was based on the reasoning that only part of the "expenses" was properly includible as an element of cost of production and consequently of the inventory value of the output. If the insured's output had consisted of a single picture frame, the costs and expenses incurred in production might conceivably have been several thousand dollars although the inventory value and market price of the single frame produced were each well under one dollar. It is noted that in the instant case, accepting as a cost of manufacture 100% of the "expenses" nevertheless yields an inventory figure far below that claimed by the insured.

The following two tables show the method employed in estimating the value of the inventory on hand at the date of the loss:

TABLE I

Estimated Value of Inventory at Date of Loss on Bases that 100%, 50%, 25%, and 0% of Expenses Were Considered to be Manufacturing Expenses

% of Expenses Treated as Manufacturing Expenses	*100*	*50*	*25*	*0*
Inventory—June 1	$ 5,700.00	$ 5,700.00	$ 5,700.00	$ 5,700.00
Add:				
Purchases, Labor, Processing, Light & Power	6,600.00	6,600.00	6,600.00	6,600.00
Expenses— (Total: $9,600.00) *				
100%	9,600.00			
50%		4,800.00		
25%			2,400.00	
0%				—
Total	$21,900.00	$17,100.00	$14,700.00	$12,300.00
Less: Cost of Sales **				
(Sales: $12,300.00)				
102%	12,500.00			
78%		9,600.00		
67%			8,200.00	
54%				6,600.00
Estimated Inventory— at Date of Loss	$ 9,400.00	$ 7,500.00	$ 6,500.00	$ 5,700.00

* Including principal officer's drawings of $5,400.00.

** See Table II.

TABLE II

Estimated Gross Profit Percentages for Years Preceding That in Which Loss Occurred—Based upon Income Tax Reports

	Year Preceding Loss	*2nd Year Preceding Loss*	*3rd Year Preceding Loss*	*Total*	*% of Average Gross Profit after Deducting "Expenses" as Indicated*
Net Income from Sales	$15,900.00	$17,700.00	$13,400.00	$47,000.00	
Gross Profit—per Income Tax Report	7,700.00	8,800.00	5,200.00	21,700.00	
Expenses	8,100.00	8,400.00	5,900.00	22,400.00	
Gross Profit Less:					
100% of Expenses *	(400.00)	400.00	(700.00)	(700.00)	(2)
50% of Expenses *	3,700.00	4,600.00	2,200.00	10,500.00	22
25% of Expenses *	5,700.00	6,700.00	3,700.00	16,100.00	33
0% of Expenses *	7,700.00	8,800.00	5,200.00	21,700.00	46

* = Figures rounded to nearest $100.00
( ) = Loss

On inspection of the merchandise and debris remaining after the loss the insurer's appraiser reported that the quantities of many items claimed to have been on hand before the loss were exaggerated. He also found numerous over-valuations of items in the insured's schedule of inventory. The following were several examples:

Item	*Value Claimed by Insured*	*Appraiser's Estimate of Value*
Oil Paintings	$ 35.00 each	$10.00 each
Paintings	100.00 each	25.00 each
Parts for Desk Sets (5 years old)	625.00 total	75.00 total

Based upon an inventory reported at $15,500.00, the net worth at the date of the loss was stated to be $15,300.00, including capital stock of $10,000.00. The insurer's representatives estimated the value of the inventory at $7,000.00. Adjusting for the difference and for a small unrecorded liability resulted in the reduction of the net worth to $6,400.00. At the date of the loss, the quick assets available (i. e., Cash and Accounts Receivable) totalled $1,700.00 as against current liabilities of $4,400.00. During the period of several months preceding the loss, a number of checks issued by the insured, in amounts ranging from $5.00 to $70.00, were returned with the notation "Insufficient Funds." During the six-week period preceding the loss the daily bank balance never exceeded $325.00; during half this period it was less than $100.00.

The date of the loss coincided with the beginning of the slow season. Had the insured not suffered the fire loss, and had the volume of $550.00 monthly (from January 1 to the date of the loss, in May) been maintained, with customers' accounts being collected promptly, the funds available would have been insufficient to meet outstanding liabilities, without making any payment whatever for new merchandise, labor, operating expenses, salaries and supplies. During the period of eleven and one-half months to the date of the loss the insured sustained a loss from operations of $3,000.00 on sales of $12,300.00, the closing inventory figure used in this computation being the estimate made by the insurer's appraiser. During the preceding year there was a loss of $350.00 on sales of $15,900.00; during the second year preceding, a gain of $500.00 was realized on sales of $17,700.00.

Case 5

Coat Lining Manufacturer: Fire

The insured entered sales returns and allowances as though they were purchases. Since the gross profit method was used in estimating the inventory on hand at the date of the loss, the claim was overstated.

Case 6

Diamond Importer: Hold-up

The claim arose through the hold-up of a salesman while he was on the road. The sales price of diamonds charged to him during the course of the trip, reduced by sales and by merchandise on memorandum with customers or deposited for safe-keeping in the hotel safe, left a loss in excess of $100,000.00 at sales price. The mark-up on sales made by the salesman was normal.

The importer's general books of account were well-kept, but the manufacturing records were deficient in that specific rough diamonds, put through the processes of cutting and polishing, were not readily identifiable throughout the period of processing. Although physical inventories were taken annually as of one month-end date, income tax returns were prepared and the books were closed on the basis of estimated inventories at a later date.

The answer supplied in the application for insurance as to the average daily amount of goods in the possession of cutters, manufacturers, customers, repairers and dealers was much too low, the amount shown having apparently been estimated rather than computed.

The company was in good financial condition; the net worth was high and the current ratio and acid test ratios were good. Despite the large volume of business, however, the net profit for the business year preceding the loss was negligible.

Case 7

Dress Shop: Fire

The insured presented numerous bills from dress manufacturers in support of purchases of dresses said to have been destroyed in the fire, which took place in March. One bill, bearing traces of alteration, read as follows:

December 15 43 dresses at $9.00—$387.00

Examination of the seller's duplicate bill book showed that the invoice had been issued undated. Based upon the sequence of dates in the book, however, the sale took place in February. The quantity actually sold was only three dresses at $9.00 each, total $27.00.

On renewed inspection of the insured's bill, it became clear that the following alterations had been made: the date *December 15* was inserted; as to the quantity sold, the figure *4* was placed before the truthful figure *3;* as to the total price, the figure *2* in the sum *$27.00* was unskillfully altered to read *8,* and the figure *3* was placed before the resulting *87* to give the new figure *$387.00.* A reproduction of this invoice is presented as Appendix B-1.

Case 8

Scrap Metal Dealer: Theft

A loaded truck, containing 25,000 pounds of pewter, tin, block tin and Babbitt metal, of a total value of $4,700.00, was said to have been stolen from the premises of the claimant, who operated a junk yard dealing in these and other metals. The insured exhibited a contract covering the sale of the above metal and calling for delivery within a week.

Visit to the premises of the buyer brought out that the contracts in the possession of buyer and seller were typewritten originals identical in text. It was ascertained that during the entire year preceding the loss, the insured had sold only $2,500.00 of metal to the buyer, and during the second year preceding, $5,500.00. The highest individual sale made to the buyer during a period of two and one-half years preceding the loss was $1,000.00; the lowest, $12.50. The buyer's records showed that no scrap tin or special mixtures containing Babbitt metal and pewter had been sold for several months before the loss. The buyer's average monthly sales during the period immediately preceding the loss were under $1,000.00. There appeared to be no need for undue haste in making the delivery, nor any need for the seller to effect delivery of the entire shipment in one truckload, an unusually heavy one for the company.

The insured's books were kept haphazardly in a foreign tongue. Details of the quantities of many items purchased from itinerant junk dealers were not available. The only evidence supporting the existence of the goods reported stolen was an alleged inventory book containing a brief list of items of merchandise. This was said to represent the inventory on hand at the date of a proposed merger with the business of a relative of the insured, which was to have taken place two months before the date of the loss. This inventory totalled $7,100.00, of which sum $5,300.00 represented tin, pewter and Babbitt metal. However, starting with the inventory values of the types of metal concerned in the loss, indicated by the records to have been on hand at the beginning of the year, and adding thereto the purchases of such metals to the date of the proposed merger, and reducing this total by the estimated cost of sales of these items during the same period, yielded a total representing the estimated inventory of pewter, tin, Babbitt metal and block tin at the date of the proposed merger, of but $3,900.00.

The financial condition of the insured was poor. Its net worth at the date of the alleged loss was estimated at less than $1,000.00. During the year preceding the loss the bank balance was never above $100.00; many checks drawn by the insured were returned unpaid, marked "Insufficient Funds."

CASE 9

Dress Manufacturer: Disappearance

This claim was for dresses which were reported to have disappeared on June 20 and 21. Each month the accountant for the insured prepared a summary showing the number of dresses on hand at the beginning of the month, the number produced during the month, the number sold and the balance which should have been on hand. He compared this balance with the end-of-month physical inventory figure furnished by the insured. Each month there were differences between the two sums, and the book figure was adjusted to agree with the number of dresses actually on hand.

The insured's accountant arrived at the figure representing the claim for disappearance by starting with the June 1 physical inventory, adding the number of dresses produced to June 20, deducting the sales to that date and comparing the result with the physical inventory on June 20. Similar procedure was followed for the June 21 claim, giving consideration, of course, to the loss claimed on June 20.

The insurer's accountant compared the daily balance in the perpetual inventory record with the insured's figures for the daily counts of dresses on hand. There were shortages or overages almost daily during a period of several months preceding the dates of the losses claimed. These daily differences indicated carelessness in record-keeping or dishonesty on the part of the insured's staff, the latter risk not being insured against under the policy. The existence of numerous overages and shortages as between perpetual inventory and physical count vitiated reliance upon the insured's records as corroboration of the quantity of dresses missing.

During the four months preceding the loss, the insured made sales amounting to $110,000.00 and realized a total net profit of $250.00; during the month preceding the loss the volume of business had been $33,000.00, and the net profit $133.00.

Case 10

Dentist: Burglary

The insured was a practising dentist, located in a congested residential district in a large eastern city. Claim was made for dental work and gold stolen at night, when the dental office was closed. The insured maintained a cash receipts book, a patients' ledger, including mouth charts, a check book, and a bank pass book. No record was kept of the quantity of gold consumed in dental work, nor did patients' ledger cards, which were kept informally, reflect in detail the work done. It was impossible, therefore, to check the accuracy of the claim for gold lost as a result of the burglary or the quantity consumed in work for patients.

The claim included an item for gold contained in customers' bridge-work, the undertaking of which work was not revealed by the patients' ledger cards. The insured stated that the bills from the dental laboratory were not retained and that no record was maintained of the names of the persons for whom such laboratory work was done.

The dentist's average gross receipts per month were $1,300.00, expenses being about $600.00 and net income, $700.00.

Case 11

Retail Dry Goods: Fire

The claimed sound value of merchandise damaged by the fire was $13,000.00. The principal records kept by the insured were a bank deposit book, a check book and a file of purchase invoices.

Items listed in the Proof of Loss were described as to type of merchandise, but their sources were not indicated. For the purpose of testing prices in the Proof of Loss, fourteen classes of goods dealt in by the insured were selected. The total sound value of such items appearing in the Proof of Loss was $6,000.00, or about 46% of the total sound value shown. Of the total in dollars of the purchase invoices presented in support of the claim, $4,000.00, or 37%, represented items in the fourteen classes of goods selected for price-testing. For twelve of the fourteen classes the highest prices claimed in the Proof of Loss were greater than the highest prices found in the purchase bills. For ten of the fourteen classes, the lowest prices in the Proof of Loss were higher than the lowest prices found in the purchase bills. Few of the valuations placed upon items in the Proof of Loss were exactly the same as prices found in the purchase bills.

Case 12

Pocketbook and Glove Retailer: Fire

The insured operated leased departments, selling pocketbooks and gloves, in several department stores. The fire took place in the insured's stockroom in one of the stores, during the month of June, which was in the slow season. The merchandise reported to have been destroyed consisted of suede and leather gloves carried over from the previous fall; the gloves were valued at $10,500.00, which was said to represent cost. The insured stated that the merchandise was staple, not being subject to hazards of style, and would have been marketable again shortly.

The claim was computed on the gross profit percentage basis. The figure for purchases was inflated, many checks for officers' salaries having been included in the ledger account for purchases. The object was to understate the amount of the salaries to the stockholder-officers, for reasons not related to the claim. A number of general journal entries were also distorted.

The insured's financial condition and operating results were unsatisfactory. It had $17,500.00 in current assets, including merchandise of $15,500.00, and owed $13,000.00 on current liabilities. The balance sheet submitted to the insurance company reflected a net worth of $13,500.00; audit of the records disclosed that figure to be but $5,000.00, which was insufficient to make possible conducting business efficiently at the units operated. The insured reported that the profit for the five-month period to the date of the fire was $4,100.00; on audit it developed that operations for that period resulted in a loss of $3,000.00. The gross profit realized by the insured was 29%, rather than the claimed gross profit of 40%.

Case 13

Fur Storage Vault: Burglary

Because of the inadequate method of record-keeping the total value of customers' furs in storage at any given date could not be determined. Every coat was reported to be insured for $100.00 except where the storage order indicated a higher valuation. Concerning several coats claimed to have been stolen, each reported by the insured at a value in excess of $100.00, it was apparent that the valuations noted upon the various copies of the storage orders had not been placed upon all the copies simultaneously.

Case 14

Spaghetti and Macaroni Manufacturer: Fire

The fire took place in January. The claim for loss and damage amounted to $5,200.00, of which $2,900.00 represented merchandise burned out of sight. The customary books of account were kept. The insured arrived at the amount of the inventory on hand at the time of the loss by adding to the alleged inventory at December 31 amounting to $7,000.00, purchases to the date of the loss, and by deducting from the total of these items the cost of sales for the same period. Recomputation of the December 31 inventory, starting with the figures for a November 30 inventory taken by the insured, adding purchases to December 31 and deducting the cost of sales for the same period, indicated an inventory at December 31 amounting to $2,800.00, rather than the figure of $7,000.00 reported.

Another test, on the basis of the weights of goods handled, revealed an excessive inventory figure as of December 31 for the raw material, semolina, and the finished product, spaghetti and macaroni. Study of the inventory of boxes indicated a similar condition. Beginning with the quantity of wooden boxes in the November 30 inventory, adding purchases for December, and deducting the number of boxes consumed in packaging during the month, revealed considerable overstatement of the quantity on hand at December 31. Although the insured reported that physical inventories had been taken every month, the detailed inventory sheets were said to have been destroyed immediately after being summarized.

The insured was in poor financial condition. Its capital and bank balances were low and the receivables due from customers were slow of collection. The gross profit earned was insufficient to cover the expenses of operation and the moderate salary drawings of the principals, who participated actively in the business. The insured reported that the rate of gross profit earned was 30%; audit demonstrated it to be but 11%.

Case 15

Retail Dry Goods: Fire

The insured did not maintain a General Ledger, nor did he use a cash register. It was his practice to remove money from the cash drawer to pay for small purchases, making no entry for the acquisition of the goods, nor the reduction of the cash. At the end of each day, the balance remaining in the cash drawer after deducting the small permanent change fund was recorded in a Sales Register as representing the day's sales, and was deposited in the bank. An estimate of purchases was made based upon the invoices appearing in the Creditors' Ledger and such other purchase invoices, statements from creditors, memoranda, and related data as were available.

Case 16

Necktie Manufacturer: Fire

Claim was made for $18,000.00 representing the loss and damage resulting from a fire which took place in December. One of the insureds presented a list of orders stated to have been taken during the course of a selling trip which was interrupted on receipt of word that a fire had taken place. Correspondence with, and visits to, the firms reported to have placed the orders indicated that almost all of the alleged orders were fictitious. Many of the firms could not be reached, letters addressed to them being returned marked, "No such address"; practically all who were reached by mail denied having placed orders. As to one company which denied the report that it had placed a $4,000.00 order, the ledger account on the insured's books reflected a number of sales only one of which was as high as $200.00, each of the others being under $100.00.

When the insurer's accountants obtained access to the records of firms which supplied merchandise to the insureds, it developed that the claim had been inflated by the presentation of numerous fraudulent purchase invoices. In many cases the claimants had apparently filled in on the blank billheads of alleged creditors, items representing purchases which had never been made; in other cases the dates of invoices of merchandise bought prior to the latest inventory taken by the insureds before the fire had been altered to read as though the items had been bought after the inventory-taking; on many invoices, quantities or prices or both had been inflated. The effect of these irregularities was to increase the total of merchandise reported to have been acquired shortly before the fire and to have been on hand when it took place.

The insured stated that none of its recent bank statements or cancelled bank vouchers survived the fire. Duplicates of the insured's monthly statements, obtained from the banks, showed charges which appeared to represent checks in the amounts of the re-dated invoices. Examination of old bank statements and cancelled vouchers included among the records remaining after the fire revealed that many of the invoices bearing altered dates had been paid about the time they were originally issued, i. e., long before the fire. Thus the insured's recent bank statements appeared to furnish indication of duplication of payment.

Access was obtained to the bank's microfilm record of checks drawn by its depositors. From these it was learned that the checks represented by the debits on the insured's bank statement during the months immediately preceding the loss were drawn to the order of the alleged sellers. The films also showed that almost all of these recent checks were cashed over the counter of the insured's bank, despite the fact that many were drawn to the order of prominent firms. In none of the cases where purchase bills were altered did the records of the suppliers show payment by the insured on or near the revised due dates of the invoices which had been altered. The obvious conclusion was that persons other than the payees actually received and cashed the checks.

Most of the current records, including the Purchase Book, General Ledger, Creditors' Ledger, Cash Receipts and Disbursements Book, bank statements and cancelled vouchers were said to have been destroyed in the fire. A photograph of the records which survived the fire is presented as Appendix B-2.

The General Ledger being missing, the insureds computed the claim by employing as a starting point figures taken from a trial balance dated a short while before the fire. The trial balance had been prepared by a certified public accountant, and was submitted on his letterhead. The accountant subsequently indicated that the document was based upon the general ledger, the figures in which were not audited by him. The trial balance apparently gave effect to all the fraudulent purchase invoices as though they were genuine; thus, the general ledger presumably contained summary postings which included all of the altered bills. Of over $30,000.00 in purchase invoices submitted in support of the figures in the trial balance and Proof of Loss, approximately $22,000.00 were either obviously irregular or were of questionable regularity.

The sources of large sums of money deposited in the insureds' bank were not explained. There was basis for the belief that these items, as well as funds said to represent capital contributions, actually represented the proceeds of the checks drawn in settlement of falsified invoices, and cashed over the counter of the insureds' bank. In Appendices B-3, B-4 and B-5 are presented reproductions of bills and checks which illustrate the methods adopted by the insureds to inflate the claim.

Case 17

Women's Coat Jobber: Burglary

The items in the claim were principally furs, including collars, used as trimmings on coats. Several trimmed and untrimmed coats were also said to have been stolen. Since the general books of account were kept poorly and the records for furs more acceptably, attention was centered on the verification of the claim for furs lost.

The supplementary records, including purchase bills, manufacturing tickets and sales orders filled, were checked. To the number of pieces of fur on hand, or attached to coats, at the beginning of the business period, was added the number of pieces of fur acquired between that date and the time of burglary. From this total was subtracted the sum of two items, the first being the furs constituting part of the trimmed coats sold, and the second, the furs remaining, either on hand or on trimmed coats. The difference represented the maximum number of fur pieces which could have been stolen.

Business was conducted on the limited capital of $1,000.00. The volume during the three and one-half month period since the founding of the business was $3,200.00. The rate of gross profit being about 15%, the estimated gross profit on sales approximated $480.00. The monthly overhead, including the principal's salary drawings at the rate of $30.00 weekly, was $215.00.

Case 18

Retailer of Groceries, Spices and Spiced Meats: Fire

The Proof of Loss enumerated 120 different items of merchandise, valued at a total of $3,400.00, reported to have been completely destroyed by fire. The insured maintained relatively few records, and those, improperly. The verification of his loss claim necessitated checking the numerous items in the Proof of Loss against the bills presented in substantiation of the quantities bought and the prices paid.

Case 19

Fruit and Vegetable Retailers: Fire

The insureds presented invoices to support their claim for damage. Visits to wholesalers indicated that the latter had furnished, for submission to the insurer, statements showing purchases exceeding in amount those actually made.

Case 20

Upholstered Furniture Manufacturer: Fire

The loss took place in May. The physical inventory last preceding was said to have been taken on February 29 of the same year and to have amounted to about $19,000.00. The inventory sheets were presented for examination. However, the insured did not produce purchase invoices nor records of merchandise received, shipped, delivered, consigned nor sold for cash. It was impossible, therefore, to trace the disposition of specific items of merchandise said to have been on hand on February 29, or acquired between then and the date of the loss.

The inventory sheets, totalling approximately $19,000.00, did not constitute a true listing of inventory. Three of the eight sheets were outright copies, as to individual items of merchandise, of other sheets, almost the only variation being that in the copies the quantities were generally either doubled or tripled; as to a few items they were merely duplicated. The total overstatement was estimated at approximately $9,000.00.

A reproduction of the inventory sheets is submitted as Appendix C. It will be noted that the items on sheet 3 are almost identical, line for line, with those on sheet 1, except that the quantities and total prices are doubled on sheet 3. Similarly, almost all the quantities and totals for the individual items on sheet 4 are double those on sheet 8. And, finally, practically all the quantities and total prices on sheet 6 are either twice or three times those on sheet 2. Question arises whether, for example, sheet 4 is a copy of sheet 8, with the quantities and amounts doubled, or whether sheet 8 is a copy of sheet 4, with the quantities and amounts reduced by one-half. For a number of reasons it was concluded that sheet 4 is a copy of sheet 8.

On sheet 8 the following items are found, in the sequence indicated:

#750	10 at	$ 9	—	$ 90.00
#930	8 at	11	—	88.00
#850	8 at	11	—	88.00

Corresponding items on sheet 4 are:

#750	20 at	$ 9	—	$180.00
#930	8 at	11	—	88.00
#850	16 at	11	—	176.00

It will be noted that on sheet 4, all items were listed at twice the quantities which are seen on sheet 8, until #930 was reached, this item being listed at the same quantity as appears on sheet 8. Item #850 was also listed on sheet 4 at the same quantity as on sheet 8, but the quantity was erased and the larger, or doubled figure, *16,* inserted in its place. It would appear that sheet 4 was intended to represent a listing of all the items on sheet 8, except that the quantities were to be doubled. But an error was made in the listing (on sheet 4) of the quantity of #930 as 8 units. This error was not repeated as to #850, since resuming with that number all the quantities on sheet 4 were doubled.

Likewise, reference is made to the item of 2 Mahogany Frames, on sheet 8, listed at prices of $40.00 for one and $35.00 for the other. On sheet 4 these appear as 4 frames at $40.00 each. It is easily understandable that if sheet 4 were a re-writing (and doubling of the values) of sheet 8, one engaged in the doubling of quantities and values, might feel it equally acceptable to merely double the quantity of the item, employing the highest price for the purpose of computation of the total price. If it were true, however, that sheet 8 was a rewriting of sheet 4, there would be little reason for showing the two mahogany frames at different prices. As further indication that sheet 4 was a copy of sheet 8, it is to be noted that the second item in column 2 of sheet 8, *viz.*, Lot #910, is omitted entirely from sheet 4.

In similar fashion it is deduced that sheet 3 was written after sheet 1, and sheet 6 after sheet 2. On sheet 3 the next to the last item in the first column, *Denim—20 yds at 50¢*, is extended as $20.00, which is twice the total of $10.00 shown for the corresponding item on sheet 1. Also, as to the last item on sheet 3, there is no corresponding item on sheet 1, but the first item on sheet 2 is undoubtedly the model or basis for the last item on sheet 3. Note that as to the seventh item on sheet 2, *Green Friezette—12 yds at 55¢*, there is no corresponding item on sheet 6.

Despite the fact that market prices had not increased between the date of the inventory-taking (February 29), and the date of the loss, the sound value of finished suites, or sets of furniture, was listed at a higher figure in the Proof of Loss than in the inventory. In some cases suites identifiable by style number had been sold recently at lower prices than those listed in the Proof of Loss. It was also noted that many frames were listed at higher prices in the Proof of Loss than in the February inventory.

The financial condition of the insured was poor. At the time of the fire its net worth was estimated at less than $4,000.00. The current ratio was 1.2 to 1. There was a bank overdraft of more than $1,500.00. The financial difficulties culminated in an involuntary petition in bankruptcy soon after the fire.

Evidence of the concealment of the insured's poor financial condition as of the date of the loss was found in the rewriting of the customers' accounts in such fashion as to show a single opening balance in place of the numerous items, long past due, which comprised this balance. The old customers' ledger sheets were then destroyed. The accounts receivable total appearing in the General Ledger was reduced from $21,000.00 to $7,000.00 by a Journal entry as of July 1, i. e., after the loss. Inquiry developed that many of the customers' accounts represented balances due on shipments made three years before the fire, the customers having been thrown into bankruptcy shortly after the sales.

According to the books of the insured a net loss of $400.00 was sustained during the year preceding the loss and a profit of $100.00 was earned during the year next preceding. Adjustment to correct the overstatement of inventory at February 29, discussed above, resulted in a net loss of approximately $9,400.00 for the year preceding the loss. The period from March 1 to the date of the loss was particularly unprofitable.

CASE 21

Fur Dealer: Fire

The loss involved dyed foxtails. The insured took no physical inventory and kept inadequate records for merchandise acquired and sold. In many cases the goods bought and sold were billed as "lots." This prevented estimating the quantity on hand at the time of the loss. In addition there were no receiving or shipping records. As a result neither the quantities said to have been received nor those reported sold could be verified. The gross profit percentage test was therefore resorted to for the purpose of estimating the maximum value of merchandise on hand at the time of the loss. The authenticity of recent bills for merchandise and for dyeing charges was confirmed by visits to fur dealers and dyers.

CASE 22

Retail Luggage and Leather Goods: Hold-up

The hold-up took place in the late afternoon, just before the customary closing hour. The loss claim included both merchandise and the proceeds of sales.

The stock consisted of luggage and other leather goods, of a total value of $10,000.00. Since the claim was a small one, and the inventory made up of hundreds of pieces, many of them small, it was impractical for the insurer to take a physical inventory. Normally, comparison of the items on hand as reflected by such inventory, with those shown by the perpetual inventory records, would indicate what items had been taken by the hold-up men.

The insured followed the practice of balancing the cash register daily, making daily deposits of collections, reduced by the amount disbursed for purchases or expenses. The money reported to have been removed from the cash register represented the proceeds of the sale of several of the most expensive items of leather goods ever carried in stock by the insured. Although these pieces had been in stock several years they were reported to have been sold on the day of the loss, at the full sales price as originally marked; inspection of leather goods of equal age still in stock revealed that such goods were faded or discolored with age.

It was the insured's custom to place in the receipt-printing device of the cash register the seller's copy of every sales check as it was paid. The serial numbers imprinted by the cash register revealed that some of the items claimed to have been sold and paid for on the date of the loss (the proceeds being claimed to have been lost in the hold-up) had apparently been sold on the previous day. It was unusual, and not in accord with the customary practice of the insured, that such funds should remain in the cash register as long as the closing hour (the time of the hold-up) of the day following that of sale.

Case 23

Wholesale Automobile Tires: Hold-up

The custodian of the insured's tire-shop was held up and a large quantity of automobile tires, worth about $5,000.00, was loaded upon a truck and removed. The insured kept a perpetual inventory record against which the physical inventory was said to have been checked daily. The insured maintained none of the customary general books of account. The amount of the claim was verified by checking into the perpetual inventory record the quantities shown by purchase and sales invoices, and reducing the totals indicated to have been on hand before the loss, by those on hand after the loss. Prices were somewhat difficult to check because of the frequent divergence by the tire manufacturers from the already-involved discount arrangements.

The financial condition of the insured was only fair. Operating results were unsatisfactory; an annual volume of $35,000.00 produced a gross profit of under $2,500.00, which was inadequate to cover the operating expenses.

Case 24

Ladies' Handbag Manufacturer and Novelty Jewelry & Ornament Jobber: Fire

The insured's claim covered ladies' handbags, and ornaments for hats, purses and dresses. The ornaments were more than three years old, representing the stock of merchandise remaining when the insured discontinued business as a jobber of such goods. Many of the old ornaments were tarnished or rusted and the glass and semi-precious stones had fallen out. The insured agreed that the line of ornaments was incomplete and that the investment of a large sum of money would be required to complete the line before the realization of value from it through sales.

The records kept did not make possible the identification of specific style numbers of bags from the time they were put into production through the time of sale. The gross profit percentage method was therefore used for the purpose of arriving at the value of bags on hand at the time of the fire. Bills evidencing the acquisition of the ornaments and jewelry had long since been discarded. The items were carried in the year-end inventories at nominal valuations per unit, in anticipation of possible return to fashion.

The insured's statement of financial condition immediately prior to the loss indicated a net worth of $14,000.00. Current assets of $16,000.00 included inventory reported at $11,500.00. Of the latter sum, however, $5,500.00 represented the ornaments and novelty jewelry referred to above; in the opinion of the insurer's appraisers the value of this merchandise was $3,000.00. On the basis of this figure current assets would be reduced to $13,500.00, and net worth to $11,500.00. Current liabilities amounted to $4,600.00.

The percentage of gross profit on sales during the business year immediately preceding the loss was 18.8; the gross profit percentage for the second year preceding was 23.2. The insured's accountant estimated the gross profit for the period from the latest inventory to the date of the loss at 20%, on the theory that the gross profit percentage of 18.8 earned during the year preceding the loss was abnormally low. The insurer took the position that the gross profit percentage was no greater than 18.8, and proposed to undertake the process of comparing such sales as were identifiable as to style, with the corresponding production costs. After discussion, the insured acquiesced in the figure 18.8%. The use of the higher gross percentage would have resulted, of course, in a greater claim for loss.

Total sales for the two-year period preceding the loss reached about $120,000.00. The net profit from operations was about 1% on sales.

Case 25

Diamond and Jewelry Importer and Wholesaler: Hold-up

The insurer's investigation indicated that the loss took place under suspicious circumstances. The claimant maintained the customary general books of account but kept no perpetual inventory records. Ascertainment of the sources and cost of items sold was impossible because the merchandise was not identified by lot number. Periodic inventories were estimated by the insurer on the basis of the estimated gross profit percentages on the sale of diamonds and other merchandise. The figures for the average value of goods held in trust, as submitted in the Application for Insurance, were considerably lower than those found on examination of the records.

The financial condition of the insured was extremely poor, chiefly as a result of difficulty in collecting outstanding accounts and notes receivable. Notes receivable were replaced at maturity by other notes whose maturities were extended for long periods. Delinquent accounts were offset by notes receivable which were themselves not honored at maturity.

Case 26

Furriers and Fur Storage Vault Operators: Burglary

The loss, involving customers' coats left for storage, took place in early fall, just before the beginning of cold weather. The principal record of interest was a series of bound books containing perforated original receipts to be delivered to customers, and permanently-bound carbon copies to be retained. Each receipt showed the name and address of the customer, the description and value of the furs stored, and the provisions of the storage contract; one of the conditions of the policy was that the insured issue to his customer a receipt containing an agreement to insure the property.

The claim included a number of expensive coats which, investigation indicated, had either been left for remodeling or were being manufactured to the order of customers. Storage receipts for such items had apparently not actually been issued to the customers, since both the originals and the carbon copies were found on the premises of the insured.

The insured's records for stored garments were planned to include a 3" x 5" index card showing the description of the furs received, their value and the ultimate disposition of the item. The system was apparently not maintained properly, there being no cards for numerous items. Finally, there was maintained on the insured's large cash register, a running total of furs in storage, based upon record made through the register of the storage receipt numbers and the valuations of items added to, or removed from, storage. This record was not complete;

although all the items stored were listed on the register, often fur coats removed from storage were omitted from the listing through inadvertence or negligence.

To facilitate ascertaining which fur garments were missing after the loss, a schedule listing the items left for storage was prepared. This schedule was based upon the bound volumes of duplicate storage receipts retained by the insured. Items indicated by the bookkeeping machine record or the index cards to have been returned, were then eliminated from the schedule, as were items on hand after the loss. The remaining items presumably represented the garments lost as a result of the burglary. The presumption was not entirely correct, since, according to the records, several of the coats unaccounted for were cheap, worn garments, extremely unlikely of selection by the burglars. The appearance of these items on the list, after the completion of the compilation process described, evidenced the inaccuracy of the record-keeping.

The financial condition of the insured was poor. Its position was not liquid because of the insufficiency of working capital. The insured's business required the outlay of a considerable sum for material, labor and overhead in connection with the storing and repairing of furs, income for which services could not be collected until the furs were removed from storage. At the time of the loss the insured's equity in land and buildings approximated its net worth. Operations during the year preceding the burglary resulted in a net loss of approximately 10 percent on the capital investment.

Case 27

Stationery & Toy Shop: Burglary

The insured operated a large, busy retail store, selling toys, games, cameras, stationery, clocks, fountain pens and related merchandise. A large lending library and a newspaper route serving well over a thousand customers were also conducted. The claimant had been engaged in this business for a very long period; it had been located for many years at the place where the loss occurred. The claim, based principally on the theft of fountain pens, automatic pencils and cameras, amounted to $1,400.00.

In this type of business it appears to be impossible to comply literally with the insurance policy requirement that records be kept in such manner that accurate determination of the loss or damage can be made therefrom by the company.

The customary books of account were maintained but there was no departmentalization of purchases or sales, nor a perpetual inventory. While annual inventory was said to have been taken, the insured could not find the latest inventory sheets. The stock of goods, consisting of hundreds of items, was said to have a value of $13,000.00. It was impractical to take physical inventory, or to attempt to check the amount of the claim through the gross profit test. To test the claim for specific items, however, bills for purchases of fountain pens, automatic pencils, clocks and cameras during the eight months preceding the loss were examined. It developed that the units reported to have been stolen were among the most expensive ones of their classes bought during the period under review. Concerning most of the items, it was clear that smaller quantities had been purchased during this period of eight months preceding the loss than were claimed to have been stolen. The insured's explanation was that the items listed as lost were taken from memory. Concerning the fountain pens, for example, the basis for decision upon the number lost was the theory that every groove in the trays in the showcase had been filled, and that, consequently, any groove remaining unfilled after the loss indicated a stolen pen.

The insured's financial position was poor. The total of current liabilities was within a thousand dollars of the total of current assets, each sum being low in five figures. The net worth was less than $5,000.00, and the net profit about 1½% on an annual volume of approximately $65,000.00.

Case 28

Manufacturer of Model Airplanes and Airplane Parts: Fire

The items sold by the insured were of small unit value, most of the sales being made directly to children. The records were kept informally. Purchase and sales books were not available. However, it had been the insured's practice to place on the pages of the the Customers' Ledger descriptions of the items and quantities sold, which made possible comparison of sales prices with prices in the Proof of Loss. The unit sales prices of many items were lower than the prices of these items in the Proof of Loss. The prices of certain items in the Proof of Loss also exceeded those in the sheets listing the physical inventory taken about five months previous to the fire.

The volume of business during the calendar year preceding the loss was said to have been $9,000.00; the volume during the first six months of the year in which the loss took place, $5,500.00. The rate of gross profit, stated to be 66⅔%, appeared excessive. It was not confirmed by the records made available, tests indicating that the sales price of certain items was never more than twice the cost. The value of the merchandise inventory at the date of the loss was stated to be $6,000.00; the insurer's appraiser estimated it at $2,100.00. Using the insured's gross profit rate of 66⅔% reflected the existence of a supply of merchandise sufficient for two years' business, at a time when merchandise was obtainable without any difficulty whatever.

Case 29

Retailer of Radio Sets, Refrigerators and Electrical Appliances: Fire

The insured claimed loss or damage of $11,000.00 to merchandise of a sound value of $12,000.00. The insurer believed the loss claim to be unusually large for the size of the store and the volume of business done. The records were kept improperly; to correct them, the claimant's accountant prepared eight pages of journal entries as of the date of the loss. Numerous bookkeeping records were reported missing after the fire loss. Among these were lists of cash sales and an analysis book listing the undeposited cash sales and the expenses paid in cash. In some cases collections on accounts receivable were listed on ledger cards; in others, on duplicate copies of the sales charge slips; in still others, they were apparently omitted entirely.

The claim included a large number of items, designated by the manufacturers' names and style numbers. Analysis of sales by type and style number indicated that as to some styles, the number of units reported lost exceeded the number which the records indicated as being on hand at the date of the loss. In other cases, items claimed lost were not found in recent inventories, purchase bills nor consignment records. As to many specific models of radio sets reported lost, certain books indicated that more such items were sold than, according to other records, could have been on hand. The inventory list as of the end of the year preceding the fire included some items not reflected by the records as ever having been acquired. Some of the discrepancies enumerated were doubtless attributable to the failure to describe, by name and style number, sets received on trade-in.

The values placed upon items lost were often much higher than recent purchase prices or values assigned in the most recent inventory. The insurer's appraiser found that a large number of items reported as new models were actually many years old. For example, a refrigerator listed at the sound value of $250.00 prior to the loss proved to be an obsolete model, the manufacturer of which had been out of business for four years.

The financial statement submitted by the insured as representing its condition immediately prior to the loss reflected a net worth of $13,000.00. On audit it developed that the insured's capital had been dissipated completely, the capital deficiency at the date of the loss amounting to more than $4,000.00. According to the books of account the insured had sustained a loss from operations of $5,000.00 during the year preceding the fire and had realized gains of $6,500.00 and $10,000.00 respectively during the second and third years preceding the loss. The corresponding annual volumes of business were $50,000.00, $92,000.00 and $96,000.00, and the corresponding gross profits earned, 11%, 23% and 26%.

Case 30

Men's Clothing Shop: Fire

The insured operated a small store. The bookkeeping records were incomplete. A number of purchase invoices and statements from creditors were submitted in support of the claim. Inspection of the records of suppliers of merchandise indicated that the claim was inflated. Many invoices covering goods received on memorandum, and subsequently returned to the shipper, were altered by the erasure of the words "On Memorandum" and the substitution of the words "Cash Sale," the invoices being submitted as evidence of purchases made. In one case, the insured stated that he had bought merchandise in the amounts of $100.00 and $700.00 from a given manufacturer. The supplier confirmed the authenticity of the first item. As to the second, the insured submitted a statement for $700.00 bearing the uncommon statement date, January 12, and containing no details as to the items of merchandise alleged to have been sold. The supplier was unwilling to permit the inspection of his records, but denied having issued the statement, characterizing it as fraudulent.

Case 31

Retail Druggist: Fire

The impossibility of checking the verity of the quantities of the specific items claimed to have been lost is apparent, it being unheard-of for a retail druggist to maintain a perpetual inventory of all the items in stock. The application of the gross profit percentage test was also impossible because the insured did not record all sales.

The customary general records were maintained. The values assigned by the insured to the items reported lost were checked against bills submitted in support of the claim. There was evidence of alteration of the dates of some of these purchase invoices. In the case of a cabinet containing packages of dyes, for which claim was made but for which no supporting invoice was available, the age of the dyes was indicated to be six years by a dated packing slip tucked away among the packages in the cabinet.

The net worth immediately prior to the loss was estimated to be less than $1,000.00. The capital stock amounted to $4,500.00, but a deficit of more than $3,500.00 had resulted from operations during the period of one and one-half years since the organization of the business. The insured's assets amounted to $12,000.00 which included $6,200.00 representing the book value of fixtures and $5,500.00, merchandise inventory.

During the fiscal year preceding the loss, the insured made sales totalling $12,000.00. After considering all items of other income, including that from a luncheonette operated by a concessionaire, and all expenses, the net loss from operations was $1,800.00.

Case 32

Retail Diamonds and Jewelry: Burglary

The claim was for jewelry lost as the result of a burglary in April. The insured maintained the customary books of account. The amount of the claim was computed based upon an improperly-kept perpetual inventory or stock book, a physical inventory taken on January 31 preceding the loss and a physical inventory taken immediately after the loss. There were many inconsistencies in these records. Numerous items bought prior to January 31 were not listed in the January 31 inventory but were nevertheless reported lost in the burglary. Other items appeared in the January 31 inventory and in the claim for loss although sales records indicated the disposal of the items before January 31.

Many items stolen in an earlier loss through window-breaking, and paid for by an insurance company, were nevertheless listed in the loss claim. Although these items were obviously not on the premises at January 31, in the perpetual inventory record they were marked with symbols (a set of quotation marks, as follows, " ") indicating that they were on hand when inventory was taken on January 31.

Some items listed in the claim for loss were also listed in the inventory of goods on hand after the loss. Certain items of merchandise delivered to the insured on memorandum, and reported stolen, appeared in the insured's claim at higher prices than those in the memorandum invoices.

Items frequently appeared in sales invoices without identification by serial number, rendering impossible the proper posting of the items to the stock book. The insured's subsequent report of "open" or available items in the stock book as having been lost resulted in inflation of the claim.

Case 33

Wholesale Rings, Mountings and Mounted Diamonds: Disappearance

The loss claim was based upon the disappearance of merchandise worth $14,000.00 from the custody of a traveling salesman during a call at a retail jewelry store. The customary bookkeeping records were maintained.

Although a Stock Book was kept, the amount of the claim was arrived at in a somewhat unusual fashion. A stock card was kept for each item of merchandise, the face of each card containing the description, source, cost and sales price of the item. Control of the amount of merchandise in the possession of a specific salesman was attempted by placing the cards representing his stock in a file drawer marked with his name. When a sale was made by the salesman, the card was removed from his file, marked "Sold," and placed in a file drawer maintained for such items.

Following the loss, the salesman prepared a list of the merchandise remaining in his possession. The elimination of the cards for these items from the file of cards representing the merchandise in his custody, presumably indicated the goods lost through disappearance. Since no control was said to have been maintained or attempted over the merchandise in the possession of the salesman, other than the segregation of cards as described above, it is apparent that the claim might readily have been inflated by placing additional cards in the drawer of the salesman from whose possession the goods had disappeared.

Except for the larger diamonds, no record was kept of the weights of diamonds placed into mounted pieces, and even for these larger diamonds no record was kept of the specific source of supply. For the smaller diamonds, the insured listed an estimated average price per diamond in its Stock Book and inventory cards; these prices were substantially correct.

The financial condition of the insured was poor; it had difficulty meeting its obligations at maturity. Post-dated checks, and notes whose maturities were extended, were offered in settlement of obligations on maturing notes, the latter notes themselves representing extensions of the maturity dates of obligations.

Case 34

Wholesale Cultured Pearls: Burglary

The loss involved a number of strings of cultured pearls stolen from a large retail shop where they had been left on consignment by the wholesaler.

The consignor based its charge to the retailer upon the weight and number of the pearls on each string, but was unwilling to make available to the insurer the calculations of the cost of the pearls. The consignee kept unsatisfactory records of the disposition of the consigned merchandise, merely striking out each item on the consignment invoice as the item was sold, without identifying such "record" of sale by invoice number. Complete checking of the records of the consignee would necessitate the examination of all of its sales invoices for the period under review, an impractical procedure since the cultured pearls represented only one of a large number of items traded in by the consignee.

Case 35

Retail Jewelry: Hold-up

The missing items consisted of diamonds and mounted jewelry stated to be worth over $100,000.00. The insured maintained the customary books of account. The details of a physical inventory taken at the close of the preceding year were unavailable. The inventory sheets were reported to have been kept in a metal box which was stolen by the hold-up men.

Purchase invoices submitted in support of the claim bore inadequate evidence of relationship to the missing diamonds and jewelry. Frequently the only characteristic which appeared to link invoices and mounted pieces was the fact that they were of the same class, i. e., watches, brooches, pins or other pieces of jewelry; no lot or other identification numbers appeared on the invoices. Nor was any record available which made possible tracing loose diamonds from the purchase invoices to the specific pieces of mounted jewelry of which they ultimately formed part.

While records of mountings put into work were kept, they were incomplete and of almost no value in checking the cost of mounted pieces. In one case a parcel of diamonds was traced from its source to a given mounting, which had been stolen. The value claimed for the item was made up of both the cost price of the diamonds and the cost, including diamonds, of the completed, mounted piece. Often items whose costs were traceable through the Mounting Book were found to be priced at figures in excess of those shown in the Mounting Book.

A loose-leaf record constituting the daily inventory of goods displayed in the showcases and otherwise accessible to the clerks was apparently inaccurate since it contained items which were discovered, through review of other records of the insured, to have been sold. Many stock numbers for rings were apparently used in duplicate. This often precluded the possibility of determining from the records which of the two items bearing a single stock number had been sold and which lost in the hold-up. On one occasion a large part of the stock of the insured was put up for sale at auction. Records were found of successful bids made on behalf of the insured, to prevent the sale of the merchandise to outsiders at unduly low prices. Under a provision generally found in the Jewelers' Block policy, reading:

> The Company shall not be liable beyond the actual cash value of the property at the time of any loss or damage and the loss or damage . . . shall in no event exceed the lowest figure put upon such property in the Assured's inventories, stock books, stock papers or lists existing at the time the loss occurred. . . .

question might arise whether the successful "bid" prices, where lower than the values claimed by the insured, might not represent the maximum recovery by the insured.

The insured's lease called for a minimum rental supplemented by a fixed percentage on all the sales over a given figure. Although the store was located in a busy, fashionable shopping center, the sales recorded were few in number, and for the most part, small in amount.

During the three years preceding the hold-up, the insured sustained operating losses ranging from a mid-four-figure point to one low in five figures. The net worth was very low in six figures based upon the inventory reported as of the date of the loss. The inventory represented over ninety per cent of the net worth.

CASE 36

Sales Agent for Manufacturer of Unleavened Bread and Related Products: Fire

The claim was made by an agent whose contract required that he insure the goods at his own expense for the benefit of his principal. Inspection of the records of the principal indicated that it earned forty-five percent gross profit. The agent received a commission of approximately fifteen percent out of which he was required to pay all expenses including trucking costs from the factory to his premises and the cost of delivery to customers. All unsold merchandise was returnable.

The agent kept a book of duplicates of sales invoices and retained copies of the consignment memoranda listing merchandise shipped to him. Because of the large volume of business done and the low unit price of the commodity dealt in, the accuracy of the claim was checked through the selection of a limited number of items for testing as to quantities received and shipped. The records appeared to be in order.

CASE 37

Night Club Operator: Fire

Although the claim was for loss and damage to leasehold alterations, fixtures and equipment rather than to merchandise, this case is presented because of its bookkeeping features.

The insured's records were incomplete. Each year a new set of records was opened, no balances being brought forward from the preceding year's books. The records of earlier years were not available for examination.

The following are abstracts from the unusual testimony of the insured's accountant at the examination under oath:

Q: How is it that there is no balance carried over from the other books?
A: We always wanted to keep a record for the season, and I always kept it that way.

. . . . .

A: Another reason, it did not make any difference to me or to them. What could there be a balance that I should carry over? If there was cash, they [the owners] probably took it out; if there were bills for liability, I had it on a slip of paper; if there was construction, it was there, it did not run away; if it was charges, our books show the charges. So there was really nothing to carry over.

The books contained no record of liabilities nor of the acquisitions of fixed assets prior to the current season. Nor did they reflect the form of business enterprise being conducted by the insured. On this point the testimony of the insured's accountant was:

Q: And you were the accountant for Club A—— and then for Club B——?
A: In that place.
Q: And after the Club B——, these two gentlemen, who are now interested in Club C——, were conducting the business as partners?
A: I don't know whether they were partners or a corporation when they began. My books don't even show that.

Case 38

Women's Underwear Manufacturer: Fire

The findings of the insurer's appraiser as to the quantities and values of, and the damage to, goods on the premises after the loss, differed considerably from the figures presented by the insured. Concerning items which the insured designated by lot numbers, the appraised sound value and the loss were found to be approximately twenty-five per cent of the corresponding values in the Proof of Loss.

The insured reported that it had maintained a full set of books, but that certain of the records, namely, the Cash Book, Purchase Book, Sales Book, Purchase Ledger, Sales Ledger, and a "small" ledger had been lost in a subway train by one of the partners. Purchase invoices, cost calculation books and other important records were unavailable but an incomplete General Ledger was submitted.

The fire took place on April 9. A financial statement as of that date, given by the insured to the Fire Department, reflected a net worth of $9,500.00. Assignments of claim subsequently filed with the insurer indicated that $3,000.00 of obligations had been omitted in reaching the net worth figure reported. Two months before the loss the insured had issued a financial statement indicating a net worth of $16,000.00; a statement issued the year before reflected a net worth of $31,000.00.

Case 39

Pocketbook Manufacturer: Fire

The fire started while the factory was in operation, a number of employees being present. The company manufactured a low-priced line of pocketbooks, its business being highly competitive. The customary records were maintained in acceptable fashion.

The insured's financial condition was precarious. The business was conducted in hand-to-mouth fashion on a capital of $1,200.00, the principals drawing only a small weekly wage for their labors. To keep the principals, who were the major workers, busy, arrangements were made for the manufacture of a special consignment of 500 dozen purses at a price of $2.75 a dozen. The completion of this $1,375.00 contract required the use of $1,000.00 of materials and necessitated three full weeks of work on the part of each of the three principals. The excess of $375.00 over the cost of materials was all that was available to cover rental and overhead expenses and the nominal wages of each of the three principals for three weeks.

Case 40

Diamond Dealer: Burglary

The insured made claim for $18,000.00 for the loss sustained as a result of the burglarizing of the premises of a loan company which held some of his diamonds as security for loans. The major record maintained was a unique bound book constituting an all-purpose record. On the even-numbered pages were recorded sales and cash receipts; on the odd-numbered pages, purchases and cash payments. It was stated that on the purchases–cash payments pages, entries in black ink represented purchases which had been paid for, and entries in red ink, purchases on credit. On the sales–cash receipts pages, entries in black ink represented receipts of cash, either for cash or time sales, and entries in red ink, sales on credit. These distinctions were not made consistently. Further, entries were frequently blurred, erased, written over or crossed out. Consequently it was impossible to interpret a large number of the entries in this record.

The insured assigned lot numbers, though not in sequence, to the various items of merchandise purchased. Frequently diamonds were removed from one numbered lot and transferred to another without record of the transfer. Identification of all the items sold was impossible because of the claimant's practice of combining parts of numerous purchases in a single sale without identifying the sources, quantities or weights of the individual items sold. In one case, where sales had been made from given lots without indication of the weights of goods sold from each, and where other sales had been made of identifiable weights and quantities of merchandise drawn from the same lots, the assembly of all of the lots of goods so interlocked revealed that purchases and sales covering 120 lots were involved.

No perpetual inventory was kept. Where sales were reported by lot numbers there were numerous errors in the numbers. Often, without the insured's making proper notation, needed merchandise which had been pledged with the loan company was replaced by other merchandise not required immediately. In many cases it was impossible to determine the cost of specific sales from the insured's records. Likewise, it was impossible to determine the total cost of sales and what specific items of merchandise remained on hand after the alleged loss.

Inconsistencies of this sort were revealed: lot numbers whose elements had apparently all been sold reappeared in inventories of later dates; lot numbers not found in the inventory at a given date, nor purchased thereafter, were reflected in the records as having been sold subsequently; lot numbers in a given inventory, or purchased after the date of the inventory, which were not sold prior to the date of the next inventory, did not appear in that inventory; lot numbers of whose acquisition there was no record, appeared in inventories; lots were recorded as having been sold on dates prior to the dates of purchase.

The use of the Gross Profit method of arriving at estimates of inventory values was not practical in this case since the insured had been in business only thirteen months prior to the loss.

Case 41

Hardware and House Furnishings Retailer: Fire

The insured's claim was based upon loss and damage to merchandise stated to be worth $5,700.00. Numerous invoices were submitted in support of the quantities and prices claimed in the list of goods reported lost or damaged. Often the prices in the invoices and in the report of claim were at variance; the principal similarity or point of relationship appeared to be that the goods were of the same general description. As a rule the quantities shown in the invoices submitted in support of the loss claim were much lower than those in the Proof of Loss.

Case 42

Necktie Manufacturers: Fire

The claim was for damage to 1,250 dozen neckties, whose cost of manufacture was said to be $2,100.00. The insureds estimated that this quantity represented between two and one-half and three weeks' output. The major part of the insureds' business was done with peddlers who paid cash for their purchases.

It was reported that there had been in existence a bound book which recorded purchases, cash disbursements, the source and amounts of cash receipts and copies of invoices for goods sold on credit but the whereabouts of this record after the loss were unknown. The claimants had no safe, and since the record was customarily kept on a shelf in the front of the store, it was reported that the book had been consumed in the fire.

The only records available were purchase bills, labor records, check books and the bank deposit book. During the period of several months preceding the loss the bank deposits averaged $1,800.00 monthly. Based upon the insureds' estimate of an average production of 400 to 500 dozen neckties weekly, and on the assumptions that all collections were deposited and that none of the deposits were from sources other than customers, the average sales price per dozen was less than one dollar. The insureds stated, however, that their price line was from $1.25 to $3.00 per dozen. The average cost price claimed for the neckties constituting the basis for the insurance claim was approximately $1.70 per dozen.

The insureds prepared a schedule listing the estimated material, labor and overhead cost for each of the five grades of ties which they manufactured. The number of higher-priced neckties contained in the claim greatly exceeded the quantity that could have been manufactured from the corresponding higher-priced materials purchased during the months preceding the loss.

The insureds operated a very small business. The total capital investment was less than $2,500.00, part of it provided through a partner's borrowing upon his life insurance policies. Bank balances were generally very low. The banks frequently charged the insureds fees for small checks which had been drawn against insufficient or uncollected balances.

Case 43

Converter and Jobber of Cotton and Rayon Yarn: Fire

The insured was engaged in the business of buying yarn, generally in hanks, winding it on spools and selling it at wholesale. Some of the yarn, bought undyed, was sent to dyers before the winding process was undertaken. The insured had engaged in this business for many years and had been located for a long period at the premises where the fire occurred. Claim was made for $14,000.00, representing loss and damage to merchandise of an alleged sound value approximately ten percent higher. An inventory taken by a representative of the insurer showed that the damaged merchandise on hand after the loss weighed approximately 7,000 pounds less than the figure claimed by the insured. This represented a reduction in value of about $6,800.00. A number of items designated by lot numbers, for which claim was made, appeared at two places in the Proof of Loss.

It was stated that a stock, or perpetual inventory, record had been kept but that it had been destroyed by the fire. Inventory sheets were available, however, listing the details of merchandise on hand about one month before the fire. The books of account showed only a few dyeing bills during the year preceding the loss. This indicated the possibility that a large part of the dyed merchandise on hand at the time of the loss was somewhat old.

Yarn was available in plentiful supply. The types and counts of the merchandise dealt in were readily identifiable by the descriptions in the inventory list and the purchase and sales books. Analysis of the purchases and sales of a number of the classes of merchandise in stock indicated the possibility that some of the yarns on hand at the time of the loss were old and perhaps unsalable at full price. For example, in the case of 40/2 yarn, purchases averaged 900 pounds per month and sales 865 pounds per month. On the basis of the quantities reported to have been on hand on December 31, the average inventory was 3,225 pounds, almost a four months' supply. In view of the plentiful supply of yarn available, the poor financial condition of the insured, and the insurance company's post-loss inventory revealing a lesser weight of damaged merchandise on hand than that claimed by the insured, there appeared to be basis for the belief that purchases of 40/2 yarn were made only in quantities to satisfy immediate requirements. The following is a schedule showing, by months, the number of pounds purchased and sold during the period of approximately a year preceding the loss:

	Purchases (Lbs.)	*Sales (Lbs.)*
January	1,389	857
February	1,609	1,213
March	1,412	1,481
April	508	675
May	731	1,084
June	1,384	928
July	84	176
August	358	492
September	965	806
October	70	648
November	1,792	1,035
December	495	988
Sub-Total	10,797	10,383
January (3 weeks)	1,091	627
Total	11,888	11,010

Inventory at December 31: 3,040 lbs.

An invoice for 377 pounds of 40/2 yarn bought on November 5 bore the notation in pencil:

Sundry Sales 11/19–12/4	337
In Stock	37–4
	374–4

This showed the disposition of the merchandise covered by the invoice, and appeared to indicate that either there was almost no inventory of 40/2 yarn on December 4, or the merchandise on hand was unsuitable for current requirements.

In the case of 60/2 yarn the purchases during the year preceding the fire amounted to 24,354 pounds, and the sales to 24,283 pounds. The inventory at December 31 was reported as 5,885 pounds. As to this item, too, it appears that the claimed inventory at December 31 was either excessive or largely unsalable. The details as to the number of pounds of 60/2 yarn purchased and sold during the period of approximately a year preceding the loss were as follows:

	Purchases (Lbs.)	*Sales (Lbs.)*
January	1,596	1,638
February	2,511	1,581

	Purchases (Lbs.)	*Sales (Lbs.)*
March	1,934	2,094
April	2,021	2,622
May	4,316	3,556
June	2,221	2,160
July	1,617	1,801
August	1,690	1,090
September	1,616	2,073
October	563	1,614
November	1,869	1,165
December	2,400	2,889
Sub-Total	24,354	24,283
January (3 weeks)	2,995	2,752
Total	27,349	27,035

Inventory at December 31: 5,885 lbs.

The insured was in poor liquid condition. Although the records indicated a net worth of $16,000.00 prior to the fire, inventory taken on behalf of the insurer and the examination of the customers' accounts indicated overvaluation of the inventory and receivables to the extent of approximately $7,000.00. After correction for this overstatement, the current assets amounted to $15,000.00, including inventory—some of it slow-moving—valued at $10,000.00 and accounts receivable of $4,500.00. Current liabilities amounted to not less than $6,500.00. According to the books of account, before adjustment, the insured's net worth fell approximately fifty percent during the period of six years preceding the loss. The insured's wife had loaned the business $2,000.00 shortly before the fire, this amount being recorded as part of the capital of the insured.

The following data relate to the insured's business operations during the years immediately preceding the loss:

Year Preceding the Loss	*Sales*	*Purchases*	*% of Gross Profit*	*% of Net Loss on Sales after Nominal Salary to Owner*
1st	$44,000.00	$38,000.00	10	10
2nd	50,000.00	40,000.00	14	4
3rd	89,000.00	72,000.00	5	10

Beginning several months before the fire the insured reduced his weekly drawings (reflected as salary in the table above) from $50.00 to

$35.00. He was required to pay interest on purchase bills because of delinquency in payment.

CASE 44

Spaghetti and Macaroni Manufacturer: Fire

The company's business was poor. The financial condition was not liquid, there being as long as 150 days' delay in paying accounts due on 30 day terms. A dividend on the capital stock was passed, and the stockholders were reported to be indignant at the management. Several days later the premises of the company were reported to have been raided by a number of men who removed some records, strewed books and papers over the floor and set fire to the plant. The insurance claim arose out of the damage caused by this fire. After the fire all the recent records were found to be missing, but numerous old records, of no use in the determination of the financial condition of the company and the results of its operations, were available.

CASE 45

Dealer in Inexpensive Furs: Disappearance

The insured made claim for 1,000 fur collars stolen from his automobile. The insurer's investigators stated that it was physically impossible for so large a quantity of fur collars to be contained in the car. The claimant's records were poor. The quantities of the various types of furs purchased were not determinable because numerous purchase bills reflected the acquisition of job lots of furs. The insured stated that he did not keep a purchase book, but conventional folio references noted upon purchase bills indicated that the bills had been entered in such record. The insured reported that much of his merchandise was paid for by checks obtained from friends and business acquaintances or by cash, since few suppliers would accept the claimant's checks.

In the insured's book of duplicate copies of sales invoices were many voided items. Only a few invoices were in carbon, the insured's explanation being that when merchandise taken to a customer for demonstration was accepted, a bill was immediately prepared, the insured's record of the bill being an original writing in the bill book which, elsewhere, would normally contain only carbon copies.

In support of his claim the insured presented a number of purchase invoices, one of them dealing with the single item "one job lot dogs $1,225.00." This invoice appeared to have been altered, the impression being confirmed by a visit to a member of the former partnership which had supplied the furs, the partnership having since gone out of business. This individual indicated that the correct amount of the sale was about $300.00, covering about 1,800 cheap fur skins at 18 cents each, and that the correct date of sale was about one year before the date appearing on the bill presented by the claimant. The supplier established the correct date readily because the sale had been made a short time before his firm went out of business. The date appearing on the bill presented to the insurer was about one year after the supplier had gone out of business.

Case 46

Owner of Fur Coat: Burglary

Although this claim was made by an individual, based upon the theft of a fur coat from an automobile, it is presented because of the use made of the retail furrier's records in checking the claim. The furrier's books did not support the insured's claim as to the price paid for the coat; they indicated that an old coat had been traded-in in part payment for the new one. It was said, however, that no records were kept of the customer's measurements, the number and prices of the skins consumed in the new coat, the estimated labor charge, nor similar information. The furrier's records for money received from customers were likewise kept very poorly.

Case 47

Women's and Children's Hat Jobber: Fire

The insured based its claim upon an alleged physical inventory at January 1, to which had been added the purchases made from then to the date of the loss; from this total the estimated cost of merchandise sold between January 1 and the date of the loss had been deducted. The original inventory sheets were said to have been lost, but the insured presented a summary of the inventory, reported to have been prepared by its accountant, which was used as the basis for the insurance claim. The summary indicated an average cost which was approximately $2.00 per dozen higher than the average cost per dozen for the eight-month period preceding the loss.

The claimant reported its net worth to be $14,000.00, which sum included $6,500.00 representing the equity in a long-held—and apparently unmarketable—$17,500.00 parcel of unimproved real estate in an undeveloped section. A financial statement issued for credit a month before the fire reflected a net worth of $35,000.00 based upon an equity in real estate of $16,500.00 (rather than the book value of $6,500.00) and accounts receivable stated at approximately $11,000.00 more than book value.

Examination of the records indicated that the 25% gross profit percentage reported by the insured for the year preceding the loss was actually somewhat lower. The gross profit percentage during the new season, which had begun only two months before the loss, was 20%. Statistics of volume, profits and drawings during the two years preceding the loss were as follows:

Year Preceding Loss	*Sales Volume*	*Net Profit*	*Partners' Drawings*	*Net Reduction in Capital*
1st	$69,000.00	$2,000.00	$5,500.00	$3,500.00
2nd	92,500.00	5,500.00	6,300.00	800.00

Case 48

Tobacco and Candy Wholesaler: Hold-up of Truck

The claim arose as a result of the hold-up of the insured's truckman and the removal of the contents of the vehicle. The customary general records were kept but no perpetual inventory was maintained.

The insured's investment in this business was $55,000.00. On this capital an annual volume of business of almost $1,000,000.00 was done. The gross profit was 2%, and the net loss, after moderate salaries to the stockholder-officers, actively engaged in the business, was about $7,000.00.

Case 49

Jewelry Wholesalers: Hold-up

The insured conducted a wholesale jewelry business carrying a stock of 5,000 to 6,000 different items, and employing a large office and stock room staff as well as a number of salesmen. The claim was based upon the hold-up of one of these salesmen while he was on the road, and the taking of the contents of a sample case of jewelry, the total loss being about $10,000.00.

The insured kept a book listing the line of samples. Every salesman carried almost the entire line of samples; notations made in the sample book, in a column provided for each salesman, indicated whether the item had been given to the man whose initials headed the column. The samples were generally used for demonstration and display only, but where additional pieces were given, to be sold, appropriate notation was made.

Mountings and diamonds were bought by the insured and both mounted and unmounted goods were sold. The mountings were identifiable by style or lot number, and could be traced to specific purchase invoices. The diamonds used were generally small ones, taken from parcels of diamonds which had been purchased. Perpetual inventory records were not maintained. There was kept, however, a record listing and describing each style of mounted and unmounted merchandise available for sale.

The company did an annual business of $500,000.00. The gross profit ranged from 33% to 25%. Net profit figures were not available.

Case 50

Hat and Cap Retailer: Fire

The insured conducted a retail hat and cap shop of moderate size in a residential section. All of the caps sold were manufactured on the premises. The insured made claim for $1,375.00 for loss and damage to his stock caused by fire.

He presented a large number of purchase bills, totalling about three times the amount of the claim for straw and soft hats, in support of the prices assigned to the items damaged or destroyed. In the case of the soft hats the highest price evidenced by the bills was $27.50 per dozen; in the Proof of Loss, however, claim was made for items costing as much as $45.00 per dozen. The lowest price evidenced by the bills was $18.00 per dozen; in the Proof of Loss the lowest price was $19.50 per dozen.

Case 51

Resident Buyer of Dresses: Fire

The insured made claim for dresses which had been destroyed or damaged by fire, the claim being based upon a physical inventory taken several weeks earlier, adjusted to give effect to purchases and sales from the date of the inventory to the date of the loss.

It developed that for reasons unrelated to the loss the insured had recorded as sales of dresses, adjustments actually representing additions to the prices billed for piece goods shipped to foreign customers. On the other hand, dresses had been given gratuitously to policemen and others, without entry reflecting the consequent reduction of the stock. As a result the insurer questioned the credibility of the perpetual inventory as a basis for the adjustment of the loss.

Case 52

Women's Hat Manufacturer: Burglary

The insured made claim for loss of $3,800.00 sustained as a result of the burglarizing of its premises. The customary books of account were kept, including one showing the alleged costs of the various styles of hats made. Sheets were available listing physical inventories reported to have been taken monthly.

Since the style or cost book did not show the actual number of pieces of straw braid required for the manufacture of the various styles of straw hats, it was impossible to determine the total number of pieces consumed in manufacture between the dates of the latest inventory and the fire. Tests were made in the presence of the insurer's auditors to determine the number of pieces of braid required to manufacture a dozen hats of each of various style numbers. The tests showed that the quantities differed from those noted in the cost book and from those reported orally by the insured's representatives. For example, as to one hat style, the cost book indicated that the production of a dozen hats required fifteen pieces of braid; the insured stated that twelve pieces were required; a test indicated that only nine and one-half pieces were needed. The greater the number of pieces required, the higher the cost of finished hats, and the lower the quantity of raw material, *viz.*, braid, on hand at the time of the loss.

The claimant explained the appearance of the high figure of fifteen pieces in the cost book with the comment that the object was to delude the salesmen into the belief that the cost of production was higher than was actually the case, so that they would refuse to grant customers concessions from the listed wholesale prices.

As to numerous styles listed in the cost calculation book, some of the elements of cost were omitted. Labor costs shown were often inaccurate because they represented estimates of cost, made prior to the settlement of rates with the union, no changes being made in the cost calculation book on the final settling of rates. Many style numbers were omitted from the book although the list of numbers for which blocks and dies were available indicated that such styles were being manufactured.

Purchase records were faulty, many of the bills bearing no indication, through initials or signature of approval, of the receipt of the merchandise. The alleged physical inventories were apparently not actual inventories. The November 30 inventory sheets, for example, included the earliest purchases of merchandise for the coming spring season. The entire amount of the invoices for such purchases was included in the inventory despite the fact that there had been some sales in November of spring merchandise manufactured from this material.

The insured's current position and general financial condition were poor. Current assets, totalling $20,000.00, were exceeded by current liabilities. The net worth, amounting to $6,000.00, was based upon the inclusion among the assets of machinery and fixtures and blocks and dies, on which no depreciation had been provided. The principal source of short-term financing was the insured's contract with its bank under the terms of which the latter advanced 75 per cent of the face value of sales invoices.

The operating results were unsatisfactory. Sales for the seven-month period preceding the loss amounted to $85,000.00, the net loss thereon amounting to $2,000.00, before provision for depreciation and obsolescence.

Case 53

Retail Men's and Boys' Clothing: Fire

The insured claimed $4,200.00 for merchandise damaged or destroyed by fire. The insurer's appraiser estimated the loss at between 25 and 30 percent of that amount. The claimant maintained few of the customary books of account. He used no general ledger nor general journal, and creditors confirmed that he had no checking account, all payments to them having been made in cash.

A study was made of $4,000.00 of purchase bills submitted in support of the prices claimed in the Proof of Loss. Comparison between the items in these purchase bills and the items in the Proof of Loss indicated the following:

Pants: 3% of the pants purchased cost $3.25 per pair or higher; 49% of the quantity claimed destroyed or damaged was reported to cost $3.25 per pair.

Suits: 1% of the suits purchased cost $17.00 each or higher; 61% of the quantity claimed destroyed or damaged was reported to cost $17.50 per suit.

Overcoats: Only 1 overcoat of a total of 55 purchased cost over $14.50, its cost being $16.00; 18 overcoats, representing about 46%

of the quantity in the Proof of Loss, were said to have cost $18.00 each.

Case 54

Necktie Manufacturer: Water Damage

The insured, located in an east-coast city, made claim for damage amounting to $2,300.00, to thirteen lots of goods of the sound value of $2,800.00. The damage was caused by the seepage of water during the extinguishment of a fire at the premises adjoining those of the insured. The loss occurred in December.

One of the thirteen lots consisted of 490 dozen silk neckties, distinctive because stamped with the emblem of a prominent fraternal organization. It was stated that the neckties had been produced during the slow months of the preceding summer on speculation, or experimentally, in anticipation of sale as novelties at the convention and parade of the fraternal organization during the following summer.

The insured maintained the customary general books of account. No inventory record was kept. Examination of the sales books indicated that immediately after being stamped with the emblem of the fraternal organization, practically the entire output of these special neckties had been shipped, billed at $3.00 per dozen, to an affiliate. This affiliated company was located in a west-coast city near that selected by the fraternal organization for its annual convention and parade. The following schedule shows the dates of stamping of the neckties and the dates of shipment to the affiliate:

Stamped		*Shipped*	
Date	*Quantity (in Doz.)*	*Date*	*Quantity (in Doz.)*
June 11	45	June 22	45½
21	32	22	32
22	38	22	38
24	94	24	94
25	36	25	36
25	34	26	34
26	23	26	20
26	55	27	58
27	86	27	86
28) 29)	36⅓	29	37
Total	479⅓	Total	480½
June 30	22		

Because of inclement weather the fraternal organization did not hold its customary annual parade. The neckties were then shipped back to the manufacturer, and were in the insured's cellar the following winter when the damage through seepage of water occurred.

No formal cost records were kept. However, the insured reported the cost of production at $3.30 per dozen, offering in support of the figure informal, though detailed, estimates of cost. An analysis of sales during the year preceding the loss indicated that, excluding the fraternal organization neckties in question, 90% of the quantity sold had been billed at $3.00 per dozen or less, 95% at $3.30 per dozen or less and 98% at $4.00 per dozen or less. The production cost per dozen of the experimental line of neckties was thus reported to be equal to or greater than the sales price per dozen of 95% of the merchandise sold during the year preceding the loss.

The insured was in fair financial position. As to business operations, the volume during the year preceding the loss was $200,000.00, the gross profit on sales being 17%. Thus, neckties whose cost of manufacture was $3.30 per dozen would normally sell at about $4.00 per dozen. The average inventory was approximately $8,000.00, indicating an unusually rapid turnover. The net profit for the year preceding the loss, prior to the deduction of drawings made by the insured, was $8,500.00.

Towards the close of the examination under oath it became clear that the insured had falsified its claim and had given untruthful testimony at the examination under oath. Apparently either because of embarrassment or fear of the possible consequences of the testimony, the insured delayed suit until it became untimely under the policy, and finally abandoned the claim.

Case 55

Glazed Fruit Manufacturer: Fire

The insured made claim for $4,700.00 representing the loss and damage caused by a fire which took place in June, to merchandise of a sound value of $5,400.00. Practically the entire stock had been acquired at nominal prices at a sheriff's sale in February. The insured maintained the customary bookkeeping records. There were also available inventories of the merchandise acquired at the sheriff's sale in February, an inventory taken on April 30, and a schedule listing merchandise said to have been on hand after the loss.

No perpetual inventory or stock records were maintained. The checking of the February inventory against the April 30 inventory, against the inventory listing items on hand after the loss, and against the Proof of Loss, revealed many discrepancies. A number of items listed in the Proof of Loss as having been burned out of sight were also reported on hand after the loss. Several items shown in the inventory of goods bought at the sheriff's sale appeared in subsequent inventories and in the Proof of Loss at very large increases in price. As to a number of items, although there was no evidence in the company's records of the acquisition of such goods, they nevertheless appeared in the inventory of goods as of the date of the loss and in the Proof of Loss.

Case 56

Women's Knitted Sportswear Manufacturer: Fire

The insured made claim for damage of $6,000.00 to merchandise of a sound value of $6,700.00. The correction of errors in arithmetic computation resulted in the reduction of the sound value to $6,100.00. The insurer's appraiser estimated the loss and damage at $1,600.00, to goods worth only $3,900.00. The claimant maintained the customary general books of account but kept neither stock nor manufacturing records.

The financial condition of the insured was poor. According to the books of account, current assets amounted to $7,500.00 and current liabilities to $9,000.00. The current assets included inventory valued at $6,100.00 by the insured; the use of the insurer's appraisal of the sound value at $3,900.00 would result in the reduction of the current assets to $5,300.00. The net worth at the time of the loss, based upon the figures shown in the books, and accepting the insured's valuation of its inventory, was approximately $6,000.00; the depreciated book value of machinery and fixtures itself exceeded this sum. Adjusting the net worth to give effect to the appraiser's estimate of the value of the merchandise would result in a net worth figure of $3,800.00.

The insured had advertised in a daily newspaper, seeking additional capital. Numerous loans were made to the business by relatives of the principals and by employees. During the business year preceding the fire a net loss of $13,000.00 was sustained on a volume of $36,000.00. The insured had advertised in the trade newspapers offering to furnish free instruction in the operation of knitting machines, the object apparently being to obtain a supply of free labor.

APPENDICES B-E

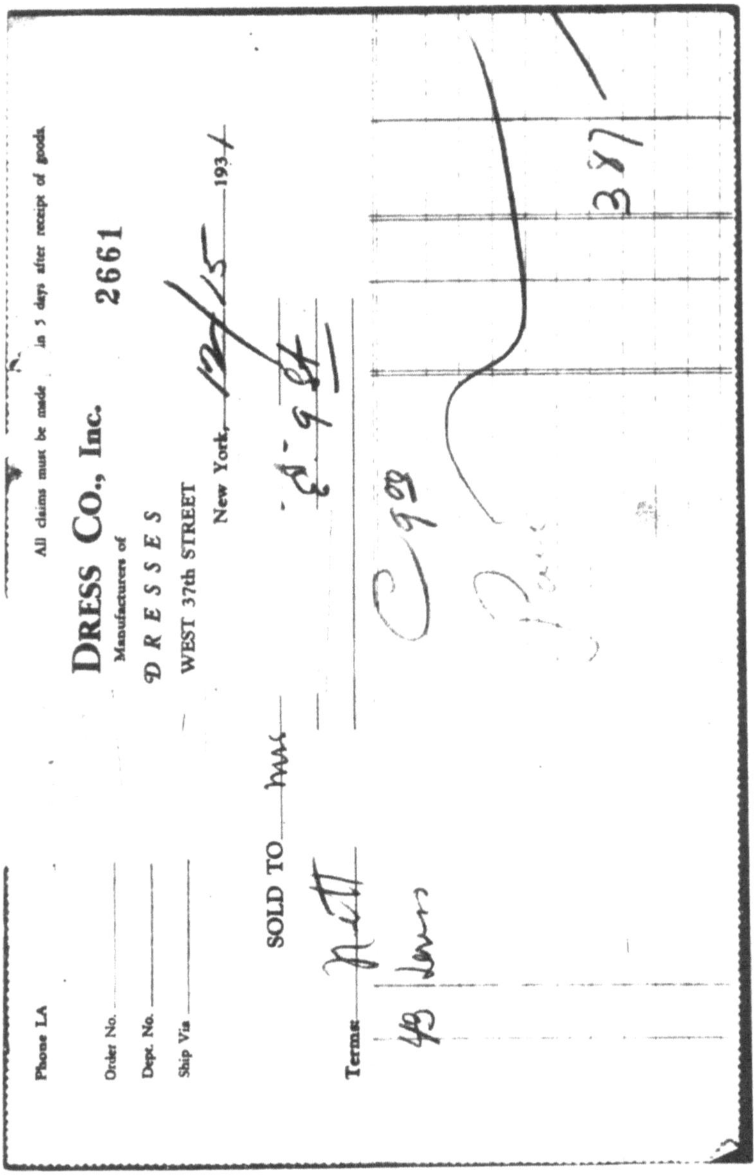

All claims must be made in 5 days after receipt of goods.

DRESS CO., Inc.

Manufacturers of

DRESSES

WEST 37th STREET

2661

New York, 12/15 193

Phone LA

Order No.

Dept. No.

Ship Via

SOLD TO

Terms

APPENDIX B-1: A FRAUDULENT INVOICE

(Source: Appendix A, Case 7)

Explanation

Invoice #2661, as originally issued, was dated February 1931, and covered 3 dresses at $9.00--Total $27.00.

The invoice was apparently altered by the insured to read as follows:

December 15, 1931 43 dresses at $9.00--$387.00

The supplier disavowed the altered invoice and permitted inspection of his carbon copy of the original sales invoice.

APPENDIX B-2

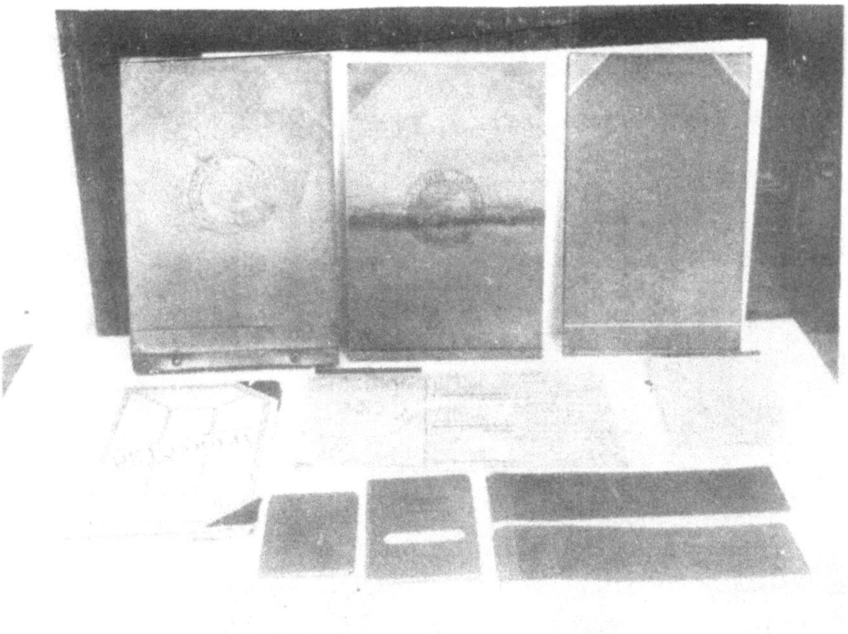

APPENDIX B-2

THE BOOKS AND RECORDS WHICH SURVIVED A FIRE

(Source: Appendix A, Case 16)

Explanation

These are photographs of the books and records which remained after a fire. The two sections at the left show how badly most of the records were burned. The undamaged records shown above were of almost no use in the assignment of determining the amount of the loss.

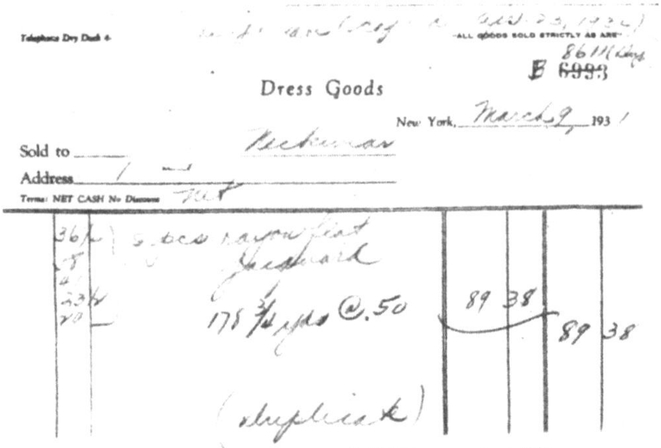

Telephone Dry Dock 4-

"ALL GOODS SOLD STRICTLY AS ARE"

8611 Days

B ~~6993~~

Dress Goods

New York, March 9, 1931

Sold to Neckwear

Address

Terms: NET CASH No Discount Net

36 1/2	5 pcs rayon flat jacquard			
	178 3/4 yds @ .50	89 38		89 38
	(duplicate)			

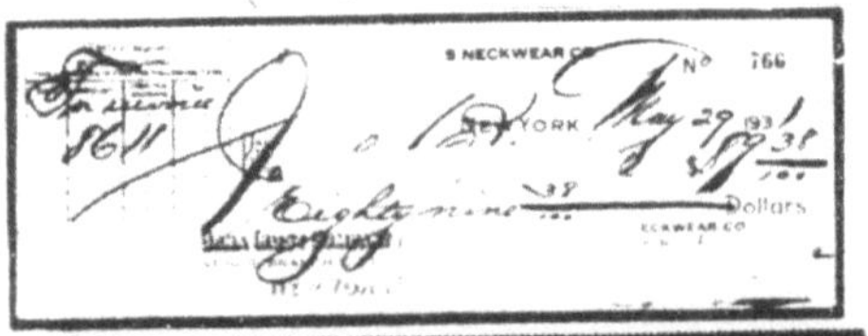

8611

S NECKWEAR CO

No 766

NEW YORK May 29 1931

$89 38/100

Eighty-nine 38/100 Dollars

NECKWEAR CO

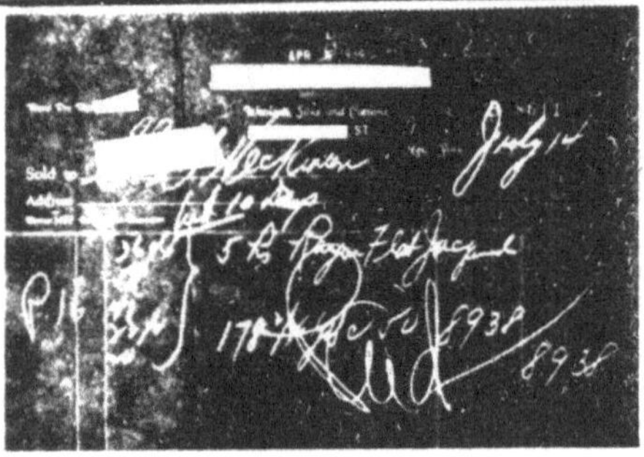

[redacted]

July 14

Sold to [redacted] Neckwear

Net 10 days

36 1/2 5 pcs Rayon Flat Jacquard

178 3/4 yds @ .50 89 38 89 38

Paid

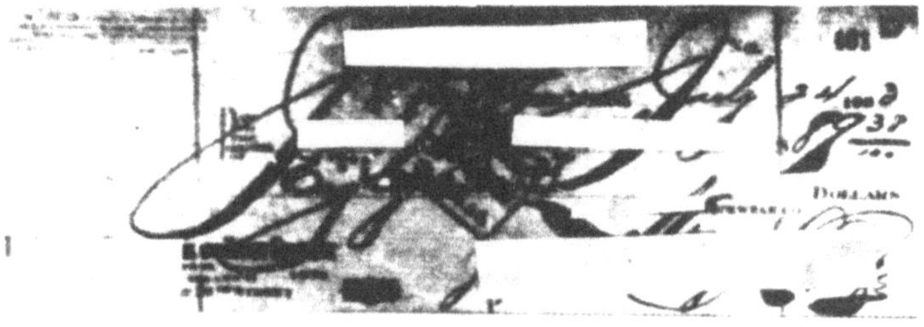

APPENDIX B-3: A FRAUDULENT INVOICE

(Source: Appendix A, Case 16)

Explanation

Invoice #B8611, dated March 9, 1931, was for 178 3/4 yards of Rayon Flat Jacquard at $.50 per yard--total $89.38. The insured paid the bill by check #766, dated May 29, 1931.

The date of the invoice was altered to July 14, 1933, and a check dated July 24, 1933, was drawn to the order of the supplier, in purported settlement of the invoice. The check was imprinted with a small rubber-stamp rectangle containing the word "Cashed," indicating that it had been cashed over the counter of the insured's bank. The supplier, disavowing the altered invoice, furnished a copy of the original and denied receipt of the 1933 check drawn to his order.

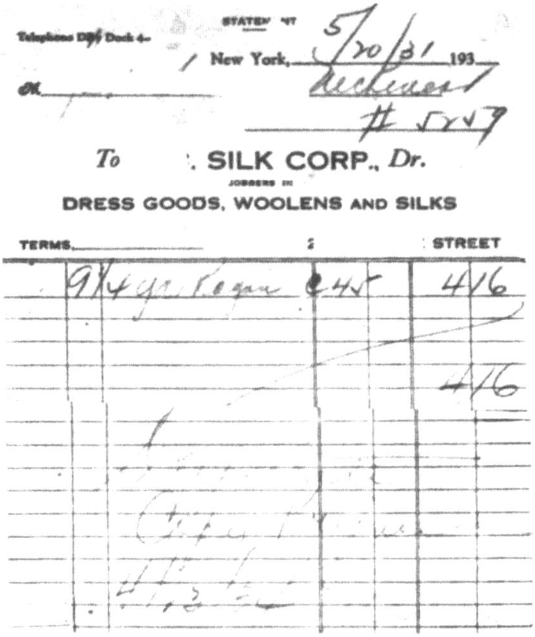

Telephone Dry Dock 4-

STATEMENT

New York, 5/20/31 193

To . SILK CORP., Dr.

JOBBERS IN

DRESS GOODS, WOOLENS AND SILKS

TERMS ______ STREET

9 1/4 yds Rayon	.45		4 16
			4 16

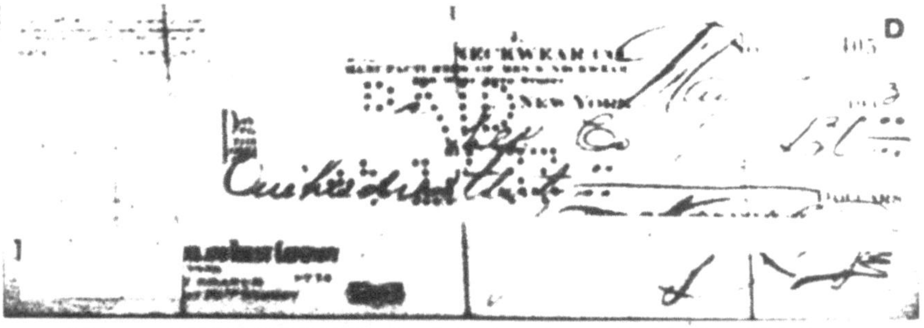

NECKWEAR INC

NEW YORK

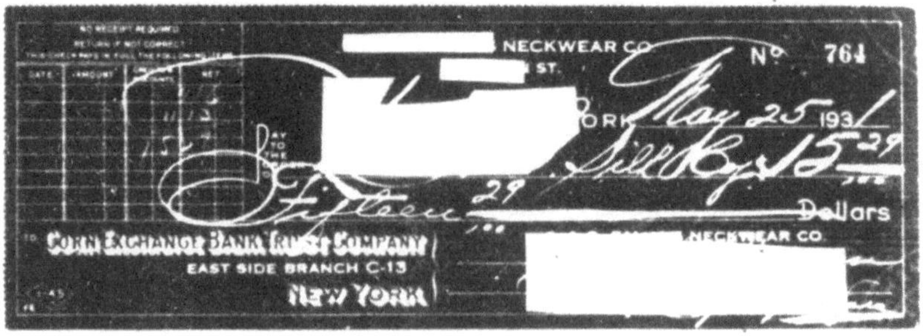

NO RECEIPT REQUIRED
RETURN IF NOT CORRECT
THIS CHECK PAYS IN FULL THE FOLLOWING ITEMS

DATE	AMOUNT		NET

[redacted] NECKWEAR CO. No 764

[redacted] ST.

[redacted] YORK May 25 1931

PAY TO THE ORDER OF [redacted] Silk Corp $15 29/100

Fifteen 29/100 Dollars

TO CORN EXCHANGE BANK TRUST COMPANY
EAST SIDE BRANCH C-13
NEW YORK

NECKWEAR CO.

[redacted]

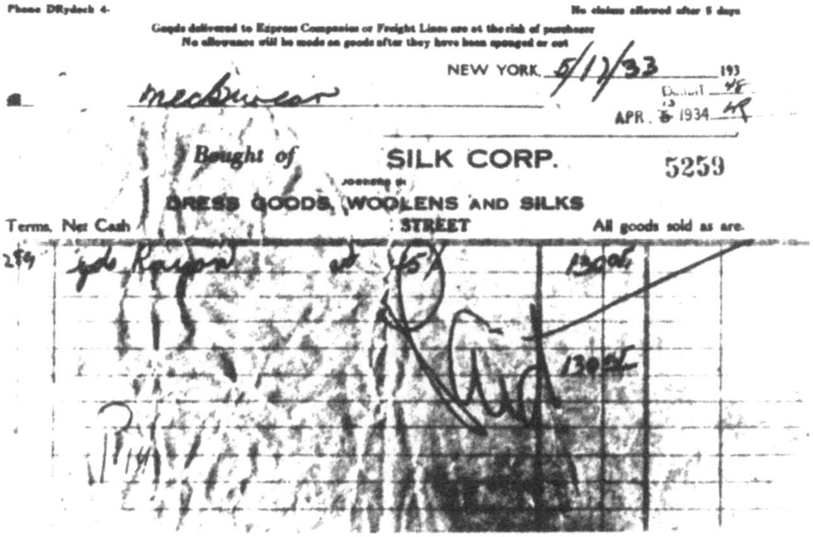

Phone DRydock 4-

No claims allowed after 5 days

Goods delivered to Express Companies or Freight Lines are at the risk of purchaser

No allowance will be made on goods after they have been sponged or cut

NEW YORK 5/17/33 193

APR . 1934

neckwear

Bought of SILK CORP. 5259

DRESS GOODS, WOOLENS AND SILKS

Terms, Net Cash STREET All goods sold as are.

289 yds Rayon at 45 130.05

130.05

APPENDIX B-4: A FRAUDULENT INVOICE

(Source: Appendix A, Case 16)

Explanation

Invoice #5259, dated May 20, 1931, was for 9 1/4 yards of Rayon at $.45 per yard--total $4.16. The invoice was altered to read as follows:

May 17, 1933 289 yds. Rayon at $.45--$130.05,

and a check dated May 17, 1933 was drawn to the order of the supplier in purported settlement of the invoice. The supplier, disavowing the altered invoice, furnished a copy of the original and denied receipt of the 1933 check drawn to his order.

The insured's files revealed that check #764, in the amount of $15.29, was issued in 1931 in settlement (according to the voucher section of the check) of two 1931 bills from the supplier, one of them for $4.16.

APPENDIX B-5: A FRAUDULENT INVOICE

(Source: Appendix A, Case 16)

Explanation

Invoice #476, dated February 22, 1931, (opposite) was for 67 1/4 yards of Rayon Crepe at $.40 per yard--total $26.90.

The invoice was altered to read as follows (see page 160):

July 12, 193(3) : 267 1/4 yds. Rayon Crepe at $.40--$109.90

and a check dated July 12, 1933 was drawn to the order of a fictitious payee in purported settlement of the invoice. The seller, disavowing the altered invoice, furnished a copy of the original bill, and denied receipt of the 1933 check.

THE CO.

SILKS & DRESS GOODS

STREET

NEW YORK, ______________ 193

Copy of Bill

476

2/22/31

Neckwear

Allen

67 1/4 yd Rayon Crepe @ .40 - 26.90

(141)

Paid

This is a copy from our bill book
made April 23 - 1984. by Co
[illegible]

(also see page 160)

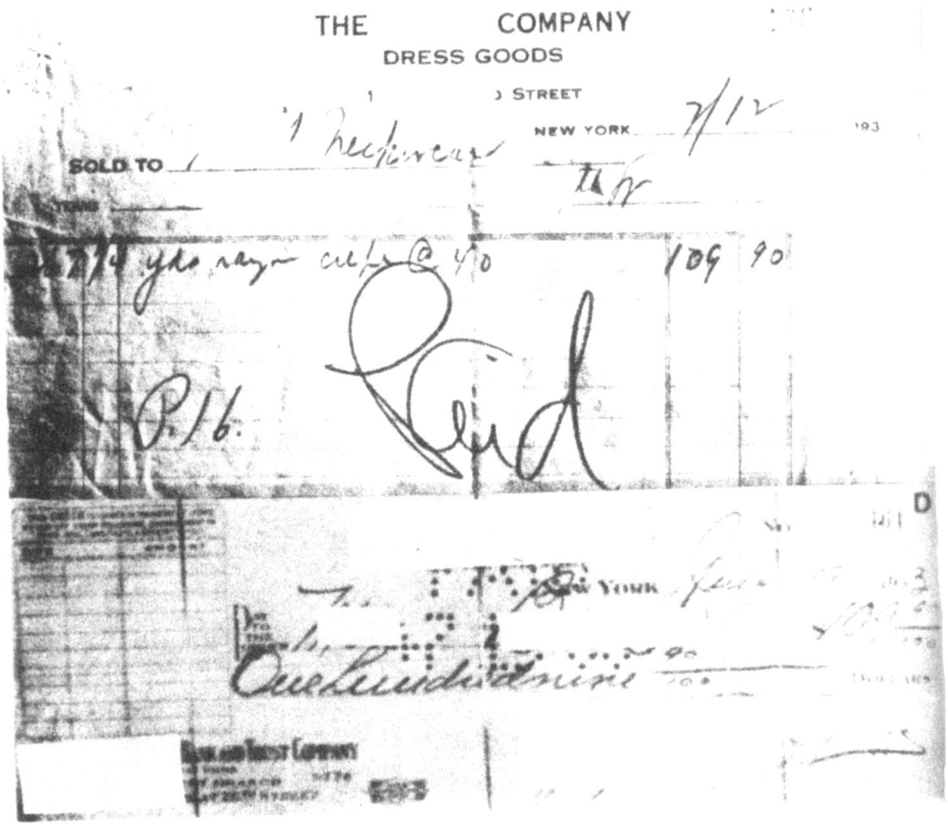

THE COMPANY

DRESS GOODS

STREET

NEW YORK 7/12 193

SOLD TO

yds rayon crepe @ .40 109 90

P.16.

Paid

NEW YORK

APPENDIX C

AN INFLATED INVENTORY SCHEDULE

(Source: Appendix A, Case 20)

Explanation

The insured's eight-sheet inventory schedule is reproduced on the following pages exactly as submitted, except that the sheets are rearranged and presented in pairs. Inspection of the reproductions indicates obvious falsification of a large part of the total inventory.

Except for a few items, sheet 3 is a copy of sheet 1, and sheet 4, a copy of sheet 8, the quantities and total prices being doubled on sheets 3 and 4. Likewise, sheet 6 is a copy of sheet 2, except that practically all the quantities and total prices on sheet 6 are either double or triple those on sheet 2. The inventory sheets are discussed further in Appendix A, Case 20.

Inc.

Manufacturers of

Distinctive Upholstered Furniture

ROCKAWAY AVENUE

BROOKLYN, N. Y.

Inventory - Feb 29. 1932

#1

MATERIAL IN STOCK

	Pr.	Yds.	$			Pr.	Yds.		
Corona Gold	2.50	25	62	50	Velour Tap.	.25	120	$30	00
Silk Mog	3	15	45	00	Green Frieze	.55	100	55	00
Silk Tap	2.25	15	33	75	Red Tap.	.85	75	63	75
Silk Frisette	1.25	30	37	50	Jacq	1.25	5	6	25
Green Tapestry	1.75	5	8	75	Rust Tapestry	1.25	50	62	50
Mog	1.75	25	35	00	Green velour	2.50	30	75	00
Green Mog	1.75	10	17	50	Rust velour	2.00	45	90	00
Tap.	75	5	3	75	Frieze	4.00	60	240	00
Mog	2.00	10	20	00	Frieze	4.00	10	40	00
Blue	1.75	5	8	75	Frieze	2.00	15	30	00
Silk Tap	1.75	10	17	50	Yale	2.50	35	87	50
Tap	1.00	28	28	00	Gold Frieze	1.00	40	40	00
Red velour	70	35	24	50	Rust Flowered	.75	90	67	50
[illegible]	70	30	21	50	Mohair	1.25	65	81	25
[illegible]	.50	20	10	00	Jacq	1.10	55	60	50
[illegible]	.80	27	21	60				1424	75

Ex. 23b-9/30/32-MEP

Inc.

Manufacturers of

Distinctive Upholstered Furniture

ROCKAWAY AVENUE

BROOKLYN, N. Y.

#3

MATERIAL IN STOCK

	@	Yds	$
[illegible] Gold	2.50	50	125.00
Silk Moq	3.00	30	90.00
Silk Tap.	2.75	30	67.50
Silk Frizette	1.25	60	75.00
Green Tapestry	1.75	10	16.00
Moq	1.75	50	70.00
Green Moq	1.75	20	35.00
Tap.	.75	10	7.50
Moq	2.00	20	40.00
Broc	1.75	10	17.50
Silk Tap	1.75	20	35.00
Tap.	1.00	56	56.00
Red velour	.70	.70	49.00
[illegible] velour	.70	60	43.00
Denim	.50	20	20.00
[illegible]	.80	54	43.20
			[illegible]016.30

[illegible]	@	Yds.	
[illegible]	.25	240	60.00
Green Frizette	.55	200	110.00
Flowered Tap	.85	150	127.50
Jacq	1.25	10	12.50
Red Tapestry	1.25	100	125.00
Green velour	2.50	60	150.00
Red velour	2.00	90	180.00
Frieze	4.00	120	480.00
Frieze	4.00	20	80.00
Frieze	2.00	30	60.00
Yale	2.50	70	175.00
Gold Frizette	1.00	80	80.00
Red Flowered	.75	180	135.00
Mohair	1.25	130	162.50
Jacq	1.10	110	120.00
Frizette	.55	290	159.50
			$2233.30

Inc.

Manufacturers of

Distinctive Upholstered Furniture

ROCKAWAY AVENUE

BROOKLYN, N. Y.

✓

MATERIAL IN STOCK

	@		$		@	yds		
Freizette	.55	145 yds	79.75	Freize	2.00	15	30	00
Fralen Jacq	1.20	51	61.20	Rust Freize	3.75	10	37	50
Jacq	1.25	15	18.75	Rust Freize	1.75	8	14	00
Jacq	1.00	25	25.00	Green Freize	2.00	5	10	00
Jacq	1.25	12	15.00	Silk Freizette	1.25	10	12	50
"	1.25	13	16.25	Green Mog	2.50	5	12	50
Green Freizette	.55	12	6.60	Silk Mog	3.00	4	12	00
Green Freizette	.75	15	11.00	Silk Tapestry	1.75	12	21	00
Fleur Freizette	.55	45	24.75	Green Freizette	.75	70	52	50
Fleur Freizette	1.10	12	13.20	Green Freizette	1.10	10	11	00
Rust Freizette	.75	85	63.75	Rust Hem-spun	.50	60	30	00
Rust Freizette	.75	12	9.00	Mog	1.15	70	80	50
Mog	2.00	60	120.00	Silk Tap	2.00	7	14	00
			~~[illegible]~~				[illegible]	60

Ex 232-1/30/32-McE.T.

Inc.

Manufacturers of

Distinctive Upholstered Furniture

ROCKAWAY AVENUE

BROOKLYN, N. Y.

MATERIAL IN STOCK

#6

	@	Yds	$		@	Yds	$
Freizette	.55	190	159.50	Freize	2.00	30	60.00
Green Jacq	1.20	153	183.60	Rust Freize	3.75	20	75.00
Jacq	1.25	45	56.25	Rust Freize	1.75	16	28.00
Jacq	1.00	75	75.00	Green Freize	2.00	15	30.00
Jacq	1.25	36	45.00	Silk Freizette	1.25	30	37.00
"	1.25	39	48.75	Green Mog	2.50	15	37.00
Green Freizette	.75	45	33.00	Silk Mog	3.00	12	36.00
Flowered Freizette	.55	135	74.25	Silk Tap.	1.75	36	63.00
Flowered Freizette	1.10	36	39.60	Green Freizette	.75	140	105.00
Rust Freizette	.75	225	191.25	Green Freizette	1.10	30	33.00
Rust Freizette	.75	36	27.00	Rust Homespun	.50	120	60.00
Mog	2.00	120	240	Mog	1.15	140	161.00
				Silk Tap	2.00	14	28.00
						15	346.50

Ex. 23 9/30/32-7458

Inc.

Manufacturers of

Distinctive Upholstered Furniture

ROCKAWAY AVENUE

BROOKLYN, N. Y.

#5

FINISHED SUITES IN STOCK

	@	Suites	$		@	Suites	$
#3	$35	4	140.00	#200	85	2	170.00
Club chairs	14	5	70.00	600	115	2	230.00
#915	35	4	140.00	601	120	1	120.00
#341	75	2	150.00	802	105	2	210.00
#502	37	10	370	Kaufman frame	100.00	2	200.00
[illegible]	50	8	400.00	#500	55	2	110.00
575	60	2	120.00	Open Top	65	1	65.00
550	75	2	150	525	110	2	220.00
700	70	2	140.00	905	115	1	115.00
920	100	2	200.00	Cushion			
260	135	2	270.00				13 420.30
175	125	2	250.00				
		11	980.30				

(x 23) – 9/30/32 – Keep

Inc.

Manufacturers of

Distinctive Upholstered Furniture

ROCKAWAY AVENUE

BROOKLYN, N. Y.

MATERIAL IN STOCK

#7

	@	yds	$			$
Tapestry	1.70	140	245.00	Trimming		25.00
Silk Tap.	1.75	12	21.00	Denim cushions		15.00
Rust Tap	1.00	75	75.00	Jag 50 yds @ 1.15		57.50
Tap	1.10	45	49.50	Stuffing cotton		200.00
Tap	1.25	14	17.25	Shellac varnish		75.00
Jag	1.25	15	18.75	paper		25.00
Black Denim	.07	300	21.00			
Denim	.09	220	28.80		16	843.45
twine	.15	90 lbs	13.50			
twine			10.00			

Inc.

Manufacturers of

Distinctive Upholstered Furniture

ROCKAWAY AVENUE

BROOKLYN, N. Y.

Tacks and springs and sundry materials on lot 118.48

FRAMES IN STOCK

1400	12	@ [illegible]	$20.00	#951	5	7	$35.00
600	7	@ 24	154.00	110	4	16	64.00
825	9	@ 12	108.00	Living Room	10	5	50.00
575	7	@ 12	84.00	800	6	15	90.00
750	10	@ 9	90.00	200	10	12	120.00
730	8	@ 11	88.00	Open Arm 804	5	11	55.00
850	8	@ 11	88.00	520	3	12	36.00
[illegible]	4	@ 18	72.00	541	6	10	60.00
1200	2	@ 27.50	55.00	Odd Frames	10	7	70.00
#2	"	8.00	40.00	Mahogany 3 Lamps	2	40 35	75.00
Chair	6	@ 2.75	16.50	Ch of [illegible] 502	4	6	24.00
905	8	@ 24	192.00	Odd Chairs	10	2.50	25.00
915	4	@ 8	32.00	#3	2	13	26.00
875	4	@ 25	100.00	950	4	7.50	30.00
[illegible]	9	@ 20	180.00	500	4	6	24.00
403	3	9	27.00	402	2	9	18.00
							18591.95

236—

Inc.

Manufacturers of

Distinctive Upholstered Furniture

ROCKAWAY AVENUE

BROOKLYN, N. Y.

FRAMES IN STOCK #4

#770	24	@$[illegible]	$770.00	Lawson frames	[illegible]	@$20	$360.00
600	14	@22	308.00	#403	6	9	54.00
825	18	12	216.00	751	10	7	70.00
575	14	12	168.00	Wing Chairs	20	$5	100.00
750	20	9	180.00	806	12	15	180.00
930	8	11	88.00	200	20	12	240.00
850	16	11	176.00	[illegible]	10	11	110.00
805	8	18	144.00	520	6	12	72.00
1260	4	27.50	110.00	541	12	10	120.00
#2	10	8.00	80.00	Odd frames	20	7	140.00
Club chairs	12	@2.75	33.00	Mahogany frames	4	40	160.00
905	16	24	384.00	Chiffonier 502	8	6	48.00
915	8	8	64.00	Odd Chairs	20	2.50	50.00
875	8	25	200.00	#3	4	13	52.00

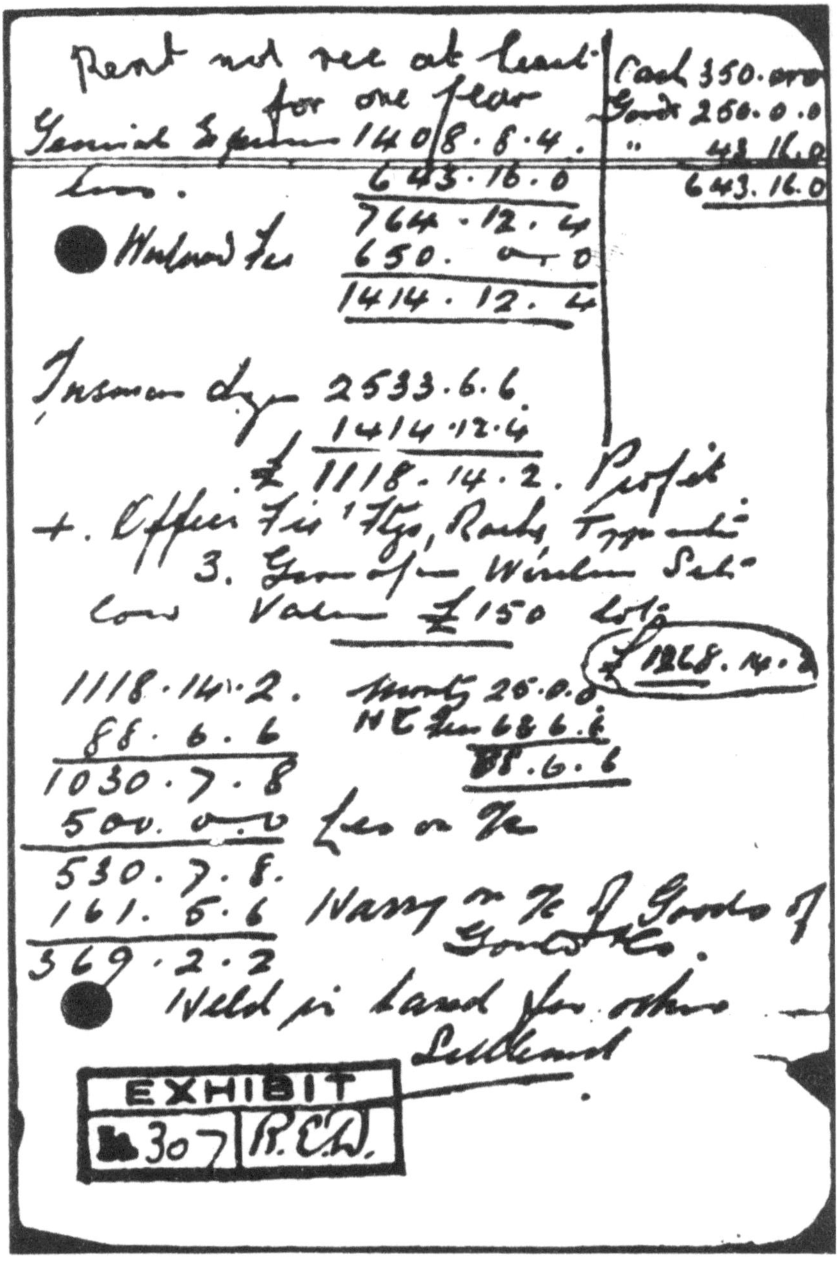

Rent not rec at least for one year

General Expenses 1408.8.4.	Cash 350.0.0
	Goods 250.0.0
	" 43.16.0
Loss. 643.16.0	643.16.0
764.12.4	
Weekend fees 650.0.0	
1414.12.4	

Insurance [illegible] 2533.6.6
1414.12.4
£ 1118.14.2. Profit
+. Office Fee [illegible], [illegible]
3. [illegible] Wireless Set
Cow Value £150 [illegible]
£ 1268.14.2

1118.14.2. [illegible] 20.0.0
88.6.6 NC fees 68.6.6
1030.7.8 88.6.6
500.0.0 fees on [illegible]
530.7.8.
161.5.6 [illegible] Goods of [illegible]
369.2.2
Held in hand for other settlement

EXHIBIT
307 R.C.D.

Source: Dearden, Harold, The Fire Raisers
(London: William Heinemann, Ltd., 1934), p. 203.
(APPENDIX D)

APPENDIX D

THE ARSONISTS' SETTLEMENT SHEET

Explanation

This sheet was prepared by the insured following the adjustment of a planned, fraudulent loss. The sheet fell into the hands of the fire investigators.

The receipt of L 2533/6/6 from the insurance company is shown. From this sum are deducted the expenses and costs of L 1414/12/4, leaving a balance of L 1118/14/2, which is clearly marked "Profit." The disposition of the major part of this profit is indicated, and a balance of L 369/2/2 is marked "Held in hand for other settlement." (See page 79 of this volume.)

APPENDIX E

QUESTIONNAIRE FORM OF THE NEW YORK BOARD OF FIRE UNDERWRITERS

Explanation

This form (see page 172) is used by the Information Bureau of the Committee on Losses and Adjustments of the New York Board of Fire Underwriters to obtain information from applicants for coverage. (See page 42 of this volume.) On the other side of the form are printed the name and address of the Board, and one of the narrow edges of the form is gummed. This facilitates the conversion of the questionnaire into an envelope, for mailing to the Board.

APPENDIX E

STATEMENT TO THE NEW YORK BOARD OF FIRE UNDERWRITERS, NEW YORK, N. Y.

Rendered by (Name of Firm, Corporation or Individual) ....

Address .... Floor ....

Line of Business .... Retail or Wholesale ....

Are you a firm (partnership), corporation or individual? .... How long in business? ....

How long at this location? .... Previous location and how long ....

Give trade names, if any .... Are they registered? ....

Give names and residence addresses of all partners or officers of your concern and previous business connections of each.

Names	Residence Addresses	Give names of all concerns with which each was previously connected, and in what capacity	
		Name of Concern	Capacity

Date of Inventory and following Financial Statement ...., 19....

ASSETS		LIABILITIES	
Cash on hand	$	Accounts payable, not due	$
Cash in bank	$	Accounts payable, past due	$
Accounts receivable, good and collectible, owing by customers, not past due (not over 4 mos. old)	$	Trade acceptances and notes payable for merchandise	$
Accounts receivable collectible, owing by customers, (over 4 mos. but not over 1 year old)	$	Notes payable to banks for borrowed money	$
Accounts and notes receivable, owing by officers, partners, employees and others not customers, whether past due or not	$	Notes and debts payable to others than to banks (including partners, officers, friends and relatives) for borrowed money	$
Trade acceptances and notes receivable, not past due	$	Money of others on deposit with us	$
Trade acceptances and notes receivable, past due	$	Chattel mortgage and other liens	$
Merchandise on hand (Market or cost whichever is lower)	$	Other liabilities	$
Machinery, fixtures and other equipment	$	Total Liabilities	$
Real estate equities	$	If individual or partnership: Net Worth	$
Other assets	$	If corporation: Capital	$
		Surplus	$
Total Assets	$	Total Liabilities and Capital	$

Annual Sales .... No contingent debts or liabilities, as endorsers or guarantors, except .... $

Do you desire the surplus to be considered as capital? ....

Have you omitted from your accounts payable any obligations for merchandise charged to you, whether delivered or undelivered, up to the date of this inventory? .... If so, how much? ....

Do you keep books of account? .... If so, state which books you keep: Sales ledger? .... Purchase ledger? .... General ledger? .... Private ledger? .... Sales book? .... Cash book? .... Stock book? .... Manufacturing book? .... Shipping book? .... Journal? .... Day book? .... Calculation book? .... Cost books? .... Check book? .... Bank deposit book? .... What books other than those enumerated above do you use? ....

How often do you take inventory? .... Have you the originals of your last and previous inventory sheets? ....

Are they kept permanently? .... Are they kept in a safe? ....

Have you sold, assigned, transferred, pledged or obtained loans on your accounts receivable, notes receivable, trade acceptances receivable or merchandise? .... If so, state names, amounts, and nature of the security given as collateral ....

Are your books regularly examined by a Certified Public Accountant or by an auditor? .... If so, by whom, and when were they last examined? Name .... Address .... Date of examination ....

State the name and location of your bank or banks ....

Have you or any partner or officer of this concern at any time been in bankruptcy or assigned for the benefit of creditors or effected a composition settlement, or been a partner or officer in any concern which was in bankruptcy or assigned for the benefit of creditors or effected a composition settlement, while so connected? .... If so, give details ....

Have you or any partner or officer of this concern at any time made a claim against a fire insurance company, or been a partner or officer in any concern which made a claim against a fire insurance company while so connected? .... If so, give details ....

Have you or any partner or officer of this concern at any time made a claim against a burglary insurance company, or been a partner or officer in any concern which made a claim against a burglary insurance company while so connected? .... If so, give details ....

Give name and address of your insurance brokers ....

State fire insurance carried on merchandise $.......... machinery and fixtures $.......... Market $.......... Building $.......... Use and Occupancy $.......... Profits $.......... Sprinkler Leakage $..........

Do you carry burglary insurance? If so, in what company, in what amount ....

Names of companies in which you carry fire insurance and amount in each: ....

(I) We herewith submit the above true and accurate statement of our assets and liabilities as shown by (my) our books on date named above and, unless (I) we notify you of any change which reduces materially (my) our pecuniary responsibility, you and they may continue to rely upon the figures herein set forth.

The undersigned has answered the above questions and has made the foregoing statement respecting my (our) financial condition from personal knowledge, certifies to the correctness of all of the information given and represents and warrants that members of your Board may rely upon the accuracy thereof in issuing insurance from time to time.

DATED, NEW YORK ...., 19....

Signed in the presence of

Name .... (Name of corporation, partnership or person seeking insurance)

Residence ....

Occupation .... (Signature of partner, officer, or individual)

Place of Business ....

Form [illegible]

BIBLIOGRAPHY

Books

Ackerman, S. B. *Insurance* (Rev. Ed., New York: Ronald Press Co., 1938).

Allen, Francis T. *General Principles of Insurance* (New York: Longmans, Green & Co., 1936).

Appleman, Earl. *Inland Marine Insurance* (New York: McGraw-Hill Book Co., Inc., 1934).

*Appleman, John Alan. *Insurance Law and Practice* (Kansas City, Mo.: Vernon Law Book Co., 1942).

*Ball, A. J. Lougborough. *Trial and Error* (London: Faber & Faber, Ltd., 1936).

Barbour, Robert P. *Agents Key to Fire Insurance* (5th. Ed., Philadelphia: The Spectator, 1939).

*Bonbright, James C. *Valuation of Property* (1st. Ed., New York: McGraw-Hill Book Co., Inc., 1937), 2 Vols., Vol. I.

Bouvier's Law Dictionary (See Rawle, Francis).

Branson, George R. "Psychology of Loss Adjustments," in Insurance Society of New York, *The Fire Insurance Contract* (Indianapolis: Rough Notes Co., 1922).

*Brown, D. C. "Adjustment of Stock Losses," in Insurance Society of New York, *The Fire Insurance Contract* (Indianapolis: Rough Notes Co., 1922).

Butzel, Ben. *A Digest of Insurance* (New York: Leonard Publishing Co., 1932).

Cady, Edwin Welling. *Law of Insurance* (3rd. Ed., Rochester, N.Y.: Lawyers Co-operative Publishing Co., 1934).

*Campbell, Alexander Colin. *Insurance and Crime* (New York & London: G. P. Putnam's Sons, 1902).

*Castenholz, William B. *Auditing Procedure* (Chicago: La Salle Extension University, 1931).

*Clark, Walter. *Photography by Infrared* (2nd. Ed., New York: John Wiley & Sons, Inc., 1946).

*Clement, George A. *Fire Insurance* (New York: Baker, Voorhis & Co., 1905).

* Indicates reference cited.

*Cleminshaw, J. M., Co. *Appraisers Manual* (Cleveland: 1937).
*Cooley, Roger W. *Briefs on the Law of Insurance* (2nd. Ed., St. Paul, Minn.: West Publishing Co.).
*Couch, George J. *Cyclopedia of Insurance Law* (Rochester, N.Y.: Lawyers Co-operative Publishing Co.).
*Cox, Henry C. *Advanced and Analytical Accounting* [Greeley, H. D. *Business Accounting,* 5 Vols., Vol. 4], (New York: Ronald Press Co., 1920).
*Crobaugh, Clyde J. *Handbook of Insurance* (New York: Prentice-Hall, Inc., 1931).
——— and Redding, Amos E. *Casualty Insurance* (New York: Prentice-Hall, Inc., 1928).
*Dargan, T. J., Jr. "Fire Loss Settlements," in Home Insurance Co., *Insurance Adjustments.* Reprint of a Series of Lectures. Lecture 1. (New York: n.d.).
*Dean, A. F. *Philosophy of Fire Insurance* (Chicago: Edward B. Hatch, 1925), 3 Vols., Vol. I.
*Dearden, Harold. *The Fire Raisers* (London: William Heinemann, Ltd., 1934).
*Dominge, Charles C. and Lincoln, Walter O. *Fire Insurance Inspection and Underwriting* (5th. Ed., Philadelphia: The Spectator, 1939).
Drewes, W. K. *Fine Arts Insurance* (New York: Underwriter Printing & Publishing Co., 1938).
*Eggleston, DeWitt Carl. *Auditing Procedure* (2nd. Ed., New York: John Wiley & Sons, Inc., 1935).
*Farrar, H. M. *Fire Insurance Racket in California* (Los Angeles: 1933).
*Faulkner, J. M. "Adjustment of Inland Marine Losses Referring Chiefly to Personal Property and the Transportation Classes," in Scott, L. J., and Faulkner, J. M. *Lectures on Insurance* (New York: Insurance Institute of America, Inc., 1936).
*Finney, H. A. *Principles of Accounting. Advanced* (3rd. Ed., New York: Prentice-Hall, Inc., 1946).
**The Forum* (Indianapolis: Rough Notes Co., 1914).
*Fox, Robert J. "The Claim—The Proof of Loss—When Is Loss Payable," in Insurance Society of New York, *The Fire Insurance Contract* (Indianapolis: Rough Notes Co., 1922).
Goldin, Abe J. *Principles of the New York Standard Fire Insurance Policy* (Philadelphia: Insurance Publishers, 1938).
——— *Law of Insurance in Pennsylvania* (2nd. Ed., Philadelphia: George T. Bisel Co., 1946), 2 Vols.
*Griswold, J. *Fire Underwriters' Text-Book* (2nd. Ed., Montreal: Insurance & Finance Chronicle Office, R. Wilson Smith, 1889).
*——— *Hand-Book of Adjustments of Loss or Damage by Fire* (3rd. Ed., New York: Insurance Monitor Office, 1894).

*Hall, Norman. *Elements of Fire Insurance Practice* (Manchester: "Policy-Holder" Journal Co., Ltd., 1928).

*Hall, Thrasher. *Adjustment of Losses from the School of Experience* (Indianapolis: Rough Notes Co., 1917).

——— "Fire Insurance Adjustments," in *Special Hazards. A Series of Ten Lectures Delivered by Experts before the Fire Insurance Club of Chicago, 1906–1907* (Indianapolis: Rough Notes Co., n.d.).

*——— *Hall on Insurance Adjustments* (1st. Rev. Ed., Indianapolis: Rough Notes Co., 1916).

*Hardy, Charles O. *Risk and Risk Bearing* (Rev. Ed., Chicago: The University of Chicago Press, 1931).

Hardy, Edward Rochie. "Fire Insurance Underwriting," in American School of Correspondence, *Cyclopedia of Fire Prevention and Insurance* (Chicago: American Technical Society, 1912), 4 Vols., Vol. 4.

*Hebard, C. F. "Audits of Exposure," in Michelbacher, G. F. *Casualty Insurance Principles* (2nd. Ed., New York: McGraw-Hill Book Co., Inc., 1942).

Hedges, J. Edward. *Practical Fire and Casualty Insurance* (2nd. Ed., Cincinnati: National Underwriter Co., 1946).

Home Insurance Company. *Insurance Adjustments* (New York: The Home Insurance Co., n.d.).

Hubbard, Clarence T. *Where Fire Insurance Leaves Off* (New York: F. S. Crofts & Co., 1930).

*Huebner, S. S. *Property Insurance* (New York: D. Appleton–Century Co., Inc., 1938).

Ingram, Dwight. *Sales Training Course in Property Insurance* (Cincinnati: National Underwriter Co., 1939).

*Insurance Society of New York. *The Fire Insurance Contract* (Indianapolis: Rough Notes Co., 1922).

*Joyce, Joseph A. *Law of Insurance* (2nd. Ed., Rochester, N.Y.: Lawyers Co-operative Publishing Co., 1917).

*Kaplan, Abraham and Berger, Samuel A. *The Dachis Case* (New York: Davidson Press, 1930).

*——— *The Wilson Warehouse Case* (New York: 1930).

*Kester, Roy B. *Advanced Accounting* (4th. Ed., New York: Ronald Press Co., 1946).

*Kulp, C. A. *Casualty Insurance* (New York: Ronald Press Co., 1928).

*——— *Casualty Insurance* (Rev. Ed., New York: Ronald Press Co., 1942).

*Long, Roland H. *Richards on the Law of Insurance* (4th. Ed., New York: Baker Voorhis & Co., 1932).

*McKenna, James A. "Ascertainment of Value and Profit from Books of Account," in Insurance Society of New York, *The Fire Insurance Contract* (Indianapolis: Rough Notes Co., 1922).

Magee, John Henry. *An Approach to the Study of Moral Hazard* (New York: Insurance Institute of America, Inc., 1933).

*——— *General Insurance* (Rev. Ed., Chicago: Richard D. Irwin, Inc., 1942).

——— *Property Insurance* (Chicago: Richard D. Irwin, Inc., 1941).

Manes, Alfred. *Insurance: Facts and Problems* (New York: Harper & Bros., 1938).

*Meade, Calvert. "Fire Loss Settlements," in Fire Underwriters' Association of the Pacific, *Lectures Delivered to the Associate Members* (San Francisco: The Association), 5 Vols., Vol. 3 (1916–1917).

*Michael, Jerome and Wechsler, Herbert. *Criminal Law and Its Administration* (Chicago: The Foundation Press, Inc., 1940).

Michelbacher, G. F. *Casualty Insurance Principles* (2nd. Ed., New York: McGraw-Hill Book Co., Inc., 1942).

*Montgomery, Robert H. *Auditing Theory and Practice* (6th. Ed., New York: Ronald Press Co., 1940).

*Moore, Francis C. *Fire Insurance and How to Build* (New York: Baker & Taylor Co., 1903).

*Mortimer, William M. *Inland Marine Insurance* (New York: Transportation Service Co., 1934).

*Mowbray, Albert H. *Insurance* (3rd. Ed., New York: McGraw-Hill Book Co., Inc., 1946).

*Myers, Laurence S. *Manufacturer and Insurance* (Rev. Ed., Cincinnati: National Underwriter Co., 1940).

*Nelson, Oscar S. *Fire Loss Adjustment Problems in the United States* (Chester, Pa., 1930).

*Newlove, George Hillis, Smith, C. Aubrey, and White, John Arch. *Intermediate Accounting* (Boston: D. C. Heath & Co., 1939).

*Patterson, Edwin W. *Cases and Materials on the Law of Insurance* (Chicago: The Foundation Press, Inc., 1947).

*——— *Cases and Other Materials on the Law of Insurance* (New York: Commerce Clearing House, Inc., 1932).

*——— *Essentials of Insurance Law* (1st. Ed., New York: McGraw-Hill Book Co., Inc., 1935).

Pitcher, William R. "Unusual and Interesting Fire Loss Claims," in Insurance Society of New York, *The Fire Insurance Contract* (Indianapolis: Rough Notes Co., 1922).

*Rawle, Francis. *Bouvier's Law Dictionary* (3rd. Revision, St. Paul, Minn.: West Publishing Co., 1914).

*Reed, Prentiss B. *Adjustment of Fire Losses* (1st. Ed., New York: McGraw-Hill Book Co., Inc., 1929).

——— *Fire Insurance Underwriting* (1st. Ed., New York: McGraw-Hill Book Co., Inc., 1940).

*Rees, Fred H. *Investigators and Adjusters Handbook* (2nd. Ed., Chicago: The Spectator Co., 1926).

Remington, Bernard C., and Hurren, Herbert G., Editors. *Dictionary of Fire Insurance* (2nd. Ed., London: Sir Isaac Pitman & Sons, Ltd., 1935).

Rethoret, Harry. *Fire Investigations* (Toronto: Recording & Statistical Corp., Ltd., 1945).

——— *Incendiarism and Accidental Fires* (Montreal: Fire Underwriters' Investigation Bureau of Canada, Inc., 1941).

*Rich, Wiley D. *Legal Responsibilities and Rights of Public Accountants* (New York: American Institute Publishing Co., Inc., 1935).

Richards on the Law of Insurance (see Long, Roland H.).

Richardson, William Payson. *Law of Evidence* (6th. Ed., Brooklyn, N.Y.: 1944).

*Riegel, Robert, and Loman, H. J. *Insurance Principles and Practices* (Rev. Ed., New York: Prentice-Hall, Inc., 1929).

Robb, Willis O. "Settlement of Losses," in Dunham, Howard P., Editor, *Business of Insurance* (New York: Ronald Press Co., 1912), 3 Vols., Vol. I.

*Royce, Josiah. *War and Insurance* (New York: The Macmillan Co., 1914).

*Rupprecht, Charles F. *Modern Fire Underwriter* (Philadelphia: The Spectator, 1940).

*Sexton, William. *Fire Insurance* (San Francisco: The Coast Review, 1915).

*Soulé, George. *Soulé's New Science and Practice of Accounts* (7th. Ed., New Orleans: 1903).

*Spicer, Ernest Evan and Pegler, Ernest C. *Book-Keeping and Accounts* (3rd. Ed., London: H. Foulks Lynch & Co., 1914).

*Steeb, Geo. Velten. *Special Agents and Adjusters Handbook* (2nd. Ed., Chicago: The Spectator Co., 1922).

*Streightoff, Frank Hatch. *Advanced Accounting* (New York & London: Harper & Bros., 1932).

Tarbell, Thomas F. *Legal Requirements and State Supervision of Fire Insurance* (New York: Insurance Society of New York, 1927).

*Thistle, Edward B. "Underwriting Burglary and Theft Risks," in *Lectures on Insurance. Intermediate Course. Casualty and Surety* (New York: Underwriter Printing & Publishing Co., 1923).

Vance, William R. *Handbook of the Law of Insurance* (2nd. Ed., St. Paul, Minn.: West Publishing Co., 1930).

*Vlachos, William. *Moral Hazard* (2nd. Ed., Philadelphia: Vlachos & Co., 1929).

Wandel, William Hamlin. *The Control of Competition in Fire Insurance* (Lancaster, Pa.: 1935).

***Webster's New International Dictionary* (2nd. Ed., unabridged, Springfield, Mass.: G. & C. Merriam Co., 1945).

*Wigmore, John Henry. *Evidence* (3rd. Ed., Boston: Little, Brown & Co., 1940).

*Willett, Allan H. *Economic Theory of Risk and Insurance,* Columbia University, Faculty of Political Science. Studies in History, Economics and Public Law, Vol. 14, No. 2 (New York: Columbia University Press, 1901).

*Williams, T. H. *Fire Insurance Contract, With Legal Decisions* (2nd. Ed., San Francisco: Underwriters' Report, 1930).

——— Editor, *Writings and Remarks of William Sexton* (Fire Underwriters Association of the Pacific, n.d.).

*Windle, Joseph J. "Adjustment of Cotton Losses and Cotton Salvage Handling," in Insurance Society of New York, *The Fire Insurance Contract* (Indianapolis: Rough Notes Co., 1922).

*Wolfe, F. E. *Principles of Property Insurance* (New York: Thomas Y. Crowell Co., 1930).

Wolfe, Louis H. *Fire Loss Adjusting in Twelve Lessons* (Multigraphed; n.d. On file in the library of The Insurance Society of New York, Inc.).

*Wright, James R. *Fire Insurance* (Toronto: Sir Isaac Pitman & Sons, Ltd., 1932).

Proceedings and Reports

Allen, C. Guy. "Adjustment Problems." Summary of Address, *Proceedings of First Fire and Casualty Insurance Conference.* April 30, 1945. Ohio State University (Columbus, O.: 1945).

*Barnard, Chester F. "Loss Management," *Proceedings of the Fifty-fourth Annual Meeting of the Fire Underwriters' Association of the Pacific* (1930).

*Beard, Roy C., "Investigation and Adjustment of Questionable Fires," *Proceedings and Papers of the Thirty-sixth Annual Convention of the National Association of Mutual Insurance Companies* (Chicago: 1931).

*Boston. Mayor's Committee on Fire Insurance Rates, *Report on the Problem of Fire Waste and Insurance Rates in the City of Boston* (Boston: 1929).

Brady, John E. "The Part Moral Hazard Plays in Fire Insurance," *Proceedings of Fifty-third Annual Meeting of the Fire Underwriters' Association of the Pacific* (1929).

*Clarke, Arthur A. "Adjustment of Losses Under Pacific and Atlantic Coast Conditions," *Proceedings of Forty-sixth Annual Meeting of the Fire Underwriters' Association of the Pacific* (1922).

Colvin, Charles A. "Moral Hazard," *Proceedings of Forty-eighth Annual Meeting of the Fire Underwriters' Association of the Pacific* (1924).

Federation of Insurance Counsel. *Proceedings.* 1938–1941.

Fire Underwriters' Association of the Pacific. *Proceedings.* 1878 to 1946.

*Grant, H. M. "Upon the Element of Estimate in Loss Adjustments," *Proceedings of Fifteenth Annual Meeting of the Fire Underwriters' Association of the Pacific* (1891).

*Lowden, William H. "Losses and Adjustments," *Proceedings of Eleventh Annual Meeting of the Fire Underwriters' Association of the Pacific* (1887).

——— "The Measure of Manufacturer's Damage," *Proceedings of Fifteenth Annual Meeting of the Fire Underwriters' Association of the Pacific* (1891).

*——— "What to Do When the Books Are Burned," *Proceedings of Fourteenth Annual Meeting of the Fire Underwriters' Association of the Pacific* (1890).

*Mayer, F. J. Alex. "Scientific Bookkeeping and the Adjustment of Book Losses. With and Without Books," *Proceedings of Twenty-ninth Annual Meeting of the Fire Underwriters' Association of the Pacific* (1905).

*Merchants Association of New York, *Report of Committee on Fire Prevention and Insurance on Incendiarism* (New York: The Association, 1913).

"Modern Insurance Developments," *Annals of the American Academy of Political and Social Science,* Vol. 161 (May 1932).

National Association of Insurance Commissioners. *Proceedings.* 1936–1945.

National Board of Fire Underwriters. *Proceedings.* 1928–1946.

*Seventy-first Annual Meeting (1937). Report of Committee on Adjustments.

*Seventy-third Annual Meeting (1939). Report of Committee on Incendiarism and Arson.

*Eightieth Annual Meeting (1946). Report of Committee on Incendiarism and Arson.

National Convention of Insurance Commissioners. *Proceedings.* 1933–1935.

New York Board of Fire Underwriters. *Annual Reports.* 1930–1941. (Subsequent reports available only to member-companies).

New York (State) Legislature. Joint Committee Appointed to Investigate Corrupt Practices in Connection with Legislation, and the Affairs of Insurance Companies, Other Than Those Doing Life Insurance Business. Report Transmitted to the Legislature February 1, 1911. (Albany: J. B. Lyon Company, State Printers, 1911).

*Ontario (Canada) Insurance Commission, "Report on [sic] Insurance Commission." The Hon. Mr. Justice Masten, Commissioner. Printed by order of the Legislative Assembly of Ontario (Toronto: A. T. Wilgress, Printer to the King's Most Excellent Majesty, 1919).

Penney, W. "Fraudulent Claims and Incendiary Fires." *Transactions of the Insurance Society of Edinburgh*, 1937–1938 (Edinburgh: H. J. Pillans & Wilson, 1938).

*Sexton, William. "Adjusting," *Proceedings of Twenty-first Annual Meeting of the Fire Underwriters' Association of the Pacific* (1897).

*——— "Adjusting Lumber Losses," *Proceedings of Thirty-second Annual Meeting of the Fire Underwriters' Association of the Pacific* (1908).

——— "Adjustment of Fire Losses," *Fire Insurance Society of San Francisco. Annual Report of Proceedings*, 1910–1911.

*Stanton, John C. "Moral Hazard," *Proceedings of Fiftieth Annual Meeting of the Fire Underwriters' Association of the Pacific* (1926).

Steinmetz, Richard C. "Unusual Arson Cases," *Proceedings of Forty-third Annual Meeting of National Fire Protection Association* (Boston: The Association, 1939).

*Stratton, G. F. "Underwriters Salvage Company and Its Relation to the Adjustment of Fire Losses," *Proceedings of Fifty-fourth Annual Meeting of the Fire Underwriters' Association of the Pacific* (1930).

*Thomas, W. P. "Losses and Adjustments," *Proceedings of Tenth Annual Meeting of the Fire Underwriters' Association of the Pacific* (1886).

*Wisconsin. Report of the Wisconsin Legislative Fire Insurance Investigating Committee of the Senate and Assembly, Made to the Governor Pursuant to Joint Resolution 130, A., and Chapter 512 of the Laws of 1911. (Madison: Democrat Printing Co., State Printer, 1913).

PAMPHLETS

American Institute of Accountants. Library and Bureau of Information. Special Bulletin No. 10. "Fire Losses." October 1921.

Barton, William F. "Forms and Clauses." Three Lectures before the Insurance Institute of America. 1919–1920. (New York: North British & Mercantile Insurance Co., 1920).

Chandor, R. M. "Moral Hazard in Its Relation to Fire Underwriting." Address before Examining Underwriters Association, New York, March 23, 1922. (Privately printed.)

**Character Inspection Services for Fire Insurance Companies* (Atlanta: Retail Credit Co., undated).

Evans, Hunt, Rees & Hanley. *Digest of Burglary Insurance Decisions. State of New York.* (New York: Evans, Hunt, Rees & Hanley, 1927).

*Foulke, Roy A. *Relativity of the Moral Hazard* (New York: Dun & Bradstreet, Inc., 1940).

*Hall, Thrasher. "Adjustment of Fire Losses." Address before Seventy-first Meeting of Central Supply Association, Chicago, June 22, 1916 (Chicago: n.d.).

**Inspector's Handbook. Burglary Insurance Underwriting and Reporting* (Rev. Ed., Atlanta: Retail Credit Co., 1934).

**Inspector's Handbook. Fire Insurance Underwriting and Reporting* (Atlanta: Retail Credit Co., 1941).

*Kleinhaus, H. I. *Retail Inventory Method in Practical Operation* (Rev. Ed., New York: Controllers' Congress, National Retail Dry Goods Association, 1941).

Lock, F. "Relation of Fire Insurance to Incendiarism." Address before International Association of Fire Engineers (New York: National Board of Fire Underwriters, 1913).

McInerney, Thomas. "Checking the Proofs of Loss and Paying the Claim." Insurance Society of New York. Howe Readings in Insurance. No. 15 (New York: The Society, 1933).

*National Board of Fire Underwriters. *Non-Concurrent Apportionments. Recommendations of the National Board of Fire Underwriters* (New York: The Board, January 1934).

*——— *Non-Concurrent Apportionments. Recommendations of the National Board of Fire Underwriters* (New York: The Board, 1942).

National Fire Protection Association. *Fireman's Responsibility in Arson Detection* (Boston: The Association, n.d. [1946?]).

*National Retail Dry Goods Association, Controllers' Congress. "The Shepard Co. Fire," Insurance Bulletin, Vol. 8, No. 3 (November 1924).

*Phillips, George H. "Underwriting from a Credit Standpoint." Insurance Society of New York. Howe Readings in Insurance. No. 14. Three Special Lectures (New York: The Society, 1932).

*Piver, Jack. *So You're New in Fire Insurance* (San Francisco: Pacific Insurance Magazine, 1946).

*Retail Credit Co. *Inspector's Handbook. Reporting Financial Information* (Atlanta: Retail Credit Co., 1941).

Shallcross, C. F. *Sketch of Fire Underwriting Practice and Conditions in the United States of America* (New York [?]: C. F. Shallcross, 1922).

*Sullivan, W. A. "Settlement of Losses without Controversy." Paper before American Management Association, Insurance Conference, New York, May 15, 1933. *American Management Series, Insurance 15* (New York: The Association, 1933).

PERIODICALS

*Aaronson, Benjamin. "Collecting Fire Losses," Pace Student, Vol. VI, No. 10 (September 1921).

*" 'Actual Cash Value' of Insured Property: The Normal Rules and Their Wartime Modifications," Notes, 91 University of Pennsylvania Law Review and American Law Register (1942), (Philadelphia: University of Pennsylvania Law School).

*American Insurance Digest and Insurance Monitor. "Current Conditions That Tend to Create Moral Hazard Fires," Vol. 72, No. 1 (January 5, 1924).

*Bachman, Roy G. "Adjustment of Losses." Chapter I of Fire and Marine Insurance—Course No. 1, Weekly Underwriter, Vol. 147, No. 19 (November 7, 1942).
*Bell, Ernest W. "Adjustment of Fire Losses," Public Accountant, Vol. 23, No. 1 (July 30, 1923).
Best's Insurance News. Casualty Edition: May–September 1938; Fire and Marine Edition: 1928–September 1938; Fire and Casualty Edition: October 1938–August 1946.
*Blacklock, Frank. "Suggestions to a Young Accountant on Adjusting a Fire Loss," Business, Vol. 18, No. 5 (May 1898).
*Bowen, Leroy. "Few Fire Claims Are Litigated," National Underwriter, Vol. 43, No. 46 (November 16, 1939).
*Brophy, Thomas P. "The Arson Racket." Lecture at Forty-third Annual Convention of International Association of Chiefs of Police, Police Journal, Vol. 13, No. 2 (April–June, 1940).
*Buenemann, J. P. "History of Fire Insurance Adjusting," Bulletin of the Insurance Club of Chicago, Inc., Vol. 19, No. 6 (May 1922).
Busby, D. A. "The Value of Accountancy to Insurance Adjusters," Our Business, Vol. 2, No. 6 (June 1941).
*Cabot, Edgar V. "Arson—An Ancient Art—Ever New," Journal of American Insurance, Vol. 13, No. 11 (November 1936).
*——— "Two Eras of Arson for Insurance," Journal of American Insurance, Vol. 14, No. 4 (April 1937).
*Caldwell, Eugene. "What Executives Should Know about Fire Insurance. Part II," American Business, Vol. 7, No. 11 (November 1937).
*Cutforth, A. E. "The Accountant as Expert Witness." Lecture Delivered to the London Members of the Institute of Chartered Accountants, October 22, 1931, The Accountant, Vol. LXXXV, No. 2972 (November 21, 1931).
*Davis, Gordon. "Provisional Insurance Loss Adjustments, "Journal of American Insurance, Vol. 22, No. 4 (April 1945).
"Determination of Losses Resulting from Fire," American Accountant, Vol. XVIII, No. 7 (July 1933).
*Dry Goods Economist. "Insurability of Merchandise at Its Counter Cost," Vol. 89, No. 5 (November 1934).
*Duncan, John C. "Property Accounting for Fire Losses," Journal of Accountancy, Vol. 5, No. 6 (April 1908); Vol. 6, No. 3 (July 1908); Vol. 7, No. 2 (December 1908).
Eastern Underwriter. 1923–June 1946.
*"Apparel Contractors' Committee Reports," Vol. 24, No. 17 (April 27, 1923).
*"Du Bois Urges Assureds to Take Advantage of Inland Marine Forms," Vol. 36, No. 15 (April 12, 1935).

*"Few Loss Crooks Can Beat Game, Say Pitcher and Tate, Adjusters," Vol. 32, No. 6 (February 6, 1931).
*"Firebug's Arrest Hits Arson Racket," Vol. 31, No. 12 (March 21, 1930).
*"Loss Committee of the New York Board," Vol. 27, No. 30 (July 23, 1926).
*"National Board Eases Loss Payment Rule," Vol. 36, No. 48 (November 8, 1935).
*"New York Board's New Way to Handle Apparel Losses," Vol. 24, No. 17 (April 27, 1923).
*"Sixteen Defendants Guilty in Great Arson Trial in London," Vol. 34, No. 35 (September 1, 1933).
*"Stewart Gives Tips on Moral Hazard Risks," Vol. 31, No. 43 (October 10, 1930).
*"Underwriting Mercantile Open Stock Insurance," Vol. 31, No. 10 (March 7, 1930).
*"Vlachos Views Fire Underwriting Problems in N.Y. City After War," Vol. 45, No. 16 (April 21, 1944).
*"W. A. Riordan Describes Vital Work of New York Board Loss Committee," Vol. 31, No. 48 (November 7, 1930).

Ehrenzweig, Albert. "Apportionment of Losses Under 'Non-concurrent' Fire Policies," Best's Insurance News, Fire and Casualty Edition, Vol. 42, No. 8 (December 1941); *Vol. 42, No. 9 (January 1942).

*Erion, Frank L. "War and Defense Measures Raise Adjustment Problems," Journal of American Insurance, Vol. 18, No. 10 (October 1941).

*Fritz, George C. "Mercantile Open Stock Burglary Insurance," in ***Budget Supplement*** (Baltimore: Maryland Casualty Co., December 1927).

*Gibson, J. D. "Excessive Insurance Brings High Loss Ratio and Is Unfair to Companies and Policyholders," Insurance Field, Fire-Casualty Edition, Vol. 61, No. 28 (April 7, 1932).

*Goble, George W. "Proposed Revision of the Standard Fire Insurance Policy with Special Reference to Hazard Clauses," Journal of American Association of University Teachers of Insurance, Vol. 4, No. 1 (March 1937).

*Greene, H. H. "Doubled Inventory Method Advanced as Means of Saving Money on Fire Loss Adjustments," Weekly Underwriter, Vol. 126, No. 2 (January 9, 1932).

*Haskins and Sells Bulletin. "The Insurance Man Speaks," Vol. XII, No. 6 (June 1929).

*Hubbard, Clarence T. "Flying Arts and Flames," Weekly Underwriter, Vol. 126, No. 10 (March 5, 1932).

Insurance Field.
Fire—Marine and Casualty Edition. 1928–1931.

Fire—Casualty Edition. 1932–June 1946.
*"Adjuster's Work Provides Background of Proof to Decide Attalla Arson Case." Vol. LXII, No. 17 (March 2, 1933).
Journal of Accountancy.
*"Correspondence" (Letter from Prentiss B. Reed), Vol. 14, No. 2 (August 1912).
*"Legal Notes," Vol. 64, No. 1 (July 1937).
*Students' Department (Letter from Geo. U. Stiff), Vol. 19, No. 6 (June 1915).
Students' Department, *Vol. 28, No. 5 (November 1919); Vol. 29, No. 4 (April 1920).
Journal of the American Association of University Teachers of Insurance. 1933–March 1946.
Journal of American Insurance. 1928–August 1946.
*Kent, George. "Trail of the Torch," Colliers, Vol. 105, No. 10 (March 9, 1940).
*McKelway, St. Clair. "Profiles. Firebug-Catcher—1," New Yorker, Vol. XI, No. 49 (January 18, 1936).
*Manes, Alfred. "Insurance Crimes," Journal of Criminal Law and Criminology, Vol. XXXV, No. 1 (May–June 1944).
*Morpeth, C. D. "Fire Loss Adjustments," Accounting, Commerce and Insurance, Vol. 10, No. 6 (September 29, 1923).
*Mortimer, William M. "Inland Marine Insurance Losses—Why Careful Investigation Is Always Necessary—Transportation, Rules and Regulations." Address before National Association of Independent Adjusters, at Washington, D.C., Weekly Underwriter, Vol. 141, No. 1 (July 1, 1939).
National Underwriter. 1928–June 1946.
*"Benefit Is Seen in Credit Work," Vol. 38, No. 16 (April 19, 1934).
*"Central Burglary Bureau Now Being Advocated," Vol. 35, No. 48 (November 26, 1931).
*"Check Points for Agents on Adjusting Losses," Vol. 45, No. 34 (August 21, 1941).
*"Insurable Values Discussed," Vol. 45, No. 44 (October 30, 1941).
*"Modified 30-day Rule Satisfactory," Vol. 38, No. 6 (February 8, 1934).
*"Moral Hazard Not Serious Fire Insurance Factor Now," Vol. 47, No. 4 (January 28, 1943).
*"P. B. Reed Suggests How to Fix Insurable Values." Vol. 43, No. 50 (December 14, 1939).
*"Psychology of Community Is Important in Underwriting," Vol. 38, No. 12 (March 22, 1934).

*"Shallcross Comments as to Sixty-Day Loss Payment Rule," Vol. 37, No. 35 (August 31, 1933).
*Neuner, John J. W. "Insurance Claims Racketeers," Journal of American Insurance, Vol. 12, No. 3 (March 1935).
New York Times.
*March 17, 1930, 1:5.
*January 12, 1932, 13:2.
*Olney, Peter B. "Accountant's Role as a Fact Finder and as a Witness," New York Certified Public Accountant, Vol. 11, No. 6 (March 1941).
*Persson, A. T. "Fire Insurance Adjusting," Journal of American Insurance, Vol. 5, No. 12 (December 1928).
*Reed, Prentiss B. "Adjusting and Paying Losses." Chapter II of Fire and Marine Insurance—Course No. 1. Weekly Underwriter, Vol. 148, No. 1 (January 2, 1943).
*——— "Loss Adjustments." Lecture before Examining Underwriters Association of New York, The Examiner, Vol. 2, No. 5 (April 1925).
*——— "Moral Hazard of Custodians," Ounce of Prevention, Vol. 2, No. 7 (April 1924).
*——— "New Factors Enter Loss Adjusting; No Fixed Rule During Wartime." Address Delivered before the Risk Research Institute, February 24, Eastern Underwriter, Vol. 44, No. 10 (March 5, 1943).
*——— "War Increases Adjuster's Problems," Weekly Underwriter, Vol. 144, No. 1 (January 4, 1941).
*Rodda, William H. "Bad Business Conditions and Incendiarism," Weekly Underwriter, Vol. 127, No. 14 (October 1, 1932).
——— "Obsolescence Versus Depreciation," Weekly Underwriter, Vol. 140, No. 9 (March 4, 1939).
*Russ, Harry D. "Claim Adjustments," Insurance Age, Vol. LIII, No. 7. (February 15, 1924).
*Scammell, E. J. "Standard Claims Manual Urged as Aid to Holding Fire and Motor Business," Weekly Underwriter, Vol. 128, No. 18 (May 6, 1933).
Spectator. 1928–June 1935.
Spectator. Property Insurance Review. July 1935–June 1946.
Stans, Maurice H. "Accounting Aspects of Fire Loss Adjustments," Our Business, Vol. 2, No. 11 (November 1941).
——— "Experience with Books of Account in Loss Adjustments." Paper Presented at a Meeting of Chicago Adjusters Association, February 14, 1946, Our Business, Vol. 7, No. 2 (April 1946).
——— "Use of Accountants in Loss Adjustment," Journal of American Insurance, Vol. 23, No. 8 (August 1946).
*Steinmetz, Richard C. "What About the Moral Hazard," Weekly Underwriter, Vol. 141, No. 23 (December 2, 1939).

*Stokes, H. F. "Fire Loss Adjustment," Best's Insurance News. Fire and Casualty Edition, Vol. 44, No. 8 (December 1943).

*Underwriter. "The Moral Hazard," Spectator, Vol. CXXVI, No. 10 (March 5, 1931).

*Van Deusen, E. A. "Bank and Insurance Stocks. This Week—Insurance Stocks," Commercial and Financial Chronicle, Vol. 160, No. 4328 (October 26, 1944).

Weekly Underwriter. 1922–June 1946.

*"Inspection Basis Changing," Vol. 106, No. 19 (May 13, 1922).

*"Jeweler's Block Is a Cover of Importance," Vol. 132, No. 17 (April 27, 1935).

Wiley, A. M. "Do You 'Service' Your Reporting Policies?" Best's Insurance News. Fire and Casualty Edition, Vol. 47, No. 4 (August 1946).

Miscellaneous References

Including Laws and Government Publications

**American Law Reports Annotated* (Rochester, N.Y.: Lawyers Co-operative Publishing Co.)

Corpus Juris (New York: American Law Book Co.).

Corpus Juris Secundum (Brooklyn, N.Y.: American Law Book Co.).

*Daly, C. L. "Loss Adjustments." Lecture before Insurance Institute of Winnipeg. Fire Course, I. March 3, 1937 (Typewritten; on file in the library of The Insurance Society of New York, Inc.).

Encyclopedia of the Social Sciences (New York: The Macmillan Co.).

Articles:

Huebner, S. S. "Fire Insurance—American."

Manes, Alfred. "Fire Insurance—European."

——— "Insurance—Principles and History."

Mowbray, A. H. "Insurance—Industry."

Patterson, Edwin W. "Insurance—Law and Regulation."

**Fire, Casualty and Surety Bulletins* (Cincinnati, O.: National Underwriter Co.).

*McLoughlin, Stephen. "Mercantile Safe and Mercantile Open Stock Burglary Insurance." Address to Second Year Casualty Students of Insurance Society of New York. February 3, 1932 (Typewritten; on file in the library of The Insurance Society of New York, Inc.).

*Maltbie, Armstrong. "Loss Adjustments from a Public Adjuster's View." April 16, 1930 (Mimeographed; probably a lecture. On file in the library of The Insurance Society of New York, Inc.).

*New York City Fire Department. Wall Exhibit, New York City Building, World's Fair of 1939, Flushing, New York.

New York State. Laws.

*Civil Practice Act, Section 374a.

*Insurance Law, Section 41.

*Laws of 1939, Chapter 882, Sections 149, 150 and 172.
*Laws of 1943, Chapter 671.
*Penal Law, Section 1202.
*New York (State) Standard Fire Insurance Policy.
U.S. Code Annotated (St. Paul, Minn.: West Publishing Co.).
*U.S. Department of Commerce, Bureau of Foreign and Domestic Commerce. Trade Promotion Series No. 152 (Revised December 1, 1934), Ramirez. Mariano H. *Trading Under the Laws of Mexico* (Washington, D.C.: U.S. Government Printing Office, 1935).
*U.S. Treasury Department, Bureau of Internal Revenue, Supplement to Regulations 111, Relating to the Income Tax Under the Internal Revenue Code (Washington, D.C.: U.S. Government Printing Office, 1946).

TABLE OF CASES

Aronson v. Maryland Casualty Co. (1926) 222 Mo. A. 490, 280 S.W. 724.
Boyle v. Hamburg-Bremen Fire Ins. Co. (1895) 169 Pa. 349.
T. J. Bruner Co. v. Fidelity & C. Co. (1917) 101 Neb. 825, 166 N.W. 242.
Claflin v. Commonwealth Ins. Co. (1883) 110 U.S. 81.
Columbian Ins. Co. v. Modern Laundry (8 Cir. 1921) 277 Fed. 355.
Crowley *et al.* v. North British & Mercantile Ins. Co., Limited (W.D.S.C., 1947) 70 Fed. Supp. 547.
Demarest v. Westchester F.I. Co. (1932) 234 App. Div. (1st Dept) 556, 255 N.Y. Supp. 325.
Fowler v. Phoenix Ins. Co. (1899) 35 Ore. 559.
Garten v. General Acc. F. & L. Assur. Corp. (1923) 206 App. Div. (4th Dept) 154, 200 N.Y. Supp. 546.
Golub v. Fidelity & Casualty Co. of New York 246 App. Div. (2d Dept) 537 (1935), 283 N.Y. Supp. 987 #1; 246 App. Div. (2d Dept) 616, 284 N.Y. Supp. 377, 269 N.Y. 679.
Ingersoll v. United Surety Co. (1910) 141 App. Div. (1st Dept) 527, 126 N.Y. Supp. 391.
Jacoby v. United States Fire Insurance Co., *et al.* 244 App. Div. (1st Dept) 781, 280 N.Y. Supp. 790 #4 (1935); 244 App. Div. (1st Dept) 798, 280 N.Y. Supp. 1016 #3 and 268 N.Y. 723.
Larner v. Commercial Union Assur. Co., Ltd., of London, Eng. (1926) 215 N.Y. Supp. 151.
Leiman v. Metropolitan Surety Co. (App. Term., 1st Dept 1908) 111 N.Y. Supp. 536.
Lenzner v. National Surety Co. (1924) 209 App. Div. (2d Dept) 464, 204 N.Y. Supp. 796.
Licht v. N.Y. Indemnity Co. (1928) 250 N.Y. 211.
Litchfield v. City of N.Y. (1926) 244 N.Y. 251, 155 N.E. 116.
Malin v. Mercantile T.M.I. Co. (1904) 105 Mo. App. 625, 80 S.W. 56.
Mass F. & M. Ins. Co. v. Schneider (5 Cir. 1928) 28 Fed. (2d) 658.
Michler v. New Amsterdam Cas. Co. (1928) 104 N.J.L. 30, 139 Atl. 725; 104 N.J.L. 663, 141 Atl. 920.
Mississippi Fire Ins. Co. v. Perdue (1928) 217 Ala. 292, 116 So. 142.

Mord v. N.Y. Indemnity Co. (1926) 216 App. Div. (2d Dept) 252, 214 N.Y. Supp. 693; 244 N.Y. 589, 155 N.E. 908.
N.Y. Underwriters' Fire Ins. Co. v. Malham & Co. (8 Cir. 1928) 25 Fed. (2d) 415.
Orenstein v. Star Ins. Co. of America (4 Cir. 1926) 10 Fed. (2d) 754.
The Spica (C.C.A. 2d, 1923) 289 Fed. 436.
Sternfeld v. Park F.I. Co. (1888) 50 Hun 262.
U.S. v. Mortimer (2 Cir. 1941) 118 Fed. (2d) 266.
Vaughan v. Virginia F. & M. Ins. Co. (1904) 102 Va. 541, 46 S.E. 692.
Wright v. Union Ins. Co. (5 Cir. 1926) 13 Fed. (2d) 612.

INDEX

Bei Fragen zur Produktsicherheit wenden Sie sich bitte an:
If you have any questions regarding product safety,
please contact:

Walter de Gruyter GmbH
Genthiner Straße 13
10785 Berlin
productsafety@degruyterbrill.com